Scottish Government and Politics

For James Kellas

Scottish Government and Politics

An Introduction

Peter Lynch

Edinburgh University Press

Edinburgh University Press Ltd
22 George Square, Edinburgh

Reprinted 2001

Typeset in 11 on 13pt Goudy
by Hewer Text Ltd, Edinburgh, and
printed and bound in Great Britain
by MPG Books Ltd, Bodmin

A CIP Record for this book is
available from the British Library

ISBN 0 7486 1287 4 (paperback)

Contents

Contents

List of tables and case studies

Preface

While this book is a text book, it did not seem so at the time of writing. The period between the establishment of the Scottish Parliament in 1999 and the completion of this book was a transitional one. It was also one in which there were very few pieces of academic research about the new institutions. As a result of these factors, this book contains a vast amount of original material and an analysis of the new institutions that should be treated as preliminary. An assessment based on the first year of an evolving devolution scheme certainly would not claim to predict the future of the Parliament and Executive although it does provide the essential contours and activities of the new system. The focus of the book is clearly institutional and intended to provide a comprehensive introduction to the Scottish Parliament, the Scottish Executive, Scottish Secretary, parties, pressure groups, media and local government. There is definitely more to Scottish politics than these institutions but time and space and the nature of an introductory text placed limits on the book.

There are a number of people who assisted me in the completion of this text. Professor James Kellas at Glasgow University was instrumental in providing encouragement in the early stages of this book. Producing a text to replace *The Scottish Political System* was in his mind as well as my own, and his book was a constant inspiration. Nicola Carr of Edinburgh University Press was also extremely supportive, as well as patient (the latter virtue was particularly welcome). I would also like to thank my head of department at Stirling, Professor Stephen Ingle, who has continually sought to provide time and space for research and writing within the department and been constantly supportive of my work.

CHAPTER I

The new Scotland

INTRODUCTION:
UNDERSTANDING THE NEW SCOTLAND

This book is, more than anything, about devolution and the resulting processes of political change. Devolution established a new Scottish Parliament and Executive. It therefore involved the creation of the Scottish political system that James Kellas talked of as far back as the 1970s. Central to the current devolution process is the notion of a 'new Scotland', which sought to garner support for a Scottish Parliament by stressing how different from Westminster the new system would be. The difference was seen to be not merely quantitative, in terms of the number of Scottish laws that could be dealt with by the Scottish Parliament compared to Westminster, but also qualitative, in terms of the way in which policy would be made. This qualitative aspect was built upon a highly negative view of the policy process at Westminster in which the government was seen to dominate policymaking through its majority in the Commons, its ability to control MPs through the whipping system, and its bureaucratic capacity in Whitehall. The governing party was seen to have untrammelled control over policy, in the face of an impotent opposition, weak backbenchers and ineffective select committee system. This view certainly exaggerated and simplified the reality of government and party control at Westminster, but fed directly into the design of the Scottish Parliament which sought to avoid the perceived pitfalls of Westminster life. More than anything, therefore, the new Scotland was to be about new institutions that were 'not Westminster'.

Two things are worth pointing out in support of the notion of the new Scotland in practice. First, it is new because it involves new institutions and policy processes. Single-party government has been replaced by coalition. Executive dominance over policymaking has been balanced by Parliamentary involvement through the committee system and through pressure group activity at various stages of the policy process. The unchallenged ability of civil servants and ministers to dominate policy has gone. Second, it is not just the process that is 'new' about the new Scotland, it is also the policy outputs. Devolution is a good example of the importance of political institutions (Lane and Ersson, 2000). It involves a vast number of new policies that would not have been instituted under previous institutional arrangements. The tiny number of Scottish bills dealt with at Westminster pale into insignificance alongside the legislative agenda of the Scottish Parliament. The type of bills passed and under consideration also offer clear examples of the different policy outputs brought about by devolution. The abolition of feudal tenure, section 2a/28, and land reform would not be expected to pass through the House of Lords at Westminster – indeed the section 28 reform did not in 2000 – so without devolution, key legislative outputs simply would not have occurred in Scotland.

Moreover, some of the legislation enacted and proposed under the devolution arrangements provide a clear picture of Scotland as a fundamentally unreformed land before the Parliament was established. Lacking its own Parliament and dependent on the legislative timetable at Westminster, large numbers of issues and problems were simply never addressed; hence the ability of feudal land laws to survive for 900 years. Devolution meant the new Parliament and Executive were swamped by demands and pressures for legislative change, resulting in the widespread legal reforms enacted and under discussion following the establishment of the Scottish Parliament: for example, legislation on incapable adults, and consultations over children's security, stalking and harrassment and the physical punishment of children, to name but a few. Scotland is playing an extremely rapid form of catch-up in many policy areas.

Consensus politics is central to devolution and the new Scotland. However, it is important to take a realistic view of this idea. Consensus politics does not mean all the parties and pressure groups sitting down and agreeing with each other about everything or making fundamental compromises on their goals and policies. What it does mean is that no single group has a majority in the Scottish Parliament and many of the Parliament's actions are open to internal and external pressure that require negotiation and compromise to retain support. Coalition is one example of consensus, the multi-party and multi-functional nature of the Parliament's committee system is another. Each necessitates consensus rather than one-party rule. Similarly, devolution involves power-sharing between government, Parliament and civic Scotland, meaning that pressure groups have their foot firmly in the door in policy discussions. This fact leads to a more consensual attitude to policymaking through the exchange of ideas and policy positions facilitated by the Parliament's inclusive process. However, this situation does not always lead to agreement or indeed to consensus. It can lead to fundamental disagreements and messy compromises that leave nobody happy – the section 2a/28 issue being a key example. Such is the nature of democratic politics.

– Continuity versus change –

Devolution involved a measure of both continuity and change in Scottish politics. Of the two, change has been the more obvious feature of devolution given the prominence of the new Parliament and Executive. However, there are also significant continuities in the previous system of government in Scotland. The Scottish Executive is essentially the Scottish Office, staffed by the same civil servants. Scotland still has a Secretary of State within the Cabinet. There is still a Scottish question time in the House of Commons, a Scottish Grand Committee and a Scottish Affairs Select Committee. Politicians such as the Chancellor of the Exchequer, Gordon Brown, remain major players within Scottish politics despite devolution. And Westminster remains responsible for vast areas of government and policy in Scotland such as the economy, foreign affairs, social security, air and rail transport, trade and commerce, employment law and the European Union. The Britishness of Scottish politics thus remains a central fact of political life after devolution. Analysis of the new Parliament therefore has to retain a UK perspective, recognising the limited nature of devolution but also the mutual interdependence of Scottish and UK government in devolved policy areas such as health, law and order and agriculture, as well as reserved policy areas. Fundamentally, devolution did not create a separate Scottish Parliament but one embedded in UK and EU governance structures. Negotiating the limits of devolution and establishing effective intergovernmental relations are two important tasks for the Parliament and Executive. Each task prevents the adoption of a purely internal perspective towards Scottish devolution.

– The return of Scotland –

Devolution signified the return of Scotland (Nairn, 2000). Here was an ancient nation – not region – regaining its national Parliament and its own government. Of course, to some extent, Scotland had been returning for some time. The rise of the political nationalism in the 1960s and the cultural renaissance in Scottish literature in the 1980s are two prominent examples of this return. The creation of the Scottish Parliament meant that Scotland had arrived as a political entity, albeit an incomplete one. This fact begs the question of what happens next? Is Scotland a region that sought regional autonomy and is now contented (the settled will) or is it a nation that sought national autonomy, meaning independence? This question is at the centre of the devolution debate and always has been. For arch devo-sceptic Tam Dalyell, devolution in the 1970s was a slippery slope to independence; by the 1990s, Dalyell saw devolution as having placed Scotland on a motorway without exits leading to independence.

The establishment of the Scottish Parliament in 1999 did not answer the essential devolution question: where is it all leading to? But it is possible to view devolution as a dynamic process which impacts upon all sorts of organisations within Scotland – political parties, media, pressure groups, government bodies – and creates considerable tensions and points of conflict between Scottish and UK institutions. Tensions over policy differences in student finance, section 2a/28, asylum seekers, UK treatment of genetically-modified foods, European funding and beef all generated intergovernmental conflicts between Scotland and the UK in the post-devolution period. But such conflicts are not merely intergovernmental in terms of existing between government institutions, they also go to the heart of Scotland's constitutional position and can be seen as tests for devolution which spark debate over independence. Although this book largely focuses on the 'small' question of what the Parliament does rather than the 'big' question of whether it will lead to independence, this latter question should still be kept in mind, especially as the new arrangements evolve.

– THE UK AS A DEVOLVED STATE –

Devolution within the UK was certainly a process rather than an event under the first Blair administration and one that substantially altered the 'sovereigntyscape' of UK politics (Nairn, 2000). While this book is concerned with assessing the devolution process in Scotland, devolution itself was more widely applied across the UK. Alongside the Scottish Parliament are the National Assembly for Wales (not merely an assembly), the Northern Ireland Assembly and cross-party Executive, and an elected Mayor for London and the Greater London Authority. Thus, four parts of the UK now enjoy devolved government. Sure enough, the level of devolution in these nations and regions is highly differentiated and asymmetrical, but it is devolution nonetheless. Moreover, the extent of devolution has brought about overarching intergovernmental bodies such as the British Irish Council and the Joint Ministerial Committees. British government AD (after devolution) is clearly not what it was BD (before devolution) and, in time, the debate over the English regions (the return of England, to paraphrase Tom Nairn) and the notion of an English Parliament may generate further institutional change. This situation means that Scottish devolution interacts with other institutions and reforms which generate their own dynamic with the capacity to create territorial conflicts and intergovernmental disputes.

– CONCLUSION –

Devolution created an ambitious new political system in Scotland, and this system faced two initial challenges. First, it had to turn a constitutional blueprint into the reality of a working government and legislature, a challenge subject to all sorts of teething problems. Second, it was faced with the task of living up to high public expectations about devolution, in a harsh media climate which was severely critical of the Parliament. Over time, these problems of establishment will be replaced by problems of performance and policy delivery: can the Parliament and Executive actually reform and improve Scottish society and the economy? Furthermore, because the Parliament was established with a clear democratic agenda of civic participation and power-sharing, it must fulfill this agenda or stand accused of betraying the aims of the founding fathers (and mothers). The Parliament will not be judged solely as a legislature in terms of making laws and holding the government to account but in terms of whether it helps to create a new Scottish democracy and moves away from elite-centred, top-down government.

CHAPTER 2

The long road to a Scottish Parliament

– INTRODUCTION –

The issue of a Scottish Parliament has been around in Scottish politics for over a century, though was seldom seen as a serious political issue for British governments. In recent times, two serious attempts were made by governments to establish a Scottish Parliament. The first, in the 1970s, ended in the ignominy of the devolution referendum of 1 March 1979. The second, in the 1990s, succeeded through the devolution referendum of 11 September 1997 and the formal establishment of the new Parliament on 1 July 1999. Of course, in a wider European perspective, the creation of a regional parliament and government in Scotland came fifty years after the West German *Länder*, twenty-nine years after Italy's regional government, twenty years after the autonomous communities of Spain, nineteen years after Belgium's regional councils and seventeen years after France established regional councils. Despite the late arrival, the significance of the Scottish Parliament is that it is a case of a Parliament being restored to a former nation-state rather than simply a region (Nairn, 2000), with the Parliament also viewed as a national Parliament. This chapter will examine the historical evolution of devolution in Scotland, in addition to providing a guide to the current devolution scheme embodied in the Scotland Act 1998 and now alive and kicking on the Mound in the shape of the Scottish Parliament and Executive.

– A CENTURY OF DEVOLUTION? –

Supporters of a Scottish Parliament promoted the issue for around 100 years, mostly without success. Organisations such as the Scottish Home Rule Association, the Scottish Convention, the Scottish Covenant Association and the Campaign for a Scottish Assembly sought to promote the issue of a

Scottish Parliament, but did so in very changing political circumstances. For example, the Scottish Home Rule Association (SHRA) campaigned for a Parliament in the 1920s, recruiting members, establishing branches, pressurising Labour MPs, and creating a constitutional convention to design a package of measures for a Parliament. However, its efforts to promote the issue largely fell on deaf ears within the two main political parties. Some Labour MPs and a number of party activists rallied to the cause, but the issue was not taken seriously by the Labour leadership or by the party as a whole (Mitchell, 1996: p. 79). Such treatment led Roland Muirhead, the leading figure within the SHRA, to consider establishing a distinct political party in favour of Home Rule which would challenge the other parties to support a Scottish Parliament through electoral pressure. In time, from 1926-7 onwards, this situation was to lead to the decline and disappearance of the SHRA and the slow formation of what was to become the SNP in 1934. Such radically different means to achieve the same end – a Scottish Parliament – have marked out the Home Rule movement for most of the past 100 years.

James Mitchell (1996) outlined four main routes through which proponents of Home Rule sought to deliver a Scottish Parliament: the creation of Home Rule pressure groups, the establishment of constitutional conventions, the use of petitions and referenda, and the creation of a political party to campaign for constitutional change. Each of these strategies for self-government was utilised by campaigners over the years, with varied success. Home Rule pressure groups sought to promote the issue among the public and to pressurise the parties into responding. Sometimes, these groups were organised by members of various parties such as the Campaign for a Scottish Assembly, comprised of Labour, SNP and Liberal activists. At other times, they were intra-party pressure groups such as Scottish Labour Action or the predominantly Labour SHRA. A number of Home Rule groups used the mechanism of a constitutional convention as a device to promote the idea of a Parliament, to design specific proposals for a Parliament and also to confer it with a degree of elite legitimacy. The first convention, the Scottish National Convention, was organised by the SHRA in the 1920s. It held a variety of meetings from 1924 to 1927, but it failed to win much support from local and civic organisations in Scotland, and the convention petered out as some of its members transferred their political attention to the establishment of the National Party of Scotland. The second convention, the Scottish National Assembly, was set up by the Scottish Convention, largely a group of individuals around John McCormick who had broken away from the SNP in 1942. The Scottish National Assembly met from 1947 to 1950, with the limited participation of local councils and civic organisations. Again, with neither the Labour government nor the Unionists showing any interest in Home Rule, the Assembly's efforts came to nothing. However, it did give birth to the Covenant Association, which gained great popularity and publicity with the National Covenant in 1951, though this initiative again failed to deliver Home Rule.

The third constitutional convention was established in 1989 following the efforts of the Campaign for a Scottish Assembly, the organisers of the Claim of Right for Scottish self-government and the political parties. The Scottish Constitutional Convention ran from 1989–95, with the involvement of Labour, Liberal Democrats, the STUC, local authorities and a range of civic organisations. Like previous conventions, it sought to popularise Home Rule but, more fundamentally, it sought to engineer elite and cross-party support for a scheme of devolution. Rather than see the pro-change parties divided by the fact they supported different varieties of Home Rule, it sought to gather all of the parties around one table to hammer out a compromise scheme they could all support. Of course, there were partisan motivations here, with Labour in particular keen to show a level of activity over the issue of a Scottish Parliament that would contain an SNP that was resurgent in the polls following its dramatic victory at the Govan by-election in November 1988 (Lynch, 1996). Nonetheless, the Convention played an important role in designing the main elements of a devolution package and, moreover, helping to create a coalition of supporters for Home Rule which contained most of Scotland's major institutions: it established a substantial Yes campaign in embryonic form. All of this was a far cry from 1979, as will be explained below.

The third strategy for achieving Home Rule involved a variety of participatory mechanisms such as referendas and petitions. The Scottish National Covenant was launched at the Scottish National Assembly in 1949. After a slow start, the number of signatories multiplied, so much so that the Covenant Association struggled to produce enough covenants to sign. Although there were disputes about the accuracy of the total number of signatories, it was estimated that about 1.7 million Scots signed the covenant (Mitchell, 1996: p. 145). However, the difficulty with the covenant is that it was merely a statement of support for Home Rule; it involved no activity, no commitment to action and it lacked follow-through. The organisers perhaps assumed that such a show of support for Home Rule would lead to a clear response from the government. However, none was forthcoming. Later efforts to hold mini-referenda on Home Rule and the campaign for a multi-option referendum in the early 1990s fell on similarly stony ground (Mitchell, 1996).

The National Covenant

We, the people of Scotland, who subscribe to this engagement, declare our belief that reform in the constitution of our country is necessary to secure good government in accordance with our Scottish traditions and to promote the spiritual and economic welfare of our nation.

We affirm that the desire for such reform is both deep and widespread through the whole community, transcending all political differences and sectional interests and we undertake to continue united in purpose for its achievement.

With that end in view, we solemnly enter into this Covenant whereby we pledge ourselves in all loyalty to the Crown and within the framework of the United Kingdom, to do everything in our power to secure for Scotland a Parliament with adequate legislative authority in Scottish affairs.

The final approach to promoting Scottish Home Rule involved the establishment of a political party specifically to act as an electoral battering-ram for a Parliament. There had been considerable debate throughout the 1920s over the merits of forming a Home Rule party, among groups such as the Scottish National Convention, the SHRA and the Scots National League (Finlay, 1994). However, the change in approach was largely attributable to the failure of the Convention and the SHRA to influence the main political parties to prioritise rather than simply express support for a Scottish Parliament. The minutes of meetings of the Convention and the SHRA in the National Library of Scotland are peppered with discussion of the need to set up a party. Quickly, from late 1927 onwards, members of the SHRA, the Glasgow University Scottish Nationalist Association, the Scots National League and the Scottish National Movement coalesced to establish the National Party of Scotland (Finlay, 1994). The National Party later merged with the Scottish Party to establish the Scottish National Party (SNP) in 1934, although it was not until the 1940s that the SNP began to emerge as a coherent political force intent on contesting elections. However, establishing a political party as a mechanism to garner support for Home Rule was not a particularly successful device. It was forty years from the formation of the SNP to its electoral breakthrough with eleven seats at Westminster.

– Devolution in the 1970s –

In the 1970s, the issue of Scottish devolution was largely driven by the electoral success of the SNP. The party's dramatic by-election victory at Hamilton in 1967 prompted Labour Prime Minister Harold Wilson to establish a Royal Commission on the Constitution in 1968. The Tories responded to the rise of the SNP with Edward Heath's Declaration of Perth in 1968, which committed the Conservatives to establish a Scottish Assembly. The combined impact of the SNP's emergence at the two general elections of 1974 – with eleven seats and 30.4 per cent of the vote in the second election – was enough to move Labour towards supporting the establishment of a Scottish Assembly. Labour's conversion to devolution was made without the support of its membership or MPs. Labour in Scotland became pro-devolution following arm-twisting by trade union leaders and the UK leadership at the party's Dalintober Street conference in Glasgow in 1974 (Marr, 1992). At Westminster, Harold Wilson's pragmatic determination to implement devolution in order to stave off electoral defeats at the hands of the Nationalists was not shared by backbench colleagues, many of whom conspired to give the Scotland and Wales Bill and subsequently the Scotland Bill a very rough time in the House of Commons (Bogdanor, 1979). As if backbench dissent were not enough, the fact that Labour became a minority administration at Westminster presented considerable obstacles to devolution and led to substantial backbench/opposition amendments to the devolution proposals. Most notably, these amendments included the insertion of clauses to hold a post-legislative referendum on a Scottish Assembly, with a requirement that 40 per cent of the Scottish electorate, rather than voters, had to vote in support of devolution for the Assembly to be created (Balsom and McAllister, 1979). This particular wrecking amendment, proposed by Labour MP George Cunningham, led directly to the 1979 referendum and the defeat of the government's devolution plans as a result of the 40 per cent rule (see Table 2.1).

Table 2.1 The 1979 devolution referendum in Scotland

	Votes (%)	Electorate (%)
Yes	51.6	32.8
No	48.4	30.8
Turnout: 63.6%		

The referendum campaign itself was characterised by deep inter-party divisions. Although Labour, the Liberals and SNP all campaigned for a Yes vote, they fought separate Yes campaigns (Bochel, Denver and Macartney, 1981). This lack of unity and the obvious differences between the parties in terms of what type of Scottish Parliament they supported effectively undermined the Yes campaign. The No campaign not only had the comfort of the 40 per cent rule, it was also comprised of Conservative and Labour MPs. The No campaign indeed had the semblance of cross-party unity that the Yes campaign lacked, and this contributed to the small majority for the Yes campaign and the overall closeness of the result.

As will become clear from the discussion below, the Scotland Act 1978 was different to that of 1998. The Assembly was to be elected using the first-past-the-post (FPTP) electoral system, meaning a likely Labour majority in the Assembly. The Assembly had no taxation powers, the Scotland Act 1978 did not deal effectively with the division of powers with Westminster, and the Secretary of State for Scotland was given a rather expansive veto role over Assembly legislation.[1] Had the Assembly been established, there would have been ample room for its operation to be hampered by an unclear division of powers, which would have been open to legal challenge. Politically, this situation would have been interesting in the early 1980s: imagine a Labour Assembly in constant dispute with a Conservative Secretary of State for Scotland and the Assembly cast as a legislative obstacle to Thatcherism.

Moreover, in contrast to the 1998 Act, the Assembly proposals were the product of only one party and were focused narrowly on creating an Assembly. The wider democratic agenda evident in the 1990s, with consensus politics, civic engagement and consultative practices, were entirely absent from the 1970s proposals. However, although the nature of the proposals and the referendum defeat were shattering blows to the Home Rule movement, proponents of change did take a number of lessons from the 1978–9 disappointments. The next time devolution was put before the Scottish electorate, the style and substance of a Scottish Parliament were a marked improvement on the previous proposals, especially in the establishment of the Scottish Constitutional Convention and decision to hold a pre-legislative referendum.

– The Scottish Constitutional Convention –

The Scottish Constitutional Convention was created in 1989 with the task of designing a scheme of devolution, and with gaining consent for this scheme from a range of Scottish organisations, including the political parties, to avoid the inter-party divisions over a Scottish Parliament that were evident at the 1979 referendum. Despite the early departure of the

SNP, Labour and the Liberal Democrats, the STUC, local authorities and the churches all persisted with the Convention. The Convention operated through two distinct periods, from its early phase from 1989–90 to its second phase in 1992–5. These periods were marked by the agreement and publication of two sets of proposals, *Towards Scotland's Parliament* in 1990 and *Scotland's Parliament, Scotland's Right* in 1995. The second set of proposals were more detailed, and followed from a special Constitutional Commission established by the Convention to examine the thorny questions of the Parliament's electoral system and the role of gender representation (Scottish Constitutional Commission, 1994). The final Convention document was more complete than the earlier version, with clear proposals for a 129-member Parliament, with seventy-three constituency and fifty-six list members, as well as proposals for tax powers, devolved responsibilities, relations with local government, and public participation in the Parliament's activities. Additionally, the Convention provided these proposals with a level of legitimacy among key Scottish institutions such as local authorities (see Chapter 12) and civic organisations. In a sense, it helped to establish a nascent Yes campaign several years in advance of the referendum itself, as well as disarming some potential opponents of a Scottish Parliament through consultation and compromise.

Of course, the role of the Convention should not be overstated. While it influenced the content of the devolution package, other actors played significant roles and the Convention did sidestep difficult issues such as the West Lothian question. For example, the Constitution Unit (a London based think-tank which produced a range of reports on constitutional reform) was effective in persuading Labour elites to ensure a clear division of powers between Scotland and Westminster in the current Scotland Act. It did so by arguing for the adoption of the former Stormont system, in which the reserved powers of Westminster were detailed in the devolution legislation, with the proviso that all other government functions were the preserve of the devolved Parliament (Constitution Unit, 1996). Civil servants and Labour ministers involved in the devolution policy cabinet committee in London were also influential in the Scotland Act, especially in ensuring a more conservative outcome that tempered some of the constitutional radicalism of the Convention's participants. Similarly, decisions about a devolution referendum were made unilaterally by the Labour leadership in 1996 without reference to the Convention at all.

Despite such influences, the Convention did play a significant role and it is possible to talk of its continuing impact on devolution. Not only did Convention proposals such as the electoral system and tax-raising powers become important parts of the Scotland Act 1998, but its democratic agenda for devolution fed its way into the design of the Parliament through the medium of the Consultative Steering Group (a committee established by the Secretary of state for Scotland in 1998 to provide the Parliament with working procedures and draft standing orders in advance of its creation). This latter group picked up many of the Convention's anti-Westminster arguments about the need for consensus politics, power-sharing, civic involvement, consultation and so on, and instituted them as features of the new Parliament's policymaking process and decisionmaking structures (Consultative Steering Group, 1999). The high expectations and demands of the Parliament in relation to new politics and public participation can be seen as the legacies of the Convention experience.

– THE DEVOLUTION REFERENDUM 1997 –

The devolution referendum of 1997 had its origins in a remarkable reversal of policy by the Labour leadership in 1996. Under pressure from Conservative attacks over the 'tartan tax' orchestrated by the Secretary of State for Scotland, Michael Forsyth, Labour sought to use the referendum issue to defuse the tax issue specifically and the devolution question generally in advance of the general election (Mitchell et al., 1998). Thus, the referendum was to be held on the principle of devolution before detailed legislation was put before the House of Commons. It also involved two questions: one on the principle of the Parliament and the second on whether it should have taxation powers. Such a pre-legislative referendum had some merit. It would provide the devolution proposals with a mandate in the Commons and the Lords and disarm opponents of devolution in both Houses. It would also schedule the referendum early in the new Parliament, meaning it would be held within the Labour government's honeymoon period and would deal with the taxation issue. However, the referendum decision was widely criticised at the time it was made. The decision was presented as a *fait accompli* to Scottish Labour by Shadow Secretary of State for Scotland George Robertson and Labour leader Tony Blair. Labour's Scottish Executive Committee was pressurised into accepting the decision, the Scottish Labour conference was side-stepped and there was considerable disquiet within the party's devolution supporters (Jones, 1996).

The referendum campaign itself was a rather one-sided affair. The Yes campaign gathered within an umbrella group, Scotland Forward, which had organised for the referendum from late 1996 onwards with discreet meetings between Labour, Liberal Democrats and the SNP. Although the SNP publicly retained its anti-devolution stance through the 1997 general election and beyond, it moved into the Yes camp following the publication of the government White Paper, Scotland's Parliament, in late July 1997. From then on, there was an active and unified Yes campaign comprising the three main political parties in Scotland. Scotland Forward had a limited campaigning capacity as it was party machines that did most of the organisational and media work, but it was significant as a body through which to coordinate the various efforts of the pro-change parties. The No campaign was dominated by Conservatives, unlike in 1979, and even then it was up to less prominent figures such as Donald Findlay, the former Rangers Vice-Chairman, to lead the campaign through the Think Twice organisation. The Conservatives' electoral wipeout in the 1997 election and the likely victory for the Yes campaign had a demotivating effect on the No campaign, especially as the Conservatives were financially drained following the election. Although there was some strong local campaigning by the Tories at the referendum, they were a spent force who knew they faced defeat. They did have the taxation question to focus on in the 1997 referendum, but even that was to prove unsuccessful.

Table 2.2 The 1997 referendum in Scotland

	Yes (%)	No (%)
Support for a Scottish Parliament	74.3	25.7
Support for taxation powers	63.3	36.4
Turnout: 60.2%		

The outcome of the 1997 referendum was an overwhelming success for the double Yes campaign (see Table 2.2), and the vote on both questions was indisputable. Local Yes campaigners attending the counts did not bother taking ballot box samples of the first vote, which could have easily have been weighed instead of counted, and concentrated on the second vote. Significantly, compared to 1979, all parts of Scotland voted for a Parliament, from Orkney and Shetland to the Borders and Dumfries and Galloway. Only on the taxation question were there some geographical differences, with Orkney and Dumfries and Galloway opposed to tax powers. Moreover, the tax issue was separated from devolution by the nature of the two-question referendum itself, which helped to preserve such a large majority for the Parliament and to provide it with geographical legitimacy the length and breadth of Scotland. Scots voted for tax powers on the expectation that they would be used, but used to improve public services; this led to their characterisation as 'welfare rationalists' (Brown, McCrone, Paterson and Surridge, 1999). The convincing referendum outcome, allied to Labour's massive Commons majority, effectively meant that devolution was guaranteed. All that was left was the publication of the

Scotland Bill on 17 December 1997 and its passage through Westminster to become the Scotland Act in 1998.

– UNDERSTANDING THE SCOTLAND ACT –

The Scotland Act 1998 stretched to 132 sections and nine schedules, over 109 pages. In contrast to the Scotland Act 1978, the current devolution legislation is fairly comprehensive, especially in relation to the legislative powers of the Scottish Parliament itself. It achieved this clarity not by listing the powers of the Parliament in the Act but by listing the powers of Westminster in Schedule 5 of the Act and allowing the Scottish Parliament to exercise government functions outside of these reserved areas. It also included details of the electoral system, the sovereignty of Westminster, the Parliament's legislative competence and financial powers. Each of these aspects of the Act will be discussed below. However, the Act did not deal with all aspects of the devolution settlement, and numerous aspects were left to the Parliament itself to decide, either through the Consultative Steering Group or through Parliamentary debates after 6 May 1999. Some of these decisions became formal rules through incorporation in the Parliament's standing orders, others developed as Parliamentary conventions. The Act also avoided dealing with intergovernmental relations. The range of concordats and inter-ministerial committees were designed after the Scotland Act (see Chapter 9) and, although mentioned in the devolution White Paper *Scotland's Parliament*, did not see the light of day until the autumn of 1999.

– THE POWERS OF THE SCOTTISH PARLIAMENT –

– THE PARLIAMENT'S POWERS –

The Scotland Act 1998 was designed in such a way as to make the powers of the devolved Parliament implicit rather than explicit. For example, anyone expecting to skim through the Act to discover the Parliament's powers will be disappointed. Instead, they will find a lengthy list of the reserved powers of Westminster and UK government. The Scotland Act 1998 sought to deal with the division of powers between Scotland and Westminster not by detailing every power of the new Parliament as it had in 1978, but by stating what the Parliament could not do. This mechanism, adopted from the Government of Ireland Act 1920, was seen to offer a clear division of powers between Scottish and UK government and to avoid conflicts over which level of government was responsible for a policy area. However, the division remains imperfect as the two sets of governments share powers in some areas. What the Parliament is responsible for is actually listed in the White Paper *Scotland's Parliament*. The list comprises most aspects of domestic policy in Scotland that were previously the preserve of the Scottish Office such as agriculture and fisheries, economic development, education, environment, health, local government, social work, civil law, criminal justice, tourism, the arts, and so on (Scottish Office, 1997).

In addition, a number of policy areas are shared between Scotland and Westminster. The Executive and Parliament are responsible for road and passenger transport, but Westminster remains responsible for air and rail transport. Scotland has control of civil and criminal law, but laws regarding drugs misuse and firearms are reserved powers at Westminster. The health service is devolved to Scotland, but regulation of the healthcare professions, medicines and genetics are reserved to Westminster. The Scotland Act 1998 also provided a list of shared competences between Scotland and Westminster, such as employment and training, financial assistance to industry, road safety information and training, and funding of scientific research.[2] One thing that is striking about the powers transferred under devolution is that they were largely those previously transferred to the Scottish Office. Devolution therefore did not involve new powers for the Scottish Parliament, but rather different institutional arrangements for designing and implementing these powers.

– RESERVED POWERS AND SCHEDULE 5 –

Schedule 5 of the Scotland Act 1998 contains a lengthy list of those powers and responsibilities reserved to Westminster after devolution, and offers a relatively clear illustration of what the Scottish versus Westminster Parliaments should do. However, it does not involve a cast-iron division of powers between the two sets of institutions, as a number of policy areas are overlapping and interlinked. Schedule 5 attempts to provide an exhaustive list of UK government functions and, in this, it is fairly successful. It contains the 'high politics' policy areas of defence, foreign affairs, currency, macroeconomic management, immigration and nationality, and trade, together with the 'low politics' areas of energy, employment and transport. Also, the level of detail in Schedule 5 is specific enough to create some interesting examples of reserved powers, with Westminster responsible for the Chiropractors Act 1994, the Osteopaths Act 1993, the Coastguard Act 1925, the Carriage by Air Act 1961 and the Hovercraft Act 1968, except for the regulation of noise and vibration caused by the hovercraft.

There are four ways of understanding the contents of Schedule 5. First, it can be seen as an indication of the power of Westminster. It contains policy responsibilities representative of the main symbols of statehood such as currency, defence and activity in international affairs. The number of powers and their importance are also indicative of the sovereignty of Westminster and the subordinate nature of the devolved institutions, as Westminster retains the most important functions such as fiscal powers and macro-economic management. Second, Schedule 5 can be understood from the point of view of administrative practicality. Many of the reserved powers are reserved in order to retain a uniform UK market or policy space that prevents crossborder conflicts. Thus employment law, consumer law and commercial law are all reserved functions in order to retain a uniform UK market in which consumers, companies and employees all operate under the same legislation. Similarly, social security was retained as a reserved power in order to prevent a situation in which different parts of the UK would set different benefit levels, creating movements of population and welfare tourism to gain the best benefits, with implications for employment markets and for government expenditure. Abortion was made a reserved power in order to prevent the possibility of different laws in Scotland and England, leading to the situation in Ireland and Northern Ireland where women regularly travel to the UK mainland for abortions, with implications for the health services involved. Third, Schedule 5 can be seen as a shopping list for government institutions outside Westminster. It contains some policy responsibilities that the Scottish Parliament would like to obtain (and the contents can be amended by ministerial orders at Westminster rather than legislation) as well as a range of functions that could be transferred upwards to the European Union, especially currency and macroeconomic management. Fourth, Schedule 5 can be seen to represent part of a written constitution for the UK, as it actually states what central government does and writes down its core functions. By implication, it suggests that devolved governments can hold all other functions in the UK, which must give encouragement to the National Assembly for Wales and the Greater London Authority.

– LEGISLATIVE COMPETENCE AND *ultra vires* –

The role of the Secretary of State for Scotland in relation to devolved legislation is substantially different in the 1998 Scotland Act compared to the 1978 Act. Then, the Scottish Secretary had an important veto role over legislation, determining whether Scottish legislation was *ultra vires* and referring it to the Judicial Committee of the Privy Council, and being responsible for submitting the bill for Royal Assent.[3] The Secretary of State had potentially wide powers to veto legislation based on an unclear division of powers between the Assembly and Westminster, and the Judicial Committee may well have tied itself in knots determining Scottish versus

UK functions given the ambiguities of the Scotland Act 1978. However, the more recent Act deals with the Parliament's legislative competence in a very different way. First, the inclusion of Schedule 5 provides a clearer division of competences in 1998 than in 1978, and it is simpler to determine devolved versus reserved powers under the current Act, although some grey areas are still possible. Second, section 31 of the Scotland Act 1998 requires both the Presiding Officer and the sponsoring minister from the Scottish Executive to provide certificates of legislative competence for legislative proposals. These certificates are issued following legislative checks by the Parliament's legal officers and they read in a deceptively simple manner when published as part of the memoranda accompanying bills:

> On 24 September 1999, the Presiding Officer (Sir David Steel) made the following statement: 'In my view, the provisions of the Abolition of Poindings and Warrant Sales Bill would be within the legislative competence of the Scottish Parliament.'[4]

Thus, two mechanisms seek to prevent conflicts over competences, one constitutional and one within the devolved institutions, before the involvement of UK ministers and structures.

Two additional checks and balances exist to prevent the Scottish Parliament from trespassing into the area of reserved powers. Sections 32 and 33 of the Scotland Act 1998 allow the Advocate General, Lord Advocate or Attorney General to refer Scottish bills to the Judicial Committee of the Privy Council if they feel that a bill is outside the legislative competence of the Scottish Parliament. Referral can take place up to four weeks after a bill is passed, and before it has received the Royal Assent. As the Advocate General is a UK minister newly created by the Scotland Act 1998, there is obviously some scope for the UK government to seek to influence Scottish legislation here, although it only occurs in the area of reserved powers. The other two law officers are officers of the Scottish Executive. The Scottish Secretary's role is to provide an additional check on the Parliament's intrusion into reserved powers and the Minister has four weeks in which to do so. Section 35 allows the Scottish Secretary to make an order preventing the Presiding Officer from submitting a bill for Royal Assent on two grounds: first, if the bill is incompatible with the UK's international obligations, defence or national security; and, second, if the bill intrudes into Westminster's reserved powers or has an adverse effect on the operation of reserved powers.

The order must be highly specific, in that it must state which part of a bill impacts upon international obligations, national security or reserved powers, and why the order is made. There is no need for the Secretary of State to refer the order to the Judicial Committee of the Privy Council, which would leave UK government with the final say in these matters rather than subject to adjudication – a potentially important limitation on the devolved Parliament. The Secretary of State for Scotland also has the ability to make orders to prevent or ensure particular actions by ministers of the Scottish Executive in relation to the UK's international obligations and Wesminster's reserved powers, in addition to exercising a similar function over subordinate legislation within the Scottish Parliament.[5]

Of course, as yet, the legislative competences of the Scottish Parliament have not been tested, nor have the powers of the Secretary of State to make orders or revise Scottish legislation. The checks and balances described above have been part of the reason: after all, they are designed to prevent ambiguity over legislative competence. Moreover, the fact that the first Scottish Executive contained Labour and the Liberal Democrats rather than the SNP was responsible for the absence of difficulties with legislative competences. Neither of the two parties of government had an interest in challenging the Parliament's competences. In future, an SNP-led administration conceivably could seek to test out some of the grey areas of legislative competences between Scotland and Westminster, for example the Scottish Independence Referendum bill, which would provide a test case for the procedures designed to resolve legislative conflicts between the two sets of governments and Parliaments. How these conflicts are resolved is difficult to see, although there is clearly scope for the Secretary of State to develop an override power in relation to the Scottish Executive and Parliament which could destabilise the devolution process itself.

– THE SOVEREIGNTY OF WESTMINSTER –

Devolution has not affected Westminster's ability to pass legislation on any Scottish issue it wishes: part of the maintenance of the sovereignty of Parliament. Section 28 (7) of the Scotland Act 1998, dealing with devolved legislation, states that devolution 'does not affect the power of the Parliament of the United Kingdom to make laws for Scotland.' This clause offers the potential for Westminster to impose legislation on Scotland, thereby reversing the intent of devolution itself. It appears as a mantra in the Scotland Act 1998 and a large number of the concordats published in 1999 (see Chapter 9). However, the two Parliaments are operating under the convention that the UK Parliament will not legislate in devolved areas without the agreement of the Scottish Parliament. The following written Parliamentary question gives an indication of the treatment of the issue:

Dr Winnie Ewing (Highlands and Islands) (SNP): To ask the Scottish Executive whether it intends to give an assurance that the Westminster Parliament will not legislate on devolved matters. (S1W–140)

Donald Dewar: As I indicated in my statement on 9 June, legislation about devolved subjects in Scotland will normally be enacted by the Scottish Parliament. From time to time, however, it may be appropriate for an Act of the United Kingdom Parliament to include provisions about such matters. That is the case, for example, for the Food Standards Bill. I also indicated that both the Scottish Executive and the United Kingdom Government intend that, by convention, the United Kingdom Parliament will not legislate about devolved matters without the consent of the Scottish Parliament.

The need for consent has not been ignored. For example, the Immigration and Asylum Act 1999 passed at Westminster had the effect of amending Scottish law that was the preserve of the devolved Parliament. The Act altered the Social Work (Scotland) Act 1968, the Mental Health (Scotland) Act 1984, the Housing (Scotland) Act 1987 and the Children (Scotland) Act 1995: all Scottish Parliamentary responsibilities.[6] 'The Act sought to disperse refugees around the UK and provide them with vouchers rather than cash to finance their living expenses. In Scotland, cash payments had been administered by local authorities, with the councils' responsibilities for housing and social work making them key actors in the placement and management of asylum seekers. Thus, Westminster's reserved powers in immigration (section B6 of Schedule 5 of the Scotland Act 1998) effectively enabled the UK Parliament to supersede the Scottish Parliament in devolved matters because of the overlap of policy competences, with Westminster responsible for making the law and Scotland responsible for implementing it. On this occasion, the Scottish Executive consulted with the Home Office in London, but accepted the new scheme for financing asylum seekers locally. Had it been minded otherwise, it could have passed its own legislation to amend the Westminster Act and retain cash payments to asylum seekers in Scotland.

Similar examples of overlapping competences occurred with the type of legislation passed at Westminster after devolution as well as during the time period involved. Some Westminster legislation was introduced before devolution and was proceeding through the Houses of Parliament after the Scottish Parliament was established, for example the Sexual Offences (Amendment) Bill 1999 to equalise the age of consent for homosexual intercourse with that for heterosexuals had been delayed by the House of Lords in April 1999. The UK government reintroduced this bill at Westminster after devolution, yet could not alter it to take account of devolution as the Parliament Act required the new bill to be introduced in an identical format to the original. The Scottish Parliament would have agreed to the new legislation at Westminster at the time, although it might have paused for thought as the section 2a/28 debate developed. Other bills introduced before the Scottish Parliament assumed its powers on 1 July 1999 included the Health Bill, which provided for the abolition of general practice fundholding, for changes in the financial arrangements for National Health Service trusts and for the imposition of a duty of quality on the NHS in Scotland: the Water Industry Bill, which established a water industry commissioner for Scotland to replace the Customers Council; and the Pollution Prevention and Control Bill to implement the EU Directive on Intergrated Pollution Prevention and Control. Scottish Executive ministers were involved in consultations on all of these bills and the Scottish Parliament was in position to amend or repeal such legislation. As the First Minister Donald Dewar, pointed out in a debate on legislative competences between Scotland and Westminster:

> the Scottish Parliament will be able to amend or repeal legislation made at Westminster in so far as its provisions fall within this Parliament's competence. That is the case for existing legislation, for this session's bills at Westminster that affect Scotland and for future acts of the UK Parliament.[7]

However, the coalition government chose not to exercise this power in the Parliament's first year.

– THE ELECTORAL SYSTEM –

Giovanni Sartori observed that 'electoral systems are the most manipulative instrument in politics' (Sartori, 1997: p. ix). This point certainly has resonance with the Scottish Parliament. If, for instance, the Scottish Parliament had been established solely with a first-past-the-post (FPTP) electoral system, it would have delivered a majority government for Labour with a clear minority of the vote: a situation easily seen from the FPTP result of the 1999 Scottish election, with fifty-six out of seventy-three seats to Labour. The decision to use a mixed electoral system with a degree of proportionality – the combined FPTP and regional list system – produced entirely different electoral outcomes. Majority government was made highly unlikely in the Scottish electoral system, with coalition or minority governments the most likely outcomes, and this scenario turned out to be the case.

The Scottish electoral system was designed by the Scottish Constitutional Convention in the 1990s. It was one of the clearest examples of the Convention's influence on the final devolution Act, as the UK government adopted the Convention's electoral system wholesale. The electoral system consists of two parts, each adapted from the electoral system in use in Germany since 1949. The Scottish system elects a total of 129 MSPs:

1. Seventy-three are elected through the FPTP system in existing Westminster constituencies, with Orkney and Shetland each given an MSP.
2. Fifty-six additional MSPs are elected through eight regional lists. The regions were based on European Parliamentary constituencies that existed before the 1999 election. Each region elected seven MSPs through a formula specified in the Scotland Act 1998:

$$\frac{\text{the total number of regional votes for a party within the region}}{\text{the number of FPTP MPs elected for the party } + 1}$$

This formula effectively reallocates seats between the parties to even out some of the imbalances of the FPTP result. It is proportional, but not completely so. For example, the whole electoral system is numerically weighted in favour of the FPTP system, and the Scotland Act 1998 contained a second formula to retain the existing balance of FPTP and regional MSPs, meaning that regardless of the size of the Parliament there should be 57 per cent of MSPs elected by FPTP and 43 per cent elected via the regional list.[8] Over time, as the FPTP party, Labour should have a structural advantage within the Scottish electoral system, although not an advantage that produces a majority. In addition, the system involves a structural disadvantage for parties that win few FPTP seats and rely on the regional list system, such as the Conservatives and SNP at the present time. The effect of the constitutional engineering behind the electoral system is open to a variety of interpretations. For some, the abandonment of the FPTP system in favour of the additional member system (AMS) is extremely damaging to Labour as it has dominated the FPTP process since the 1960s and would hold a comfortable majority in the Scottish Parliament under that system (Dyer, 1997). Labour has therefore given up exclusive power with devolution. Others see the AMS system operating as a safety-net for Labour, ensuring it gains large numbers of list seats in a bad Scottish election that coincides with mid-term unpopularity (Curtice, 1997). Similarly, the electoral system makes it difficult for any party to gain a majority in the Scottish Parliament, and therefore presents real problems for the SNP and the pursuit of independence.

The Parliament is elected for a fixed term of four years, with elections held on the first Thursday in May. The Parliament can be dissolved and a general election held if MSPs vote for dissolution with a two-thirds majority or if the Parliament fails to elect a First Minister. If a First

Minister is not chosen after an election or if he/she resigns or the post becomes vacant, there is a twenty-eight-day period for nominations to be made and a new First Minister appointed before an election is held.[9] When vacancies arise in the Parliament, they are filled by two different mechanisms. First-past-the-post vacancies, such as the resignation of the MSP for Ayr, Ian Welsh, in 1999, result in a by-election in the constituency within three months of the vacancy. Vacancies on the regional lists are filled by the election of the next person from that party on the list. The regional returning officer is charged with the task of identifying the next candidate and determining whether they are willing to serve as an MSP. If the MSP who vacated the list was an individual, then the post will remain vacant until the Scottish election.

– Financing the Scottish Parliament –

Vernon Bogdanor (1999: p. 235) described finance as 'the spinal cord of devolution', which would determine the actual autonomy of the devolved institutions. Control of the block grant by UK government, in addition to Treasury control of tax and spending and macroeconomic management, has left the Scottish Parliament extremely weak. Indeed, although the Parliament has one tax power, to vary income tax by 3 per cent, the fact that it has not used this means it effectively has no fiscal autonomy, and this will significantly constrain the impact of the Executive and Parliament within Scotland (Mitchell, 1998). The Executive can choose to allocate its block grant between different policy areas, just as the Scottish Office did, and allocate more to health and education and less to economic development and local government, but this is a low level of autonomy. The Scottish Parliament has limited sources of revenue compared to some other regional governments: Canadian provinces have provincial sales taxes, Spanish autonomous communities were given a significant share of their local income tax in the 1990s, the three Belgian regions also receive a share of locally-raised income tax (Keating, 1998: pp. 121–2). Admittedly, most of these regional governments still depend on block grant mechanisms and transfers from central government but they do have some sources of independent taxation. The difficulty for the Scottish Parliament is that in reality it has no independent source of funds.

The block grant from Westminster is determined by two mechanisms. First, it is produced incrementally using the previous year's budget as a starting-point. Second, the annual increase in the block is determined by the Barnett formula and/or by negotiated increases by the UK government, such as the Comprehensive Spending Review. The Barnett formula was introduced in 1978 as part of the devolution package, and it is used to allocate increased expenditure to Scotland automatically as a proportion of increases in comparable English expenditure increases. Thus, if England receives increased health spending, Scotland will receive a proportional increase in health spending which is added to the existing block grant. The formula used for the proportional allocation is 10.66 per cent, so that Scottish spending will increase by 10.66 per cent of the English increase. The formula is based solely on population, rather than on economic or policy needs or any other rational criteria, and its use is seen to have some benefits for public spending in Scotland. First, there is no need for Scottish ministers, either before or after devolution, to involve themselves in bruising spending battles in Whitehall, although it does mean they are dependent on the negotiating efforts of UK ministers. Second, the Barnett formula and the block grant system are seen to deliver higher levels of public spending in Scotland, something which has irked some English MPs. The Treasury Select Committee, English Tory MPs and even candidates for the post of London mayor all criticised Scotland's public expenditure advantage compared to England. Third, while Barnett delivers spending increases based on increases in English spending in, say, health, the Scottish Executive does not have to spend the increase in the same area but can switch it between departments and policy areas.

Regardless of the merits of the Barnett formula, it is the main mechanism for allocating increased expenditure in Scotland. Besides the block grant, the Parliament lacks fiscal autonomy, and this situation feeds into the limited policy autonomy of the Parliament itself. It can change policy in various ways, but cannot undertake more ambitious initiatives that involve significant changes to tax and spending. It is dependent upon Westminster for revenue and could easily use this fiscal dependency as a means of blaming UK government for limited policy choices or expenditure cuts. Given the manner in which some English politicians honed in on the perceived Scottish spending advantage, the politicisation of Barnett and the block grant process is inevitable. Although it has been contained by Labour holding office in Scotland and Westminster, such containment will not survive a change in government in either institution.

The power to vary Scottish income tax – the 'tartan tax' – is the sole fiscal power available to the Parliament within the Scotland Act 1998. The Executive and Parliament can use local government block grants as a form of revenue-raising, but this is not the same as a tax power. For instance, the Parliament could decide to cut its block grant to local government and reallocate the funds to health. However, this would lead to council tax increases, and these would be resisted by the Executive using its capping powers, leading to cuts in local government services. To some extent, this was what the government did from 1997 to 2000, with increased funds for education and health and less for local government. However, this practice does not necessarily involve new money, just reshuffling of existing funds between budget headings. It also has the essential facet of robbing Peter to pay Paul, as most Scottish local authorities will testify.

The tax power itself is complex and not particularly effective as a revenue-raising mechanism. Indeed, it exists more as a symbol than an effective financing scheme. Rather than utilise sales taxes, property taxes or licences, the Scottish Parliament was saddled with income tax, the most politicised form of taxation in British politics over the last two decades. Since both main British parties engaged in an income-tax cutting auction at the general election, while pushing up indirect taxes, utilisation of the Scottish Parliament's tax power was unlikely. The only party that pledged to use the Parliament's tax powers at the 1999 Scottish election was the SNP. The post-election Labour-Liberal Democrat coalition pledged not to use the tax powers for the first term of the Parliament, but benefitted to some extent from increased spending through UK Chancellor Gordon Brown's Comprehensive Spending Review. The SNP's decision to raise income tax by 1 per cent would have brought an increase in annual spending of £230 million – not a great increase in a Scottish Executive annual budget of £15 billion in 1999–2000, but the only revenue-raising game in town nonetheless.

Using the tax power is a complex exercise in any case, and a costly one. The costs of setting up the mechanisms to collect the tartan tax were estimated at £10 million, with annual running costs of £8 million (Scottish Office, 1997: p. 24). It was also estimated that employers would face costs of up to £50 million to collect the tartan tax through their PAYE schemes. Such expenditures were required in order to identify who Scottish taxpayers actually were. The Scotland Act 1998 contained a number of sections that sought to define a Scottish taxpayer for the purposes of implementing the new tax power: a Scottish taxpayer would be someone who was a UK resident in the tax year in which the tax was levied, and for whom Scotland was the part of the UK with which they had the closest connection in that tax year. The latter criteria would be calculated according to the number of days spent in Scotland versus other parts of the UK and whether their principal residence was in Scotland.[10] The complexity of implementing the tax-varying power, alongside its limited gains and political unpopularity, make it an unlikely policy option for current and future Scottish Executives. The fiscal weakness of the devolved Parliament and its financial dependency on central government look set to continue.

– CONCLUSION –

A political movement supportive of a Scottish Parliament existed for over 100 years before its hopes came to fruition. However, when devolution did finally occur, it did so extremely quickly. Following the 1970s débâcle, the transition from the devolution White Paper to the referendum to the Scotland Act 1998 and the 1999 election was rapid. The scheme proposed in the White Paper in July 1997 was very close to that delivered following the 6 May 1999 election. Assessing the workings of the new devolved arrangements, especially the relationship between Scotland and UK government, remains premature because of the short-lived nature of the new political system, although sections of this text will seek to make preliminary assessments. However, three initial conclusions can be made about the Scotland Act in action.

First, the Act helped to create a more complex system of elections in Scotland as well as one that would produce different electoral outcomes to the FPTP system. The AMS system co-exists with FPTP for Westminster elections, party-list PR for European elections, and the proposed single transferable vote (STV) system for future local elections (Renewing Local Democracy Working Group, 2000). The new Scottish system was also notable in that it made all parties minorities in the Parliament and necessitated a coalition in order to establish a government with a majority on the Mound. Second, the new Parliament is fiscally weak. The lack of independent taxation powers undermines the devolution settlement by limiting the financial and policy autonomy of the Parliament. In time, given changes of government in Scotland and Westminster, this situation will become a problem. Third, the political composition of the Scottish and UK governments means there has been little testing of the overlapping functions of the two sets of Parliaments or testing of Westminster's reserved powers. Again, this is likely to change following future elections, with new governments in office.

– NOTES –

1. Scotland Act 1978, section 38, p. 17.
2. Scotland Act 1998, section 56, pp. 24–5.
3. Scotland Act 1978, section 18, p. 8.
4. Abolition of Poindings and Warrant Sales Bill, *Financial Memorandum*, 24 September 1999.
5. Scotland Act 1998, section 58, p. 26.
6. Subordinate Legislation Committee, *Official Report*, 29 June 1999.
7. Scottish Parliament, *Official Report*, 9 June 1999, vol. 1, no 8, col. 360.

8. Scotland Act 1998 Schedule 1, section 7, p. 67.
9. Scotland Act 1998, section 3, p. 2 and section 46, pp. 20–1.
10. See the complex set of criteria in the Scotland Act 1998, section 75, pp. 34–5, which would become a tax lawyers' playground if the tartan tax was levied.

CHAPTER 3

The Scottish Executive: government and administration after devolution

– INTRODUCTION –

Devolution involved the creation of a new Scottish government in addition to a Scottish Parliament. This new government was named the Scottish Executive and comprises ministers and civil servants. The establishment of the Executive was not a difficult operation as it merely involved transferring the existing Scottish Office from UK government to the new devolved government. Thus, instead of being faced with starting from scratch in terms of creating a bureaucracy, finding premises and recruiting civil servants as the Parliament had to, the creation of the Scottish Executive was relatively simple. The existence and growth of the Scottish Office since the late twentieth century meant that Scotland enjoyed its own government institutions long before devolution. It was even argued that the centralisation of the Scottish Office in Edinburgh in 1939 had provided Scotland with a proto-government of its own, that would facilitate self-government (Hanham, 1969).

While the prior existence of the Scottish Office greatly assisted the Scottish Executive post-devolution, it was also significant for the changes it brought to Scottish society. The Scottish Office was not merely a government bureaucracy but a forum for political action. It became the focus for pressure groups and social organisations and assisted in the maintenance of a distinctive Scottish civil society. Much of the business of the Scottish Office was associated with the historic institutions of Scotland, such as education and the legal system, which involved a wide range of organisations such as the Scottish teacher's union, the Educational Institute for Scotland (EIS) and the Law Society of Scotland, as well as local government. With the growth of government in the twentieth century, the Scottish Office moved into agriculture, economic development, the environment, health and social services, housing, planning and transport. It therefore became a forum for lobbying and policy negotiation with the National Farmers Union of Scotland, a wide range of business organisations and trades unions, housing associations, and environmental organisations such as Friends of the Earth and the World Wide Fund for Nature. As the Scottish Office gained functions, pressure groups associated with those functions gathered around it, and it also reacted to its increased functions by seeking dialogue with a wide range of groups, in addition to widening the role of government in Scotland through the creation of a large number of quangos that will be discussed below. Such developments were the background to the establishment of the new Scottish Executive and Parliament, with the Executive inheriting a government bureaucracy, quangos and a range of interactions with pressure groups from the existing Scottish Office.

– FORMING THE FIRST SCOTTISH EXECUTIVE –

In contrast to the usual, straightforward post-election developments associated with British politics – the prospective Prime Minister visiting the Palace and appointing the Cabinet – the period after the Scottish election was filled with a week of coalition negotiations. These negotiations were not as protracted as they could have been because the election result itself removed the SNP from any coalition role. Similarly, the Conservatives had ruled out participation in any coalition administration in the Scottish parliament. Therefore, rather than the post-election negotiations offering three coalition scenarios – a Labour-Liberal Democrat coalition, SNP-Liberal Democrat coalition, or minority administration – there was only the prospect of a Labour minority administration or a coalition deal between Labour and the Liberal Democrats.

The Scottish election campaign featured a good deal of discussion and speculation about the formation of a coalition government after 6 May 1999. On frequent occasions in the media, and especially in televised party debates, Liberal Democrat figures were challenged over the coalition issue in terms of their potential coalition partner and the policy agreements which were likely to occur. While the SNP had appeared a possible coalition partner for the Liberal Democrats before the election campaign, the party's weak poll ratings during the election rendered it an unlikely coalition partner. However, as the SNP's coalition hopes receded, it sought to stress its areas of policy convergence with the Liberal Democrats and amplify the policy distance between the Liberal Democrats and Labour in the hope of dissuading the party from negotiating a coalition with Labour.

One thing that was clear about the Liberal Democrats' approach to coalition was that the party had accepted the logic of its electoral situation, especially given the nature of the electoral system which the party had helped to design in the Constitutional Convention. The Liberal Democrats discussed and agreed the party's approach to coalition negotiations at its Executive meeting on 30 January 1999, and the *Coalition Framework* document clearly mapped out the party's approach to coalition discussions after the election. Therefore, following the election, the party had a clear process for coalition talks, which had been agreed in advance of the election. As a result, the party appeared prepared for coalition, rather than merely being rushed into rapid discussions. Such preparation was especially important because of the need to manage intra-party relations, especially potential divisions between the leadership and negotiating team and the rest of the party, particularly Liberal Democrat activists.

The *Coalition Framework* document indicated that the Liberal Democrats would initially seek to undertake coalition discussions with the party with the largest number of seats in the parliament. If no formal understanding could be reached, then discussions would take place with the second largest party. If such discussions did not bear fruit, then the Liberal Democrats would not participate in the Scottish Executive, but would promote the party's position outside the government (Scottish Liberal Democrats, 1999b). The documents also outlined two main facets of the negotiation process. First, the Liberal Democrats would only enter a coalition if there was agreement over a joint programme for government which would run for the full four years of the parliament. Second, the party would hold a consultation process before determining whether it would enter into the coalition agreement. In terms of the timescale for coalition negotiations, the Liberal Democrat MSPs were scheduled to meet on Saturday 8 May to establish a negotiating team and discuss proposals for the joint programme for government. On Sunday 9 May, the MSPs met with the party's Scottish Executive and Policy Committee to discuss coalition terms and appoint a negotiating team. It comprised the party leader, Jim Wallace; three MSPs, Nicol Stephen, Ross Finnie and Iain Smith; two representatives of the party's Scottish Executive, Denis Robertson Sullivan and Andy Myles; and the party convenor, Ian Yuill. This group was whittled down to just five in the face-to-face negotiations with Labour, although they also met with the wider negotiating team and any coalition agreement had to be agreed by the party's MSPs and executive and involved consultations with a range of party organisations.

The coalition negotiations took place very quickly and the process was completed within a week, despite various hitches along the way. When one reflects upon the fact that coalition arrangements in some European states have taken months to negotiate, the speed of government formation in the

Scottish Parliament is evident. Labour's Donald Dewar and the Liberal Democrats' Jim Wallace had a brief telephone conversation as early as 7 May 1999. It was followed by a head-to-head meeting over the format for coalition discussions on the morning of Sunday 9 May, then by a meeting of the key negotiators that evening to outline key areas for coalition discussion (*Sunday Times Scotland*, 16 May 1999). There then followed three days of negotiations over issues such as tuition fees, which were a continuous stumbling block, the Private Finance Initiative, tolls for the Skye Bridge, and proportional representation for local government elections (Finnie and McLeish, 1999). The two negotiating teams drafted the Partnership document on Thursday 13 May, gained agreement from their Scottish Parliamentary colleagues, and the two party leaders signed the document at the press launch in the National Museum of Scotland on Friday 14 May: exactly a week after the election result was known. Of course, the fact that the Liberal Democrats had voted with Labour to elect Donald Dewar as First minister on 13 May was an indication that the coalition was up and running, in addition to the earlier election of Sir David Steel as Presiding Officer. Dewar was elected with a combined total of seventy-one votes, with only one Liberal Democrat MSP, Keith Raffan, failing to support him.

The coalition discussions took place under certain internal and external pressures. Internally, the parties were under pressure not to concede certain policy stances, the most notable case being the Liberal Democrats and the issue of student tuition fees, with pressure from MSPs, party officials and members. Externally, the parties were pressurised into a deal by their UK leaders, with each being seen to encourage a coalition deal. Liberal Democrat leader Paddy Ashdown was thought to be encouraging a deal with Labour in Scotland to ensure the continuation of Labour-Liberal Democrat cooperation at Westminster (*Scotland on Sunday*, 16 May 1999). Labour's stance in the coalition talks was seen to be guided by London and the hand of the Prime Minister and his office, following a statement from his Press Secretary that the Prime Minister was involved in the coalition talks (*The Herald*, 11 May 1999). There were also indications that coalition discussions between Labour and the Liberal Democrats had actually taken place before the 1997 election (McIntyre, 1999).

As a result of the coalition agreement, the Liberal Democrats faced three different government/opposition roles in Britain: constructive opponents at Westminster, government in Scotland, and opposition and then coalition in the Welsh Assembly. Each involved a delicate political balance involving potential conflicts. The Liberal Democrats could easily be opposing legislation in one parliament or assembly that they were supporting in another. This development is, of course, the logic of devolution, but it does place pressures of consistency upon the party. It might find itself supporting a Labour policy in Scotland, which it 'constructively' opposes in London and vetoed in Cardiff. Student tuition fees and EU funding were two obvious examples. Also, the need to retain Lib-Lab cooperation at Westminster in the hope of implementing the Jenkins Commission report on electoral reform for Westminster elections was a constant pressure on coalition relations within the Scottish Executive. Clearly, there was a bigger political game being played out at Westminster than merely sustaining the Labour-Liberal Democrat coalition in Edinburgh.[1]

THE COALITION AGREEMENT: THE PARTNERSHIP FOR SCOTLAND

The coalition agreement, published on 14 May 1999, contained the broad framework of policies and operating arrangements for the new Labour-Liberal Democrat government. It outlined the main objectives of the government in the various policy areas of the Scottish Executive such as education, health, enterprise, open government and justice. The winners and losers from the coalition agreement are difficult to discern. For example, Labour's Scottish election manifesto was extremely limited in terms of clear policy goals and financial commitments, and it was merely committed to five policies: 20,000 modern apprenticeships, a Scottish Drugs Enforcement Agency, 100 new school developments and at least four modern computers for every Scottish class, eight new hospital developments and a twenty-four-hour NHS helpline, and no rise in income tax in the first term of the Scottish Parliament. The Liberal Democrat manifesto was more detailed, yet there was scope for agreement in many areas. Two areas of conflict stood out: student finance and the use of the tax powers of the Parliament.

The Liberal Democrats' commitment to remove tuition fees was frequently trumpeted at the 1999 election, and the party leader, Jim Wallace, made unequivocal statements that tuition fees would be abolished after the 6 May election. Coalition negotiations with a Labour Party committed to retain student tuition fees was therefore a major stumbling block to coalition formation. The escape route agreed by the two parties involved the establishment, as part of the partnership agreement, of the Cubie Committee to review student finance and access to education. Throughout the period of the committee's existence and following its report, there was enormous pressure on the Liberal Democrats to retain their pre-election commitment, which they did in their submission to the Cubie Committee.[2] The party was frequently criticised for selling out its principles in exchange for government office, and the tuition fees issue was a permanent problem that threatened to disrupt and bring down the coalition government during its first eight months in office. When the Cubie Committee reported in December 1999, it made fifty-one recommendations for student finance and university funding (Independent Committee of Inquiry into Student Finance, 1999).

It was up to the Scottish Executive to determine how it responded to these proposals, and it established a special ministerial committee to discuss student finance. This comprised three Labour ministers – Donald Dewar, Finance Minister Jack McConnell and Minister for Enterprise and Lifelong Learning Henry McLeish – while the Liberal Democrats were represented by party leader and Deputy First Minister Jim Wallace, Rural Affairs Minister Ross Finnie and Deputy Minister for Lifelong Learning Nicol Stephen. The committee met on a number of occasions before producing its own proposals for student finance (Scottish Executive, 2000). Some of these proposals were different enough from the Cubie Report for critics to wonder why the Scottish Executive had bothered to hold an independent inquiry in the first place. However, the Executive's proposals were agreed between the two parties and the coalition survived.

The second major policy difficulty for the coalition government involved the financing of the Scottish Executive's programme and the use of the Parliament's tax powers. The Liberal Democrats' manifesto had included the option of using the tax powers to raise extra revenue for funding public services. The party had fought successive Westminster elections committed to raising income tax by 1p to fund education. It committed itself to review the financial situation in advance of the first Scottish budget in spring 2000, with the option of using the tax powers if it was felt necessary to boost spending on health and education. Aside from the tax issue, the party was committed to increasing the health budget by £80 million in 2000–1 and then by £100 million in each successive year, as well as boosting the education budget by £170 million for each year of the Parliament (Scottish Liberal Democrats, 1999a: p. 35). The partnership agreement revealed that an extra £80 million would be allocated to the education budget, although it said nothing on increased health expenditure. The partnership document also stated that the coalition government would not use the Parliament's tax powers for the first term of the Parliament (Scottish Liberal Democrats, 1999c: p. 10). Therefore, the Liberal Democrats gained some increase in funding for education, but had to agree to rule out the use of the tax power, leaving the Scottish Executive reliant on the block grant for Westminster as its sole source of finance for 1999–2003. In time, the Treasury-controlled Comprehensive Spending Review was also to deliver more resources for the Scottish Executive, particularly in the area of health spending.

– MINISTERS AND THE FIRST SCOTTISH EXECUTIVE –

The Scottish Executive comprises twelve members, supplemented by ten deputy ministers, which includes two legal officers: the Lord Advocate and the Solicitor General. The Scottish Executive contains a number of distinctive features, partly as a result of the establishment of a coalition government after the 6 May elections. First, the Labour-Liberal Democrat coalition necessitated a balanced Executive, with places for Liberal Democrat MSPs. The Liberal Democrats sought Executive posts in the coalition negotiations and were adamant about holding power within the Executive rather than merely supporting Labour ministers and legislation. The allocation of ministerial posts in the Executive was balanced to reflect the relative popularity of Labour and the Liberal Democrats at the election. This situation gave the Liberal Democrats around a fifth of the ministerial posts on both the twelve member Executive and the government total when taking into account the deputy ministers: rather more proportionally than the party gained at the Scottish election.

Second, the allocation of portfolios and places had to reflect Liberal Democrat as well as Labour policy preferences, and involved some innovations. The most obvious innovation involved Jim Wallace's appointment as Deputy First Minister. This post was not included in the Scotland Act, which only mentioned a First Minister with powers to establish a range of ministerial posts within the Scottish Executive, but was established to signify Wallace's role as the joint leader of the coalition partnership. The Deputy First Minister was given the Justice portfolio, but was also capable of playing a wider-ranging role within the Executive to ensure that the Liberal Democrats were represented across all aspects of the coalition's work. The post would also function as a mechanism for conflict resolution and coalition management within the Executive. The coalition agreement *Partnership for Scotland* gave the following definition of the Deputy First Minister's role within the overall Executive:

> It is essential that the Deputy First Minister is kept fully informed across the range of Executive business so that he can engage in any issue where he considers that appropriate. The procedures to be established for handling business within the Executive will require officials to copy all relevant material to the offices of the leaders of both parties in the Executive. The Deputy First Minister will have appropriate official, political and specialist support to enable him to discharge his role effectively.
>
> (Scottish Liberal Democrats, 1999c: p. 11)

Of course, expecting Jim Wallace to act as Minister for Justice and to play a wide-ranging watching brief over all other policy areas within the Executive is a demanding task. Despite the appointment of a Deputy Minister for Justice and the promise of official, political and specialist support within the Executive, it will be difficult for the Liberal Democrat leader to cover the red boxes dealing with the Justice department, let alone those of all others in the Scottish Executive. Similarly, making the Liberal Democrat leader the Deputy First Minister had implications for Labour in two ways. First, had Labour formed the Scottish Executive on its own, the post would have identified Donald Dewar's deputy within the party and therefore his successor as Labour leader, and not being able to use the position created something of a succession crisis. Second, the fact that the First Minister had to stand down from office with heart trouble for some months in 2000 meant that the Deputy First Minister became the Acting First Minister. Thus, the Liberal Democrat minority chaired the Scottish cabinet, answered First Minister's questions in the chamber on behalf of the government and was effectively the leader of the Executive. Although Wallace's spell as Acting First Minister was a success, for Labour MSPs it was perhaps too much a case of the tail wagging the dog.

Coalition meant that the composition of the first Executive involved internal balances of ministerial portfolios, with Labour's Henry McLeish balanced as Enterprise and Lifelong Learning Minister by the Liberal Democrats' Nicol Stephen as a means of reconciling inter-party differences and concerns over student tuition fees. The Minister for Rural Affairs, Liberal Democrat Ross Finnie, was balanced by his deputy, Labour's John Home Robertson, in the area of Fisheries, although the notion of appointing a distinctive Minister for fishing was an attractive one, especially as a challenge to the SNP who had become the most vocal supporters of the Scottish fishing industry. The allocation and balancing of ministerial portfolios also followed some interesting lines, for example Labour gained sole control of key domestic policy areas such as social inclusion, health, primary and secondary education and local government. Meanwhile, the Liberal Democrats' control of Justice gave them influence over freedom of information, while the Rural Affairs portfolio assisted their position as the party of rural Scotland – although this is balanced by the fact that the Deputy Minister for the Highlands and Islands was Labour. The new Executive announced in October 2000 also balanced portfolios, with Justice, Rural Affairs and Education all balanced between the two coalition parties.

Table 3.1 Scottish Executive ministers October 2000–

<u>Scottish Executive Cabinet</u>

First Minister	Henry McLeish
Deputy First Minister and Minister for Justice	Jim Wallace
Minister for Finance and Local Government	Angus MacKay
Minister for Health and Community Care	Susan Deacon
Minister for Social Justice	Jackie Baillie
Minister for Transport	Sarah Boyack
Minister for Enterprise and Lifelong Learning	Wendy Alexander
Minister for Rural Affairs	Ross Finnie
Minister for Education, Europe and External Affairs	Jack McConnell
Minister for the Environment	Sam Galbraith
Minister for Parliament	Tom McCabe
Lord Advocate	Lord Boyd

<u>Deputy Ministers</u>

Deputy to Minister for Justice	Iain Gray
Deputy to Minister for Health and Community Care	Malcolm Chisholm
Deputy Minister for Enterprise and Lifelong Learning	Alasdair Morrison
Deputy Minister for Social Justice	Margaret Curran
Deputy Minister for Rural Development	Rhona Brankin
Deputy Minister for Education, Europe and External Affairs	Nicol Stephen
Deputy Minister for Finance and Local Government	Peter Peacock
Deputy Minister for Parliament	Tavish Scott
Solicitor General	Iain Davidson

As both the Scottish Executive and Parliament were only recently established, the issue of ministerial career patterns has not been to the fore. However, over the longer term the composition of the Scottish Executive must change. At Westminster, ministers usually last from two to two and a half years in their posts before being reshuffled, and in time the Scottish Executive must face a similar situation, with ministers promoted, sacked, demoted or forced to resign. In time, it will be possible to identify the extent of ministerial careers, although there is obviously only a small number of politicians available for service within the Scottish Executive as a result of the limited size of the Parliament itself. For example, the current parliament of 129 MSPs does not include 129 potential ministers. The Presiding Officer and his team of two deputies, and the four members of the Scottish Parliamentary Corporate Body (see Chapter 4) reduce the number of potential ministers to 121. Election results and government composition limits the available number even further to the seventy-one Labour and Liberal Democrat MSPs (not including the Presiding Officer). Thus, the current coalition government needed to appoint twenty ministers out of a total of only seventy-two MSPs. The chances of office were thus high for MSPs within the coalition, with reshuffles holding the potential for promotion for backbenchers or for junior ministers. In addition, the ministerial and parliamentary career ladders could present opportunities for gamekeepers to turn into poachers and vice versa, with committee convenors in some policy areas becoming ministers, and former ministers taking command of particular policy areas through their appointment as a committee convenor in the Parliament. Such developments will doubtless occur in such a small Parliament, especially one that is set to shrink in size in the future as the number of Scottish seats is reduced in order to address the West Lothian question (Curtice, 1998).

Not surprisingly, most ministers in the Executive have never previously held government office. Henry McLeish and Sam Galbraith were formerly ministers at the Scottish Office and Lord Hardie was previously Lord Advocate, but the remaining ministers were novices. Tom McCabe and Peter Peacock had previously run major local authorities, but most of the remaining ministers were elected to their first public office in 1999. Experience at Westminster was not a guide to elevation to the Scottish Executive, with a number of dual-mandate members, for example John McAllion, Malcolm Chisholm and Mike Watson kept out of the Executive though Chisholm became a minister in October 2000. Some MSPs were given the opportunity to serve as committee convenors, which was a useful substitute for ministerial office. However, the initial composition of the Scottish Executive has created some longer-term problems. First, the age profile of the senior and junior ministers is extremely youthful – fact that irritated a number of older MSPs on the Labour and Liberal Democrat backbenchers who saw themselves usurped by the young turks – and sustaining this age profile may be difficult to achieve. Second, the quality and experience of some MSPs elected in 1999 was open to question, and many were perhaps too inexperienced to hold government office: hence the mishandling of the section 2a/28 issue. However, this situation will change as the current crop of MSPs and ministers grow into their role.

– THE SCOTTISH EXECUTIVE CABINET –

The internal workings of the Scottish Executive were not a prominent feature of the government's first year in office. Weekly Cabinet meetings of the Executive and patterns of Cabinet discussions await further academic investigation. However, like the UK Cabinet, the Scottish Executive Cabinet divided into a range of sub-cabinets to deal with particular issues. The Executive did not replicate the UK Cabinet's permanent committees, but established short-term and semi-permanent ministerial groups in a number of distinct areas, largely organised around key policy goals rather than policy areas (see Table 3.2). Some groups were highly specific and lasted a matter of months, such as those dealing with student finance and section 2a/28; others were intended as longer-term bodies such as that dealing with the Scottish budget. All are capable of making decisions with the authority of the full Scottish Executive Cabinet and involve the full range of junior ministers. The need for Liberal Democrat representation across all of these committees doubtless stretched the party's ministers in the Executive.

The Cabinet itself is comprised of the First Minister, the Deputy First Minister, nine senior ministers and the Lord Advocate (see Table 3.1). Cabinet business can involve any area of collective responsibility within the Scottish Executive, but discussion usually revolves around sensitive policy issues, changes to the government's policy or objectives, changes to the Executive's spending plans, or policies which require primary legislation.[3] In addition, Cabinet exists as a forum for the resolution of policy disputes that have not been settled in ministerial committees, although this is not always successful. For example, it was reported that the section 2a/28 issue so heavily divided the Labour members of the Cabinet that Liberal Democrats were asked to vacate the meeting so that Labour could agree its political line before it was put to full Cabinet (Sunday Herald, 27 February 2000). Finally, the agenda for the weekly cabinet meetings has to be agreed by the First

Minister and Deputy First Minister, providing a further monitoring role for the Liberal Democrats at the heart of government.

Table 3.2 Ministerial committees and working groups 1999–2000 (pre-reshuffle)[4]

Student Finance	Donald Dewar (chair), Jack McConnell, Henry McLeish, Jim Wallace, Ross Finnie, Nicol Stephen
Poverty and Inclusion Task Force	Wendy Alexander (chair), Sam Galbraith, Susan Deacon, Henry McLeish, Jack McConnell, Ross Finnie, Jackie Baillie
Digital Scotland	Sam Galbraith (chair), Henry McLeish, Wendy Alexander, Ross Finnie, Jack McConnell, Peter Peacock, Susan Deacon
Budget	Tom McCabe (chair), Jack McConnell, Ross Finnie
Section 28	Tom McCabe (chair), Wendy Alexander, Sam Galbraith, Ross Finnie

– COLLECTIVE RESPONSIBILITY –

The Scottish Executive operates on the principle of collective responsibility in a similar way to the UK Cabinet, with all ministers required to support Executive policy and decisions. However, there is one significant difference: Scotland has a coalition government. Therefore arrangements for collective responsibility have to bridge party boundaries and ensure that policy discussion and decisionmaking would take account of both sides of the coalition. Equally, it is important for arrangements to operate to prevent policy disputes escalating into party splits within the Scottish Executive that would damage the coalition's existence. The First Minister and Deputy First Minister have an important role in ensuring that collective responsibility functions effectively within the coalition Executive. Ministers are required to keep the two leading ministers informed of sensitive decisions and policy advice, with the First Minister and Deputy First Minister able to intervene in policy areas when they consider it necessary.[5] Such intervention can involve memoranda, ad hoc meetings of ministers or full discussion of an issue at Scottish Cabinet. More generally, decisionmaking between ministers relies upon the flow of information and correspondence between ministers, with the Permanent Secretary of the Scottish Executive and the Executive Secretariat responsible for ensuring that ministerial decisions remain consistent with overall government policy and objectives.

– The executive secretariat –

Analysis of the 'core executive' has been a prominent feature of recent studies of British government, with examination of the Cabinet Office and Number 10 Policy Unit as examples of the core of UK government decisionmaking (Smith, 1999). Within the devolved administration in Scotland, the Executive Secretariat is the nearest the Scottish Executive has to a Cabinet Office. It acts as a coordinating mechanism for the Executive across the areas of finance, legal support, personnel and so on, and also operates as the body responsible for liaising with the Scottish Parliament and coordinating relations with UK government and the European Union: administering the various concordats, the Joint Ministerial Committees, Scottish participation in the British-Irish Council, and the operation of Scotland House in Brussels. It is comprised of policy divisions such as the External Relations Division, the Constitutional Policy and Parliamentary Liaison Division, and the Cabinet Secretariat. The Executive Secretariat has a coordinating role within the Scottish Executive, monitoring Ministerial committees and arranging ad hoc meetings on sensitive issues. It also services the Cabinet and the range of ministerial committees established by the Executive.

– Special advisers –

One area of great controversy within the Scottish Executive in its first year involved the role of special advisers. The Executive was able to recruit up to twelve special advisers to staff its Policy Unit, which was intended to operate on two levels. First, it was intended to act as a collective body for ministers in relation to policy and communications advice. Here, it was designed as a shared resource – rather than each minister having his/her own spin doctors and policy advisers, the Policy Unit was intended to provide a central source of advice to prevent inter ministerial briefings (although this was not successful). Second, it was intended to be an institution responsible for briefing ministers on the big issues of government, such as examining long-term social and economic trends affecting the Scottish Executive's objectives. However, the Policy Unit quickly became controversial as a result of the cost of special advisers and the various sackings and resignations within the unit in its first year of operation. The controversy centred around disputes between the Unit's chief of staff, John Rafferty, and chief media spokesperson David Whitton, the subsequent high-profile sacking of Rafferty by First Minister Donald Dewar, and the resignation of its strategic communications adviser, Philip Chalmers, over drink-driving convictions. The new chief of staff, Brian Fitzpatrick, was also accused of seeking to influence judicial appointments through the Policy Unit. Whether the new advisors appointed by First Minister Henry McLeish courted similar controversy remains to be seen.

– THE SCOTTISH ADMINISTRATION POST-DEVOLUTION –

Although the new Scottish Executive involved some reorganisation of the previous Scottish Office administrative structure, such reorganisation was not particularly extensive. For example, the Scottish Office was organised into five main departments before devolution: Agriculture, Environment and Fisheries; Development; Education and Industry; Health; and Home; as well as a Central Services department. This structure has not changed very much with devolution: the Scottish Executive comprises Corporate Services; Development; Education; Enterprise and Lifelong Learning; Finance; Health; Justice; and Rural Affairs, as well as the Executive Secretariat. The structure is remarkably similar to the former Scottish Office administration, as is the fact that ministerial portfolios do not follow departmental boundaries. In the pre-devolution Scottish Office, ministers often balanced large numbers of policy portfolios crossing departmental boundaries; under devolution, some ministers of the Scottish Executive can be identified with specific departments, acting as heads of departments in some cases, while others cannot. For example, the Education, Enterprise and Lifelong Learning, Finance, Justice and Rural Affairs ministers all have their own departments. However, the Minister for Social Justice shares the Development Department with the Ministers for Environment and Transport.

Geographically, the Scottish Executive is located in Edinburgh, as was the former Scottish Office; the only department outside Edinburgh is the Department for Enterprise and Lifelong Learning which is in Glasgow. This situation led to some dissatisfaction in other parts of Scotland, with Edinburgh seen as the sole beneficiary of the economic boom associated with devolution, and there was pressure to relocate Scottish Executive departments around Scotland. The dispersal of Scottish Executive departments was popularised by the Conservatives at the 1999 election, but was not adopted by the coalition government, because it believed that retaining the existing geographical locations of the administration had three benefits. First, it allowed the administration to remain close to the Parliament, facilitating parliamentary access to civil servants and ministers. Second, the dispersal of departments would have clashed with the reorganisation of the Scottish Office into the Scottish Executive, with the changes to departments and new ministerial portfolios that followed the elections of 1999. Third, the geographical proximity of departments prevented the fragmentation of the Scottish Executive and the unnecessary promotion of departmental rivalries. For many years, the Scottish Office had existed as a federal administration, with few central links or coordination between departments, and various reorganisations of the Scottish Office's structure had sought to promote a more corporate culture within government (Parry, 1987). Departmental dispersal could well have fragmented the corporate approach to decisionmaking, during a period in which interdepartmental coordination and more 'holistic government' (Leicester and MacKay, 1998), were seen to be important hallmarks of the new, devolved government.

– THE CIVIL SERVICE AND THE SCOTTISH EXECUTIVE –

The establishment of a Scottish Executive and Parliament did not involve the creation of a separate Scottish civil service. Significantly, the Scottish administration remains staffed by UK civil servants, which resulted from the fact that the Scottish Office was transferred from the central government to the Scottish Executive: a much simpler step than having to establish a Scottish administration from scratch. Like its predecessor in 1978, the Scotland Act 1998 retained Scottish Executive civil servants within the home civil service rather than establishing a separate Scottish civil service. This situation was seen to be beneficial for senior civil servants, maintaining their expanded sphere of activity within the wider UK civil service, and giving them opportunities to serve in Whitehall departments such as the Foreign Office, Trade and Industry, and the Treasury. Such service would allow the transfer of policy expertise into the Scottish Executive administration as well as allowing a wider pool of potential staff for the Scottish Executive than existing Scottish Office civil servants (Constitution Unit, 1996: p. 115).

The retention of an integrated UK civil service also assisted the Scottish Executive in maintaining links with UK government. While the Scottish Office/Executive civil service has its distinctions within UK administration, remaining a part of the home civil service should retain a common ethos and working practices to assist the devolution process. Civil servants certainly act as an important communications network on policy initiatives between Edinburgh and London, although they might also act as a conservative force in this area. Indeed, one question for civil servants will be how they operate under different political regimes. Currently civil servants within the Scottish Executive and UK government operate under Labour administrations, so that their UK status as civil servants is unimportant. But how would they behave under an SNP administration, given their UK civil

Table 3.3 Scottish Executive departments and responsibilities 2000

Scottish Executive Development Department

Ministers: Sarah Boyack, Jackie Baillie, Margaret Curran
Head of Department: Kenneth MacKenzie

Responsibilities

Building control
Housing
Local government
Planning
Social inclusion
Transport
EU structural funds management

Scottish Executive Education Department

Ministers: Jack McConnell, Nicol Stephen, Alisdair Morrison, Allan Wilson
Head of Department: John Elvidge

Responsibilities

Primary and secondary
Schooling
Children and young people
Arts
Culture
Sport
Gaelic
Broadcasting
Social work
Children's panels

Scottish Executive Finance Department

Ministers: Angus MacKay, Peter Peacock
Head of Department: Peter Collings

Responsibilities

Budget allocation
Accounts
Internal audit
Regulation of public bodies

Scottish Executive Enterprise and Lifelong Learning Department

Ministers: Wendy Alexander, Alasdair Morrison
Head of Department: Eddie Frizzell

Responsibilities

Economic development
Inward investment
Exports
Small business
Information technology
Regional Selective Assistance
Local Enterprise Companies
Tourism
Further and higher education
Locate in Scotland
SAAS
SHEFCE
SQA
Scottish Trade International
Scottish Enterprise and HIE

Scottish Executive Health Department

Ministers: Susan Deacon, Malcolm Chisholm
Head of Department: vacant

Responsibilities

Community Care
The National Health Service
Social work
Voluntary sector

Scottish Executive Justice Department

Ministers: Jim Wallace, Iain Gray
Head of Department: Jim Gallagher

Responsibilities

Civil law
Criminal justice
Scottish court administration
Fire
Police
Prison service
Emergency planning
Legal Aid system
Scottish Land Court
Scottish Prison Service
Scottish Court Service

Scottish Executive Rural Affairs Department

Ministers: Ross Finnie, Sam Galbraith, Rhona Brankin
Head of Department: John Graham

Responsibilities

Agriculture
Environment
Fisheries

service status and the fact that senior civil servants are ultimately respon-sible to the Prime Minister of the UK government rather than to the First Minister of the Scottish Executive? Clearly, there is potential for divided civil service loyalties in future, although, the fact that government depart-ments were given more autonomy over their civil servants in the 1990s has lessened central controls over the Scottish Executive bureaucracy (Con-stitution Unit, 1996: p. 115).

The senior civil servants within the Scottish Executive administration exhibit considerable levels of continuity with the former Scottish Office and with the civil service machine generally. The Permanent Secretary of the Scottish Executive, Muir Russell, is a career civil servant who joined the Scottish Office in 1970 and became Permanent Secretary before devolu-tion. The other nine heads of department at the time of the formation of the Scottish Executive were also career civil servants with their roots in the Scottish Office. Jim Gallagher joined the Scottish Office in 1976 and worked in the Home, Development and Science departments before becoming Head of the Justice Department in 2000; Geoff Scaife was chief executive of the NHS in Scotland both before and after devolution (until mid-2000), and originally joined the civil service in London in 1968; John Graham joined the Scottish Office in 1972 and was Head of Agriculture, Environment and Fisheries before taking over at Rural Affairs; Kenneth MacKenzie joined the Scottish Office in 1965, and served in all Scottish Office departments, as well as the Cabinet Office in London, before becoming Head of the Development Department of the Scottish Office, and he continued in this role in the Scottish Executive; Agnes Robson joined the Scottish Office in 1985 and became Principal Establishment Officer responsible for Corporate Services in 2000; Peter Collings joined the UK civil service in 1975, moved to the Scottish Office in 1977 and became Head of Finance in 1998; finally, Robert Gordon joined the Scottish Office in 1973 and was appointed to the new position of Head of the Executive Secretariat in 1999. While most Scottish Office senior civil servants exhibit close continuity with the previous Scottish Office structure, there were some changes with devolution. For example, Eddie Frizzell joined the Scottish Office in 1976 and then gained experience in executive agencies such as Locate in Scotland and the Scottish Prison Service before becoming Head of Enterprise and Lifelong Learning in 1999.

The senior Scottish Office civil servants had a number of common characteristics. First, they were all career civil servants within the Scottish Office, serving in different Scottish Office departments before it was transferred to the Scottish Executive. Second, none of them had any private sector experience: although some had experience in executive agencies/quangos such as Scottish Homes, Locate in Scotland and the Scottish Development Agency, experience has been gained solely within the public sector. There were also some differences between the senior civil servants. Although they were all members of the Scottish Office for substantial periods of time, only half were educated at Scottish universities; indeed, three of the senior civil servants had an Oxbridge background. Only five out of ten senior civil servants had civil service experience in London, of whom two were involved in the Cabinet Office under Labour and provided a strong link to the central administrative structures associated with the devolution arrangements of course, all of the others would have had frequent dealings with UK government departments in London as part of their Scottish Office work, but they did reflect an established trend for civil servants to spend most of their careers moving around the different Scottish Office departments rather than between Scotland and Whitehall (Kellas, 1984: p. 74). Devolution may deepen this trend; it is certainly unlikely to reverse it.

Of course, devolution is not the only development set to affect civil servants in the Scottish Executive: both the Scottish and UK governments are committed to modernising the civil service. The civil service component of the Scottish Executive was criticised for being too conservative, burdened by Westminster conventions and practices, and lacking public management experience outside the Scottish Office: features that would not assist devolution's need for a more innovative and adaptable civil service (MacKay, 1999). There has been encouragement for a recruitment revolution in the Scottish Executive, with five-year contracts, secondments, reintegration of quangos into the Executive, and new training practices (MacKay, 1999). Such reforms were intended to produce a more effective civil service machinery through an interchange of staff and ideas across the public and private sectors that contrasted with the relatively closed world of Scottish civil servants that revolved around the former Scottish Office. The Scottish Executive initiated debate on its agenda for modernising government in February 2000, and the then Finance Minister, Jack McConnell, also announced a £25 million fund to encourage the modernisation of government across the public sector. Modernisation stretched from greater use of information technology to get government on-line, to use of smart cards, and one-stop offices for government services to suggestions of fundamental reforms of the senior civil service within the Scottish Executive.[6] In connection with devolution, such developments will bring substantial change to the civil service in the Scottish Executive.

– THE SCOTTISH EXECUTIVE AND PUBLIC BODIES –

Scottish administration does not merely include the main departments of the Scottish Executive, but also a number of executive agencies or quangos for which it Executive is directly responsible. These agencies are funded and tasked by the Scottish Executive but are largely autonomous of its control. Some of these bodies are historic, others were established from the late 1980s onwards by the Conservative government in order to bring about a division between core policymaking departments and policy delivery agencies. Responsibility for service delivery was transferred to autonomous agencies that would operate on more private-sector principles – examples of the latter phenomenon included the Benefits Agency and the Employment Service. Scottish Executive departments have executive agencies, just as the Scottish Office did before devolution: the Rural Affairs Department is responsible for executive agencies such as the Scottish Agricultural Science Agency, Fisheries Research Services and Scottish Fisheries Protection Service, while the Justice Department has executive agencies such as the Scottish Prison Service and the Scottish Courts Service.

Besides agencies that were hived off from civil service departments, there are a large number of quangos or non-departmental public bodies (NDPBs) active in Scotland. They involve a broad range of organisations, with some attached to the Scottish Executive, some part of UK government and some floating between the two spheres of governance (Hogwood, 1999). Some are executive bodies with significant policy and expenditure powers such as Historic Scotland, the Scottish Arts Council, the Scottish Higher Education Funding Council and Sport Scotland; others are advisory bodies or tribunals, and these different types of quangos have quite varied roles, evident from their different size in terms of personnel and budgets. For example, there is a substantial difference between an executive NDPB such as Scottish Enterprise, which employed around 1,500 people and received government funding of £404 million in 1998–9, and an advisory NDPB such as the Historic Buildings Council for Scotland which had twelve part-time members and a budget of £15,000. Executive NDPBs were responsible for £1.9 billion of expenditure in 1998–9.

In this way, NDPBs are an extremely varied species in Scotland, partly the product of administrative devolution to the Scottish Office in the twentieth century, and the Scottish Executive is responsible for a total of eighty-three different NDPBs in a range of different categories (see Table 3.4). Examples of the nationalised industries associated with the Scottish Executive include Caledonian MacBrayne and Highlands and Islands Airports. The public corporations relate to the three regional water authorities, with substantial budgets and staffing. The advisory NDPBs involve part-time boards of members in organisations such as the General Teaching Council, the Royal Fine Art Commission, the Building Standards Advisory Committee, and the Advisory Committee on Scotland's Travelling People. They also include multiple organsations such as the thirty-two Justices of the Peace advisory committees, with 169 members. Similarly, among the tribunal NDPBs there are the thirty two children's panels, with 2,275 members. The NHS bodies involve fifteen health boards and twenty-eight NHS trusts.

Table 3.4 Non-departmental public bodies in Scotland 1999

Type	Number
Nationalised industries	3
Public corporations	3
Executive NDPBs	38
Advisory NDPBs	25
Tribunals	5
NHS bodies	9

Source: Cabinet Office, *Public Bodies* (HMSO, 1999). Includes one advisory NDPB and two tribunal NDPBs from the Scottish Courts group.

One fundamental point about quangos is that they are the responsibility of the Scottish Executive rather than the Scottish Parliament. The Scotland Act transferred Scottish Office quangos to Scottish Executive ministers, but nothing more, and the issue of quangos seldom has featured in the Scottish Parliament since devolution. When it was pursued, it was in the form of an MSP's bill on appointments to quangos by the SNP's Alex Neil,[7] and in questions over the appointment of a former Scottish Office civil servant, Harold Mills, to chair Caledonian MacBrayne. Ministers are required to make public appointments in line with the Code of Practice for Public Appointments (Parry, 1999b), but there has been continued disquiet over the procedures for quango appointments as well as the pattern of appointments, for example, the appointments process allowed no scope for parliamentary oversight of the Executive's 3,815 ministerial appointments (Cabinet Office, 1999: p. 175). Similarly, the pattern of public appointments was highly unrepresentative: appointments in 1998–9 involved only twenty two people from ethnic minorities (0.6 per cent of the total appointees) and only 28 per cent of appointees on Executive boards and 30 per cent on advisory boards were women. However, 56 per cent of appointees on tribunals were women, largely due to children's panels (Cabinet Office, 1999: p. 173). As a result, the Scottish Executive announced a review of the arrangements for quango appointments in February 2000, and the then Finance Minister, Jack McConnell, launched a consultation paper on appointments to NDPBs, with the intention of producing a more open, accountable system of appointments.[8] This process involved discussion about the role of the Scottish Parliament in examining Executive appointments and the possible establishment of a Scottish Parliamentary Commissioner for Public Appointments.[9]

Of course, while the Scottish Parliament had a limited role in overseeing quango appointments, it developed a major role in overseeing quango activities. Such bodies existed at arm's length from government for many years, but begun to be heavily scrutinised by the Parliament post-devolution. Both through their own agendas and guided by public petitions, the Parliamentary committees focused their attention on quango performance in delivering public services. Greater Glasgow Health Board, the Scottish Ambulance Service, the Scottish Arts Council and Scottish Further Education Colleges were all examples of public bodies that were investigated in the first year of the Parliament's existence. More will certainly follow.

– CONCLUSION –

The Scottish Executive was quickly conceived out of the former Scottish Office, and the new government structure contains elements of the familiar and the new. It has a new name and some changed departments and a large complement of ministers and deputies, but it is still clearly recognisable from the previous Scottish Office structure. The main difference is the political environment in which the new Executive lives and breathes. Its ministers and civil servants must operate within close scrutiny compared to the previous Scottish Office: the Parliament, its committee system and the media are all keenly interested in the work of the Executive. To some extent, and naturally enough, the Executive struggled to cope with this scrutiny in its first year, in relation to demands from MSPs for information and replies to Parliamentary questions. The Scottish Executive as a whole – Ministers, departments, civil servants – all face a transition to accommodate the new politics of the Scottish Parliament in all its aspects, such as pre-legislative consultation, committee scrutiny and the demands for more open, accessible government. The modernisation of the civil service and reforms of quango appointments also suggest that change will be an ongoing process for government bodies in Scotland.

In addition, because of the existence of a coalition in the Scottish Executive, government in Scotland has changed. The coalition government faced difficult issues, including the potentially terminal issue of student tuition fees, but has survived intact. Indeed, the divisions within the Executive in its first year largely took place within the Labour ministerial team rather than between the two parties. Effective management of difficult questions such as local government electoral reform remain a necessity to ensure coalition survival, although European experiences of coalitions offer numerous examples of coalition breakdown.

– NOTES –

1. The week of coalition negotiations was punctuated by speculation about the role of UK party leaders. For example, *Scotland on Sunday's* front page on 16 May 1999 stated, 'Ashdown tells Lib Dems "Sell out to Labour" – London leader intervenes to protect long-term relationship with Blair.'
2. Scottish Liberal Democrats, *Towards Free Education: Submission to the Inquiry into Student Funding*, Autumn 1999.
3. Scottish Executive, *The Scottish Executive: A Guide to Collective Decisionmaking*, 1999, p. 5.
4. This table is comprised of ministerial working groups for which membership was publicly available; other Cabinet subcommittees do exist, such as that on Sustainable Scotland.
5. Scottish Executive, *The Scottish Executive: A Guide to Collective Decisionmaking*, 1999, p. 1.
6. Scottish Parliament, *Official Report*, 23 February 2000.
7. The proposed Public Appointments Confirmation Bill 1999
8. Scottish Executive, *Appointments to Public Bodies in Scotland: Modernising the System*, February 2000.
9. Scottish Parliament, *Official Report*, 9 February 2000, col. 846.

CHAPTER 4

Life on the Mound: MSPs and the operation of the Scottish Parliament

– INTRODUCTION –

The Scottish Parliament was established following the election on Thursday, 6 May 1999. MSPs began registering at the Parliament on the Saturday after the election and various parties held meetings to discuss their strategies for the new institution. The Parliament met for the first time on Wednesday 12 May and on numerous occasions from then until the formal opening on 1 July, when the powers of the Parliament were formally transferred from Westminster. This chapter covers some of the aspects of the new institution which were developed during its early phase, in addition to discussing the characteristics of the 129 MSPs. It also explores aspects of MSPs' activities in the new Parliament. As an institution, the Parliament produced two main arenas for MSP activity: the committee system (see Chapter 5) and a range of individual mechanisms for MSP influence in the Parliament such as Members' motions, question times, participation in cross-party groups and holding the Executive to account. Each of these mechanisms, which can be seen as opportunities for backbench activism, is explored below.

– THE MSPs –

In terms of political experience and social characteristics, the MSPs are a mixed bunch. While the electoral system meant that the Scottish Parliament resembled voter preferences in a more accurate way than Westminster, the actual composition of the Parliament has a number of distinctive elements such as the number of female MSPs, the age profile of the MSPs and their varied political experiences.

– ETHNIC MINORITIES –

Significantly, while the Parliament is socially and geographically mixed, it is not ethnically mixed. All the MSPs are white and the Parliament contains no ethnic minorities. The parties did field candidates from the ethnic minorities, but none was successful, largely because none contested a winnable seat, for example, Labour did not select any ethnic minority candidates for its FPTP seats. The SNP had two ethnic minority candidates: Kaukab Stewart fought Glasgow Anniesland as a FPTP candidate and was placed eighth in the Glasgow regional list, next to Bashir Ahmed, who was placed ninth on the Glasgow list. The Liberal Democrats fielded two candidates from ethnic minorities: Mohammed Aslam Khan fought Glasgow Govan and was third on the list in Glasgow, and Dr Gurudeo Saluja, eighth on the list in North East Scotland. Lastly, the Conservatives fielded two ethnic minority candidates out of seventy-three, with Tasmina Ahmed-Sheikh in Glasgow Govan and Assad Rasul in Glasgow Kelvin, ranked second and sixth respectively on the Glasgow regional list. Given her position on the list, Tasmina Ahmed-Sheikh was the most likely ethnic minority candidate to be elected in Scotland, which would have been somewhat ironic in the light of the Conservatives' limited electoral appeal among Scotland's ethnic minorities compared to Labour and the SNP. Her election would also have constituted a considerable image change for Scottish Tories, helping to broaden the party's appeal across different social groups, especially ethnic minorities, the young and women. However, she was not elected in 1999 and defected to the SNP in 2000. One means of rectifying the absence of MSPs representing ethnic minorities was the proposal for the Parliament's Equal Opportunities Committee to consider co-opting representatives of Scotland's ethnic minorities onto the committee.[1] However, the proposal was not adopted.

– GENDER –

The need to make the Scottish Parliament more representative of Scottish society was one of the key debates over devolution from the late 1980s onwards (Brown, McCrone and Paterson, 1998). The Scottish Constitutional Convention and three of the four main political parties debated the need for special measures to ensure gender equality after devolution, although only Labour introduced measures to bring about positive discrimination in candidate selection in order to improve the election of women candidates. Although Labour's twinning procedures for FPTP seats came unstuck in several areas, the twinning of seats to ensure an equal number of women and men stood as candidates was overwhelmingly successful. For example, of the fifty-six Labour MSPs elected on 6 May 1999, twenty-eight were men and twenty-eight were women. In contrast, the SNP, which did not institute gender balance measures in the selection process, gained twenty male MSPs and fifteen female, broadly similar to Labour. Thus, positive discrimination helped Labour women, but the absence of positive discrimination within the SNP did not disadvantage SNP women. Significantly, it was the Conservatives and Liberal Democrats who were the least representative of Scottish society on gender issues, with only two women among the eighteen Conservative MSPs and three women among the Liberal Democrats seventeen MSPs. The success of John Scott at the Ayr by-election in 2000 did not improve the Conservatives' gender balance, although it did mean that Labour had more female than male MSPs.

Overall, women constitute forty-eight of the 129 MSPs, which represents 37 per cent of the total. This figure compares very favourably with many other elected institutions, for example, after the 1997 general election only 16.6 per cent of Scottish MPs were women compared to 18.2 per cent at Westminster as a whole. The increase in women's representation in the Scottish Parliament was also significant because it placed Scotland's level of women legislators ahead of Denmark and Finland and almost on a par with Norway and Sweden, which contain the largest number of women members in Western Europe (Brown, McCrone and Paterson, 1998: p. 174). The first Scottish Executive comprised only five women, with three acting as ministers and two as deputy ministers, which increased to four and two in 2000, all from Labour and none from the Liberal Democrats. Nevertheless, given previously low levels of women's representation in Scotland, the levels of gender balance provided by the Scottish Parliament do indicate a considerable sea change.

– AGE –

In terms of age profile at the 1999 election, the MSPs in the Parliament were decidedly middle-aged, rather than old. At the extremes, seven of the MSPs were in their twenties while only nine were in their sixties. The largest age group was of MSPs in their forties, who comprised 39 per cent of the Parliament, compared to 23 per cent in their thirties and 24.5 per cent in their fifties. The average age of the MSPs was forty-five (excluding Dorothy Grace Elder who kept her age a secret), compared to forty-nine among Scottish MPs at Westminster (Hassan and Warhurst 2000). The age profiles of the parties were all relatively similar. The average age of Labour MSPs was forty-three, compared to the SNP's average of forty-five (again minus Dorothy Grace Elder) and the Conservative and Liberal Democrat average of forty-nine. The age profile of the MSPs fed its way into the Scottish Executive in terms of ministerial posts: with a large number of 30-something ministers such as Wendy Alexander, Jackie Baillie, Sarah Boyack, Jack McConnell, Angus MacKay, Alasdair Morrison and Tavish Scott. The ability of this younger cohort to leapfrog older MSPs, especially those with local authority or Westminster experience, was striking.

– POLITICAL EXPERIENCE –

The political experience of MSPs was mixed. While there was a large number of first-time candidates and MSPs who had held no previous office, there was also a range of MSPs with experience of Parliamentary institutions. Most obviously, fourteen MSPs were sitting Westminster MPs (see Table 4.1). The new Parliament also contained one former MEP, Winnie Ewing, and two former MPs who had become peers after the last general election: Lord Watson (Mike Watson, MP for Glasgow Central 1989–97) and Lord Steel of Aikwood (former Liberal leader David Steel who represented his Borders constituency from 1965–97). In addition, a number of former MPs were also elected to the Scottish Parliament. On the SNP benches, George Reid was MP for Clackmannan and East Stirlingshire (1974–9), Winnie Ewing was MP for Hamilton (1967–70) and Moray (1974–9), and Margo MacDonald was MP for Glasgow Govan (1973–4). Among the Conservatives, Phil Gallie was MP for Ayr (1992–97) and Lord James Douglas-Hamilton was MP for Edinburgh West (1974–97). On the Liberal Democrat side, Keith Raffan was a former Conservative MP for Delyn in North Wales (1983–92) while Nicol Stephen was a Liberal Democrat MP for Kincardine and Deeside (1991–2).

The Parliament also contained thirty-nine existing or former local authority councillors from a variety of authorities and political parties. Prominent among these were the Labour MSPs Frank McAveety, MSP for Glasgow Shettleston, who had been leader of Glasgow City Council; Peter Peacock, elected at the top of Labour's list in the Highlands and Islands, who was a former independent Convenor of Highland Council; Kate McLean, MSP for Dundee West and former leader of Dundee City Council; and Hugh Henry, MSP for Paisley South and former leader of Renfrewshire Council. From the Liberal Democrats came John Farquhar-Munro, MSP for Ross, Skye and Inverness, leader of the Liberal Democrat group on Highland Council. In the SNP, Bruce Crawford, elected to the Mid-Scotland and Fife regional list, was leader of Perth and Kinross Council from 1996 to 1999. In the Conservatives, Keith Harding, elected to the Mid-Scotland and Fife regional list, was a former Conservative leader of Stirling Council.

Table 4.1 Dual-mandate Members of the Scottish Parliament at 1999 Election

MSP	Westminster constituency	Scottish constituency
Malcolm Chisholm (Lab)	Edinburgh North and Leith	Edinburgh North and Leith
Donald Dewar (Lab)	Glasgow Anniesland	Glasgow Anniesland
Sam Galbraith (Lab)	Strathkelvin and Bearsden	Strathkelvin and Bearsden
John Home-Robertson (Lab)	East Lothian	East Lothian
Henry McLeish (Lab)	Fife Central	Fife Central
John McAllion (Lab)	Dundee East	Dundee East
Roseanna Cunningham (SNP)	Perth	Perth
Margaret Ewing (SNP)	Moray	Moray
Alasdair Morgan (SNP)	Galloway and Upper Nithsdale	Galloway and Upper Nithsdale
Alex Salmond (SNP)	Banff and Buchan	Banff and Buchan
John Swinney (SNP)	Tayside North	Tayside North
Andrew Welsh (SNP)	Angus	Angus
Donald Gorrie (Lib Dem)	Edinburgh West	Central Scotland
Jim Wallace (Lib Dem)	Orkney and Shetland	Orkney

– Two classes of MSPs? –

The Scotland Act 1998 effectively created two different types of MSPs: constituency and list MSPs. Little attention was paid to the differences between these MSPs until the Parliament was up and running in May 1999. After that, the differences between the MSPs became prominent, particularly as there was a party division to the constituency-list question: fifty-three of the fifty-six Labour MSPs were elected by FPTP in constituencies, while twenty-eight of the thirty-five SNP MSPs were elected from the list. Such a pattern helped to fuel traditional hostilities between Labour and the Nationalists in a variety of ways. Inter-party conflicts over Parliamentary allowances, constituency offices, and the handling of constituency grievances by constituency and list MSPs soon helped to create two classes of MSP, and these two groups of MSPs developed an uneasy relationship in the Parliament, especially over constituency representation functions (McCabe and McCormick, 2000).

The arrangements for MSPs' office and staffing allowances were one of the first big inter-party conflicts to develop within the new Parliament. In advance of the Scottish elections, it had been assumed that all MSPs would be equal, regardless of whether they were elected from FPTP constituencies or from regional party lists. However, the allowances debate clearly indicated that Labour regarded the two types of MSPs as different and wished to use the allowances to reflect this belief. Labour sought to draw a clear distinction between the two sets of MSPs on the grounds that constituency members' roles as local representatives would lead to greater workloads through constituency business whilst list MSPs would not have direct contact with individual constituencies and would not deal with much casework. This situation was seen to be a determinant in the staffing and office allowances for individual MSPs: FPTP MSPs needed greater finance for staff and offices because of their constituency caseloads; list MSPs needed less funds for staff and offices because they lacked constituency caseloads. Of course, this view avoided the fact that list MSPs quickly acquired caseloads within their wider regional constituencies, especially as many had fought FPTP constituencies within the region.

This argument was not the sole issue at stake here. Additionally, there was a determination by Labour to monopolise the constituency representation function to prevent the SNP from establishing local offices in the constituencies to challenge sitting Labour MSPs. For example, Labour MSPs for Glasgow Govan, Ochil and Dundee East could easily have seen rival offices opened by SNP MSPs who had contested these seats unsuccessfully at the 1999 election. Thus, while the SNP proposed equal allowances for the two types of MSPs,[2] and would have proceeded with opening local offices, Labour proposed a system of allowances in which regional MSPs would gain set percentages of the allowances of FPTP members. Labour proposed that list members would receive 60 per cent of the £36,000 available to FPTP members for staffing and 60 per cent of the £10,000 office allowance.[3]

Labour's proposal was defeated by the combined efforts of the SNP, Liberal Democrats, Conservatives, Greens, Scottish Socialist Party and the Member for Falkirk West (the former Labour MP for Falkirk West who successfully stood as an independent after Labour failed to select him as a candidate for the Scottish election). The Liberal Democrats proposed a different set of arrangements for MSPs' allowances which was accepted by the coalition partners but opposed by the Conservatives and SNP. Under this proposal, each type of MSP was awarded the full staffing costs of £36,000, but the office allowances for regional members were to be calculated using a formula which meant that regional members would need to share constituency offices. In regions in which a party has several list MSPs, the office allowance would operate as follows: the first MSP would receive the full £10,000 allowance, other MSPs would receive 30 per cent of

£10,000 each; these two sets of figures would be added together and then divided by the number of regional members to gain the total office allowance.[4]

This particular proposal was entirely suitable to the Liberal Democrats, which had only one list MSP per region, and would therefore qualify for the full office allowance of £10,000 and be able to open an office for their sole use. The arrangement was not particularly suitable for the Conservatives and SNP who would have to pool their resources and MSPs together under such an arrangement. This would not be problematic in urban areas such as Lothians and Glasgow, but would be more difficult in the North East, Mid-Scotland and Fife, South of Scotland, and Highlands and Islands.

Relations between constituency and list MSPs were also problematic in the area of constituency cases. Indeed, given the predominant pattern of Labour constituency MSPs competing with SNP list MSPs across much of central Scotland, inter-MSP conflict was a likely development. This conflict also extended to relations between MPs and MSPs, with a developing turf war over involvement in local issues in parts of the West of Scotland. The most prominent inter-party 'turf war' involved Labour MPs and MSPs in Cunninghame North and South, and SNP MSPs elected from South of Scotland the regional list. The conflict developed over participation in meetings with Ayrshire and Arran Health Board, which Labour wished to restrict to constituency MSPs and the SNP wished to include list MSPs (*The Herald*, 16 November 1999). This conflict contributed to the creation of a Parliamentary working group under the Deputy Presiding Officer, George Reid, to determine a set of rules and procedures to govern relations between the two different types of MSPs. The Reid Committee set out four principles to guide relations between constituency and list MSPs:

1. Scotland has a multi-member system of representation and each constituent is represented by eight MSPs. A constituent can choose any of these eight MSPs as their representative. Regional MSPs should inform constituency MSPs when they take up a case.
2. All MSPs are equal – whether they are from a constituency or the regional list.
3. MSPs should not 'poach' cases from each other: regional MSPs can only deal with cases from their region, constituency MSPs can only deal with cases from their constituencies.
4. The wishes and interests of individual constituents and their locality should determine the allocation of representational duties, and whether a constituency or list MSPs becomes involved.[5]

MSPs would be able to approach the Presiding Officer if they felt that these four principles were not being enforced, with the Standards Committee available as a forum for dealing with serious disputes. However, these principles were not agreed at the time of publication and the management of inter-MSP disputes is likely to remain problematic given the partisan dimension to the pattern of constituency and list MSPs.

– MANAGING THE SCOTTISH PARLIAMENT –

The Parliament does not merely involve 129 MSPs, but also a range of organisational structures to manage Parliamentary business and debates. These range from traditional positions such as the Presiding Officer (the speaker of the Parliament) to other institutions such as the Scottish Parliamentary Corporate Body, the Parliamentary Bureau and the Parliamentary Convenors' Liaison Committee. Each of these bodies plays an important and occasionally controversial role within the life of the Parliament.

– THE PRESIDING OFFICER –

One of the Parliament's earliest tasks involved the election of the Presiding Officer, whose existence and tasks were detailed in the Scotland Act 1998. The Presiding Officer is responsible for chairing sessions of the Parliament, administering oaths in the Parliament (the swearing-in of MSPs following the election), checking that legislative proposals fall within the competence of the Parliament and submitting successful bills for Royal Assent. In addition, he or she is responsible for chairing the Scottish Parliamentary Corporate Body, which is responsible for the operation of the Parliament in the areas of staffing, salaries, facilities, and so on. The Presiding officer was therefore responsible for the Holyrood building project to replace the temporary chamber on the Mound, arrangements for the Parliament's opening ceremony on 1 July 1999, and the temporary removal of the Parliament's meetings to Glasgow during the General Assembly of the Church of Scotland's reoccupation of the chambers on the Mound in 2000.

The Presiding Officer and Deputy Presiding Officers are also responsible for a range of functions within the Parliament's standing orders, such as presiding over plenary meetings, convening and chairing the Parliamentary bureau (the business committee), interpreting and issuing rulings on standing orders, and representing the Parliament in relations with other bodies.[6] The tasks of the Presiding Officer's team can be seen as never-ending, with some chairing the committee of Parliamentary Convenors, overseeing arrangements for committees to travel around Scotland, and attending meetings with US state legislators and EU regional governments.

The current Presiding Officer, Sir David Steel, was elected by the Parliament on 12 May 1999. Steel's election was largely facilitated by the coalition deal between Labour and the Liberal Democrats. Although the Presiding Officer's election was conducted by secret ballot, the pattern of voting between Steel (eighty-two votes) and his opponent, the SNP's George Reid (forty-four votes), seemed to indicate that Labour and Liberal Democrat MSPs had voted for Steel, SNP MSPs had supported Reid, and the Conservatives had divided their votes between the two candidates. The fact that Labour avoided nominating a candidate for Presiding Officer also indicated that a deal had been struck. Subsequently, the Parliament elected two Deputy Presiding Officers, George Reid (SNP) and Patricia Ferguson (Labour).

– THE SCOTTISH PARLIAMENTARY CORPORATE BODY –

The SPCB comprises four MSPs plus the Presiding Officer of the Parliament. It was created by the Scotland Act 1998, with the express task of running the Parliament's finances and staffing and overseeing its offices. It is comprised of an MSP from each of the main political parties in the Parliament: Robert Brown of the Liberal Democrats, Des McNulty of Labour, Andrew Welsh of the SNP and John Young of the Conservatives. Although it was an obscure body for most of the first year of the Parliament's existence, it came to prominence during debates on the Holyrood building project. It is the SPCB which is responsible for the new Holyrood building and it bore some of the criticism in early 2000 for the expanded costs and delayed timetable for the new building.

– THE PARLIAMENTARY BUREAU –

The Parliamentary Bureau exists at the centre of the Parliament's work. In the early weeks of the Parliament's life, it acted as a forum for discussion about Parliamentary arrangements between the four parties and the Parliament's senior officers. The Bureau is comprised of the business managers (see Table 4.2) of parties which have at least five MSPs,[7] and it is chaired by the Presiding Officer or Deputy Presiding Officer, who has a casting vote on the committee. Independents and/or smaller parties are able to group together to participate on the committee if they have at least five MSPs, although this threshold was not reached at the 1999 election. The individual business managers are key figures within their parties and act as surrogates for their party leaders in negotiations over Parliamentary business.

The Parliamentary Bureau has four distinctive functions: preparing the business of Parliament, time tabling the daily order of business for plenary sessions, designing the timetable for the progress of legislation through committees, and proposing the remit, membership, duration and budget of Parliamentary committees (Consultative Steering Group, 1999: p. 27). The Bureau can also conduct any other tasks related to the functioning of the Parliament. It therefore plays a role similar to the combined functions of the Speaker at Westminster, the Leader and Shadow Leader of the House, and what are usually referred to as 'the usual channels'. It also acts as a considerable negotiating forum for issues between the parties. The fact that the four business managers on the committee are effectively surrogates of their party leaders has meant that the Bureau exists as one of the key institutions within the Parliament, where conflicts are raised and resolved on a range of issues and problems.

Table 4.2 The Parliament's business managers

Tom McCabe	Labour Minister for Parliament
Tavish Scott	Liberal Democrat Deputy Minister for Parliament
Lord James Douglas-Hamilton	Conservative Business Manager
Tricia Marwick	SNP Business Manager

– THE CONVENORS' LIAISON GROUP –

The Consultative Steering Group blueprint in 1999 did not foresee the development of the Convenors' Liaison Group. It was established by the sixteen committee convenors as a mechanism for effective management of the Parliamentary process and can also be interpreted as an assertion of Parliamentary authority and independence. Rather than simply allowing the Parliamentary Bureau and the whips to determine the legislative timetable, the Convenors' Liaison Group allows the committees to seek to promote their interests within the Parliamentary structure. This situation was particularly important given the pace of legislation proposed by the Executive and also the limited budgets available to committees. The group can be understood as something of a pressure group for the committee system, which, given its centrality to the Parliament, is vital to the functioning of the legislature. The group meets in private most weeks and its meetings are chaired by the Deputy Presiding Officer George Reid.

– THE PARLIAMENT IN ACTION –

The Scottish Parliament has two main components: plenary sessions of the full Parliament in the chamber, and committee meetings of the Parliament's sixteen committees. The plenary sessions attract most media attention and are those which come most readily to the public's mind. Set-piece debates in the chamber and ministerial question times are familiar to most people from television news, whereas committee meetings are not.

To a certain extent, the conduct of plenary business has been designed to escape Westminster's language and procedures and to make it more intelligible to the public. MSPs are referred to by their name and ministers by their ministerial post, and there are no Honourable or Right Honourable friends in the Scottish Parliament. Speakers are allocated specific times during debates and many contributions are kept short, from two to four minutes on some occasions. Therefore, most debates avoid Westminster's rambling quality, although they can appear rather short and plain as a result. The Parliament only meets for one and a half days a week in plenary session and media coverage of these events tends to concentrate on ministerial question times.

– Ministerial question time –

Scottish Executive ministers are subject to a question time on Thursday afternoons in the chamber, and this period is followed by First Minister's question time. The combined question time period is about one hour, held on a weekly basis, and it is the main opportunity for MSPs to question ministers and for the opposition leaders to challenge the First Minister. MSPs must submit their written questions in advance of the plenary session. Initially, questions had to be submitted eight days in advance of the Thursday session, but this time scale was deemed highly unsatisfactory as it meant that topical issues – such as those that had occurred in the week before the question time – were seldom raised. Thus MSPs were asking out-of-date questions, and were unable to raise more recent issues with ministers. These arrangements were altered in late 1999 so that from 13 January 2000 question time operated on a different timetable. The deadline for questions was reduced to 2.00 on Monday afternoons, and the Presiding Officer was also given the latitude to choose emergency questions at question times to introduce more topicality into debates. Finally, there were changes to the length and format of First Minister's questions, and from January, the FM dealt with more questions and supplementary questions than before. The significant thing about First Minister's question time is that the First Minister fields questions on a wide range of issues across the whole work of the Scottish Executive. The written questions are dealt with in responses supplied by civil servants, but when it comes to the supplementary questions, the First Minister is on his own, on any subject – an opportunity for the opposition to attack and try to score points.

Table 4.3 Members' motions debated May–July 2000

Subject	MSP	Date
Highlands and Islands University	George Lyon (Lib Dem)	6 July 2000
West Kilbride – National Craft Town	Allan Wilson (Lab)	5 July 2000
Emergency 999 calls	Linda Fabiani (SNP)	29 June 2000
Sexual crimes trials	Johann Lamont (Lab)	28 June 2000
Milestone House	David McLetchie (Con)	22 June 2000
Edinburgh Folk Festival	Roseanna Cunningham (SNP)	21 June 2000
Greenock Morton FC	Duncan McNeil (Lab)	15 June 2000
Disabled people's housing	Robert Brown (Lib Dem)	14 June 2000
Womens' pay	Elaine Thomson (Lab)	8 June 2000
Standard Life	Margo MacDonald (SNP)	7 June 2000
Bell Baxter High School	Keith Harding (Con)	1 June 2000
Dyspraxia	Duncan Hamilton (SNP)	25 May 2000
Construction industry employment	Johann Lamont (Lab)	24 May 2000
Prisons slopping out	Dorothy Grace Elder (SNP)	18 May 2000
Epilepsy	Mike Watson (Lab)	17 May 2000
The Black Cuillin	John Munro (Lib Dem)	11 May 2000
A90 road upgrade	David Davidson (Con)	10 May 2000

– BACKBENCH ACTIVISM –

Committees are the foremost arena for backbench MSPs to influence the work of the Parliament. However, four other avenues exist: motions for debate, raising specific issues in the chamber, MSPs' bills, and involvement in cross-party groups. The Parliament's standing orders allow MSPs to submit motions for debates which are timetabled for thirty minutes at 5.00 on Wednesday and Thursday afternoons and allow MSPs to use Parliamentary time to debate a particular issue. The motions for debate are chosen by the Presiding Officer and the Parliamentary Bureau and have afforded MSPs a range of opportunities to raise local or national issues. Examples have included the motion by Alasdair Morgan on Wigtown (Scotland's national book town) on 15 September 1999, George Lyon's motion on the Kintyre economy on 25 November 1999, Sylvia Jackson's motion on Cornton Vale Prison near Stirling on 16 December 1999, and David Mundell's motion on rural sub-post offices on 27 January 2000. Motions come from all parties, sometimes from committee convenors and also from one of the opposition leaders (see Table 4.3). Of course, many more motions are lodged than are ever debated and the party's business managers have considerable influence over the choice of motion debated. However, the procedure allows MSPs to debate important local and regional issues, which is particularly important for regional list MSPs without local constituencies. The motions for debate are designed to generate local and regional media coverage (see Chapter 11), which explains their distinctly local themes. On most occasions, ministers will attend the session dealing with members' motions and respond to the debate, for example, the relevant minister and deputy ministers responded to all the debates listed in Table 4.3, with the exception of the motion on construction industry employment. MSPs thus use Members' motions not merely to push an issue into the local media, but to pressurise the Executive.

Individual MSPs have also been active in some areas. First, one can point to the two dissenting Liberal Democrat MSPs, Donald Gorrie and Keith Raffan, who have been active in the chamber, committees and the media in promoting a range of initiatives such as opposition to the coalition deal with Labour; opposition to tuition fees; and the cost of the Parliament building at Holyrood. SNP MSP Margo McDonald was also involved with Donald Gorrie over the Holyrood project, while Labour's Mike Watson and the SNP's Tricia Marwick were active in co-sponsoring legislation to ban some types of fox-hunting in Scotland. A number of other MSPs from all parties have been active in publishing MSPs' bills in 1999–2000 (see Chapter 6).

– CROSS-PARTY GROUPS –

Cross-party groups also began to emerge as an arena for backbench activity in the Parliament's first year of operation. Backbenchers were able to join a number of cross-party groups organised into specific subject areas to discuss policy in a defined area. Such groups are regulated by the Parliament's Standards Committee, which instituted a register for cross-party groups.[8] To be recognised, a group has to be open to members of all parties, comprise at least five MSPs and include an MSP from each of the four main parties. A group can contain non-MSPs, but must involve MSPs, who must convene the group. Groups are not allowed to draw on the resources of the Parliament itself and are subject to the code of conduct and standards applicable to MSPs. Thus, for example, financial support provided to groups by outside bodies has to be registered and publicly available. Groups are established in a variety of policy areas (see Case study 1). Some dealt with economic and regional interests that crossed the boundaries of the Parliament's powers into reserved areas such as the oil and gas industry, media and shipbuilding (see Table 4.4). Other groups are more directly concerned with policies for which the Scottish Parliament is responsible. Cross-party groups were one area of backbench activity that mushroomed in 2000 once the groups were recognised by the Parliament, with a number of proposed groups awaiting approval by the Standards Committee at the close of the 1999–2000 Parliamentary year.

Table 4.4 Cross-party groups in the Scottish Parliament, 7 July 2000

Agriculture and horticulture
Sports
Tobacco control
Crofting
Borders rail
Children
Citizenship, income, economy and society
Drug misuse
Epilepsy
Information, knowledge and enlightenment
Oil and gas
Women
Media
Shipbuilding
Older people, age and aging
Palliative care
Strategic rail services
Gaelic
Animal welfare
Refugees and asylum seekers
Renewable energy
Men's violence against women and children

Source: Register of Cross-Party Groups in the Scottish Parliament

---

Case study 1 Cross-party group on Borders rail

Sixteen MSPs were members of the Borders rail group, the vast majority either constituency MSPs from the area or list MSPs from the South of Scotland. Thus the group comprised Labour MSPs from Clydesdale and Dumfries, SNP MSPs from the regional list and Galloway and Upper Nithsdale, as well as the two Liberal Democrat MSPs for the Borders constituencies and Tory MSPs from the South of Scotland list. The group was convened in order to promote rail links to the Borders but also to work towards the reopening of the Edinburgh–Carlisle railway line – in this way its reach extended beyond the Borders rail link itself. The group's membership also reached out into the community to include leading figures on Scottish Borders Council and local campaigners for the rail link.

– GOVERNMENT AND OPPOSITION –

The Scottish Parliament involved two new and significant developments: a formal coalition between Labour and the Liberal Democrats and the emergence of a Nationalist opposition. The fact that the SNP emerged as the official opposition in the Scottish Parliament was clearly a new departure. The arrival of the SNP Scottish Parliamentary group for their first post-election meeting indicated a considerable change in the party's political status. A party which had previously peaked at eleven elected members in October 1974 now had thirty-five MSPs. It thus became a leading Parliamentary group that arrived at its first meeting in fourteen taxis instead of the usual one or two. How the party performed in this new role of official opposition remained to be seen since it involved a considerable transformation in the party's fortunes and status. The fact that the new Parliament was a multi-party system rather than a simple two-party system meant that the SNP could not monopolise the role of opposition (Dahl, 1966), but had to share this function with the Conservatives, some dissident Liberal Democrat MSPs, the Green Party, Scottish Socialist Party, and the MSP for Falkirk West. In addition, the SNP opposition operated next to activist backbenchers from all parties acting through the Parliament's committee system and within an institutional design which shares power between parties and MSPs at different levels.

The Conservatives, meanwhile, experienced exactly the opposite transformation in their status, even though the election provided them with their first nationally elected representation in Scotland since their disastrous 1997 general election performance. Devolution combined with opposition status formed a dual challenge to the Scottish Conservatives, especially as the party was cast into opposition alongside the Nationalists. This latter reality meant that Conservative MSPs often combined with the SNP in votes in the Parliament, something that cannot have been entirely comfortable. Indeed, in time a pattern emerged in voting in plenary which involved SNP and Conservative members abstaining on each other's amendments and resolutions instead of supporting them.

The opposition parties have some latitude for action within the Parliament. They are able to present motions for debate in the time allocated to them within the Parliament's standing orders: sixteen half-days each year.[9] The SNP has used such occasions for debates on education on 30 September 1999 and the Act of Settlement by SNP on 16 December 1999. The Conservatives have used them to debate issues such as Scottish Enterprise and section 2a (clause 28) of the Local Government Act 1986 on 10 February 2000. Opposition leaders also have a special role at First Minister's question time and most debates in the plenary of the Parliament are balanced between government and opposition speakers.

– MSPs and parliamentary accountability –

MSPs also have a range of 'inquisitorial' functions to deliver accountability within the Parliament. Written and oral questions to ministers, members' motions and intervention in debates all exist as mechanisms of accountability. In Parliamentary debates, frontbenchers are able to dominate to some extent through their ability to open and close the debates, but there has tended to be ample time for backbench involvement in government and opposition debates and motions. Questions and debates do not necessarily influence government ministers in terms of shaping or reversing policy, but they do make them account for their actions and defend their policy decisions. Moreover, the members' motions debated at the end of plenary sessions allow individual MSPs to raise issues of concern to their constituents and generally exercise an agenda-setting role. Such efforts may seem relatively minor compared to motions of no confidence or committee inquisitions of Ministers, but they do allow MSPs to exercise accountability through political pressure and campaigning (Meny, 1993: p. 223). Donald Gorrie and Margo McDonald's efforts to shed some light on the financial failings of the Holyrood project illustrate that persistent questioning and pursuit of an issue can deliver accountable government. MSPs' use of written questions and correspondence to ministers in 1999–2000 was also considerable, presenting problems for the Scottish Executive in processing requests. For example, MSPs lodged 460 questions in October 1999, followed by 534 in November and 537 in December. In March 2000, more than, 1,000 questions were lodged. Similarly, the amount of correspondence between MSPs and ministers generated 12,207 letters from 1 July 1999 to 31 March 2000, thousands more than before devolution.[10] Such volumes of paperwork may seem excessive, but do indicate the extent to which MSPs have sought to make the Executive accountable for its actions.

– Regulating MSP behaviour –

MSPs are subject to both a code of conduct and a register of members' interests, designed by the Parliament and implemented by the Standards Committee. The manner in which MPs at Westminster were implicated in 'cash for questions' scandals along with other allegations of MSPs' misconduct led the Scottish Parliament to implement a standards regime in its first year of existence. The MSPs' code of conduct was intended to regulate MSP behaviour in a number of areas in order to deal with conflicts of interests between the MSPs' role as Parliamentarians and their financial interests. In particular, there was concern to limit the potential for MSPs to act as paid advocates for pressure groups or businesses, although this issue was controversial in some cases. The MSPs were effectively prevented from 'paid advocacy', meaning they could not seek to use their position to advance the interests of an individual or organisation that provided them with funding. Thus, MSPs could not act as paid lobbyists for organisations through asking Parliamentary questions, lodging motions, introducing a bill or seeking to amend bills. They were also banned from acting as Parliamentary strategists or advisers for lobbying companies, and taking on paid lobbying functions for organisations or individuals, and they were also given strict rules on the acceptance of hospitality or other benefits from individuals and organisations. Sifting through such rules and requirements to determine whether MSPs had contravened the rules was the job of the Standards Committee. MSPs could refer complaints to this committee which was left to pursue them using its complaints procedure and code of conduct. The Standards Committee investigated two cases in 1999: the 'Lobbygate' affair (see Case study 2) and a complaint against Mike Watson in relation to his bill against fox-hunting (see Chapter 6).

The MSPs' code of conduct included arrangements for the establishment and maintenance of a register of members' interests. The register was to be regularly updated and accessible to the public – for example, it is available on the Parliament's website. Members are required to make regular written statements of financial interests in particular and to declare interests verbally during committee and plenary debates where appropriate. Interests include any employment for which an MSP has received payment, election expenses paid for by donations from companies, individuals or organisations, financial sponsorship, gifts, overseas visits, shareholdings and property.[11] If MSPs contravene the rules regarding the register, they can be excluded from the Parliament, and members would be reported to the Presiding Officer for non-compliance. The Parliament also discussed the idea of appointing its own Standards Commissioner similar to Westminster but reached no conclusion on the issue, although it did seek to appoint an adviser to the Standards Committee.

Case study 2 Lobbygate

The Lobbygate affair emerged in the autumn of 1999, and involved allegations that lobbyists had gained preferential access to MSPs. *The Observer* newspaper had videotaped a meeting between lobbyists from Beattie Media and a fictional company in which the lobbyists claimed they had preferential access to ministers of the Scottish Executive, were able to arrange access on behalf of clients, and could influence the diary of the Finance Minister, Jack McConnell, on behalf of clients. The fact that one of the lobbyists involved, Kevin Reid, was the son of the Secretary of State for Scotland, John Reid, and that the Finance Minister and his personal assistant had previously worked for Beattie Media made the allegations extremely serious. Allegations of preferential access were also made in relation to other Labour ministers in the Scottish Executive and the former Scottish Office. The affair was damaging to Labour, especially as the First Minister changed his position over the need for an inquiry, and Labour MSPs on the Standards Committee were reluctant to sanction an inquiry. Lobby-gate was the first 'live' standards issue experienced by the Parliament and, to a certain extent, it was flying blind on the issue. The Standards Committee was under extreme political and media pressure and initially struggled to deal with the nature of the investigation. The right of the committee to take evidence on the affair in private was controversial and challenged in the courts by *The Scotsman* newspaper. The Standards Committee's inquiry determined that the Parliament's code of conduct had not been breached, but the affair was damaging to the public image of the new institution and to the company and MSPs concerned. The affair did have the benefit of feeding into the final code of conduct for MSPs and the development of an official complaints procedure as it offered a test for such procedures in advance of their adoption.

– CONCLUSION –

MSPs obviously faced considerable challenges in the first year of the Scottish Parliament because of the newness of the system. They were unfamiliar with the procedures, some of which were emerging in practice, and took time to settle into their roles and activities. The growth of backbench activism in relation to members' motions, cross-party groups and questions to Ministers were all illustrations that MSPs were getting to grips with the potentialities of the Parliament in relation to active rather than passive behaviour. Rather than existing as lobby fodder, many MSPs were taking advantage of parliamentary structures to make an impact – given the way in which the Parliament is structured, it would have been surprising if MSPs behaved in any other way. One recurrent difficulty the MSPs face, however, involves the partisan rather than practical divisions between the constituency and regional list MSPs. Despite attempts to produce a set of rules to ease relations between the two sets of MSPs, the fact that they represent the two main parties in Scotland locked in intense competition means inter-MSP conflicts will become a permanent, if manageable, feature of MSP behaviour in the Parliament.

– Notes –

1. Alex Salmond MSP, Scottish Parliament, *Official Report*, 8 June 1999, vol. 1, no. 7, col. 275.
2. Motion SIM–40, Scottish Parliament, *Official Report*, 8 June 1999, vol. 1, no. 7, col. 275.
3. Amendment SIM–40.1, Scottish Parliament, *Official Report*, 8 June 1999, vol. 1, no. 7, col. 275.
4. Amendment SIM–40.2, Scottish Parliament, *Official Report*, 8 June 1999, vol. 1, no. 7, col. 275.
5. Ad Hoc Liaison Group, *Relationships Between MSPs: Initial Report*, 18 November 1999.
6. *Scottish Parliament Standing Orders*, 3.1, 1999, p. 15.
7. *Scottish Parliament Standing Orders*, 5.2, 1999, p. 22.
8. Standards Committee Second Report 1999: *Regulation of Cross-Party Groups*.
9. *Scottish Parliament Standing Orders*, 5.6, 1999, p. 24.
10. Michael Lugton, Scottish Executive Constitutional Policy and Parliamentary Liaison Group, Procedures Committee, *Official Report*, 23 May 2000, col. 374.
11. Scottish Parliament, *Code of Conduct for Members*.

CHAPTER 5

The committee system of the Scottish Parliament

– INTRODUCTION –

The Scottish Parliament was designed as a unicameral, committee-based legislature. It was a deliberate reversal of the Westminster norm, where the committee system was seen to be weak and contributed to executive dominance and a lack of effective legislative scrutiny. The Scottish solution to such problems was to design a system of committees which combined both legislative and scrutiny functions. Thus, individual committees became responsible for scrutinising the work of Scottish government along the lines of Westminster select committees, while also considering legislative proposals similar to Westminster standing committees. Since committees were to be established for the four-year session of a Parliament, it was anticipated that MSPs would become experts in the policy areas associated with their committees and better able to scrutinise government legislation and policy. However, the design of a committee system on paper can differ from a committee system in practice. Therefore this chapter will provide an assessment of the performance of the committees as they juggle their legislative and scrutiny functions.

– THE ROLE AND FUNCTIONS OF COMMITTEES –

The Consultative Steering Group's report on the functioning of the Parliament gave six specific functions to committees (1999: p. 5):

1. to consider and report on the policy and administration of the Scottish administration
2. to conduct inquiries into such matters or issues as the Parliament may require
3. to scrutinise primary and secondary legislation and proposed European Union legislation

4. to initiate legislation
5. to scrutinise financial proposals and administration of the Scottish Executive
6. to scrutinise procedures relating to the Parliament and its Members.

With the exception of initiating legislation, each of these functions was practised by committees in their first year of existence, although not necessarily by all committees. Indeed, committee activity was often closely conditioned by the nature and pace of Executive legislation, the progress of MSPs' bills and the amount of petitions and subordinate legislation which required attention. Moreover, as will be discussed below, some committees were better able to control their agenda and workload than others, as a consequence of the aforementioned factors.

The establishment of a unicameral Parliament brought particular challenges for the Scottish Parliament and its elected members. As there was no second chamber to act as a revising chamber in relation to government legislation, such as the House of Lords, Senate or Bundesrat, it was up to the Parliament's committees to fulfil this function. However, this particular function is problematic given the fact that MSPs are elected at the same time, to the same institution, along party lines. For example, MSPs are responsible for considering legislation at all stages but are supposed to forget their party affiliations at the committee stage of the legislative process in order to suggest improvements to government proposals. The MSPs are therefore somewhat schizophrenic, expected to act as Burkean representatives independently dealing with government legislation on its merits in committees, yet to vote on party lines as directed by the whips in plenary sessions in the chamber. This situation is further influenced by the potential intervention of the party whips when committees scrutinise legislation to support/oppose particular amendments to bills. Behaving as independent backbenchers in committee is relatively easy for opposition MSPs, but less simple for the two coalition parties, whose MSPs are required to support their government. Despite this difficult balancing act, committee decisions were achieved by consensus rather than by divisions and voting. However, votes were held on a number of committees in the Parliament's first year and they tended to occur along party lines, although not always on coalition lines. There was also a tendency for the MSPs to sit in party groups in committees, reinforcing the partisan dimension within the committees. The Finance committee took the conscious decision to arrange MSPs' seating by alphabetical order rather than party group, a clear attempt to make the committee less partisan.[1]

In addition, MSPs are able to attend all committee meetings, whether a member of the committee or not. They are able to speak and propose amendments to legislation at all committee meetings but are not able to vote.[2]

The committees themselves can be divided into two groups: subject committees which are responsible for legislation and scrutiny functions over particular policy areas associated with Ministers, and mandatory committees which are responsible for the functioning of the Parliament itself as well as specific government activities. The second set of committees was adopted upon the recommendation of the Consultative Steering Group (1999). The subject committees were determined by inter-party negotiation through the Parliamentary Bureau (see Chapter 4), which established committees to reflect the pattern of ministers and policy areas of the first Scottish Executive.

Table 5.1 The committee system of the Scottish Parliament

Subject committees (eleven members each)
Justice and Home Affairs Committee (Convenor: Alisdair Morgan, SNP)
Education, Culture and Sport Committee (Convenor: Mary Mulligan, Labour)
Social Inclusion, Housing and Voluntary Sector Committee (Convenor: not appointed at time of going to press, Labour)
Enterprise and Lifelong Learning Committee (Convenor: Alex Neil, SNP)
Health and Community Care Committee (Convenor: Margaret Smith, Liberal Democrat)
Transport and the Environment Committee (Convenor: Andy Kerr, Labour)
Rural Affairs Committee (Convenor: Alex Johnstone, Conservative)
Local Government Committee (Convenor: Trish Godman, Labour)

Mandatory committees
Standards Committee (seven members) (Convenor: Mike Rumbles, Liberal Democrat)
Procedures Committee (seven members) (Convenor: Murray Tosh, Conservative)
Audit Committee (eleven members) (Convenor: Andrew Welsh, SNP)
Finance Committee (eleven members) (Convenor: Mike Watson, Labour)
European Committee (thirteen members) (Convenor: Hugh Henry, Labour)
Equal Opportunities Committee (thirteen members) (Convenor: Kate McLean, Labour)
Public Petitions Committee (seven members) (Convenor: John McAllion, Labour)
Subordinate Legislation Committee (seven members) (Convenor: Kenny McAskill, SNP)

– COMMITTEE COMPOSITION –

The composition of committees was decided using a modified d'Hondt formula, which more closely reflected party balance in the Scottish Parliament than the arrangements for committee convenors. Had the pure d'Hondt formula been used, it would have provided Labour with a majority on some committees,[3] despite the fact that it lacked a majority in the Parliament. Negotiations between the parties through the medium of the Parliamentary Bureau succeeded in compromises that agreed a slightly modified d'Hondt formula and reduced some party claims for representation on committees to manageable levels. The formula adopted for the sets of committees operated as follows: in a committee of eleven members, five places would be allocated to Labour, three to the SNP, and either one or two members to the Conservatives and Liberal Democrats depending on the committee involved; in a committee of seven members, three places would be allocated to Labour, two to the SNP, one to the Conservatives and one to the Liberal Democrats.[4] Thus, Labour did not have a majority on any committees on its own, but would have a functioning majority in each through its partnership coalition with the Liberal Democrats. The combined impact of these factors was to produce a politically mixed committee system, which meant that committees reflected the composition of the Parliament at the level of ordinary MSPs.

The allocation of committee convenors was slightly different, and it worked to Labour's advantage at the expense of the SNP. For example, Labour holds half of the sixteen committee convenors in the Parliament: 50 per cent of committee convenors based on 43 per cent of seats in the Parliament and 39 per cent of first votes in 1999. The SNP, by contrast, has four committee convenors (25 per cent) based on 27 per cent of seats in the Parliament and 29 per cent of first votes. Both the Conservatives and the Liberal Democrats are broadly level in terms of their allocation of committee convenors. The Conservatives gained two committee convenors (12.5 per cent), based on 14 per cent of the seats and 16 per cent of first votes. The Liberal Democrats also received two committee convenors, which is broadly comparable to the fact that they gained 13 per cent of the seats and 14 per cent of first votes in 1999.

Politically, the partisan affiliation of convenors is unimportant as they rely on the consensus of their committee colleagues and cannot act against their wishes, in addition to being bound by the Parliament's standing orders and rules for convenors. The committee convenors are responsible for chairing the committees, conducting votes, determining the agenda and circulating documents in tandem with the committee clerk, handling the amendments to legislation at stage two and acting as the main media spokesperson.[5] Such a workload is considerable and therefore the convenors are backed by a system of deputy convenors, which spreads the partisan leadership of individual committees in many cases as well as assisting the workload of the convenors. Such assistance is particularly relevant as thirteen of the sixteen convenors are members of other committees of the Parliament, and also have party and constituency matters to deal with.

Agreement on the organisation of committees was problematic, in spite of the efforts of party managers to reach compromise on these issues within the confines of the Parliamentary Bureau. First, there was a row over the exclusion (because they had no representation on the Parliamentary Bureau) of Denis Canavan, Robin Harper and Tommy Sheridan from their preferred committees, which created the impression that these three MSPs would not be allowed any subject committee involvement at all. During negotiations, various parties offered to give up places on committees to facilitate the involvement of the three MSPs in committee work, a compromise which seemed to have suffered from a breakdown in communications between the Parliamentary Bureau and the three MSPs. In the end, the MSPs were allocated rights to committee membership, as the main parties had vacated places on the European, Transport and Environment and Equal Opportunities Committees to assist the three MSPs. However, the affair was not a good advert for the new politics associated with the Parliament.

Second, there were disputes over the party balance of committee memberships as Labour sought to ensure party majorities on committees that did not reflect its position in the chamber. This was clearly an attempt at gamesmanship in advance of the agreement on committee composition. Third, there was a dispute between Labour and the SNP over the Nationalists' 1999 decision to allocate two of its subject committee convenors in Justice and Home Affairs and Enterprise and Lifelong Learning to senior frontbench spokespersons Roseanna Cunningham and John Swinney. Labour wished convenors to be backbenchers to prevent conflicts of interest between committees and party spokespersons. The dispute spread to the Conservatives, whose rural affairs spokesperson, Alex Johnstone, was also convenor of the Parliament's Rural Affairs Committee. The Scottish Executive was concerned that there would not be sufficient distinction between these MSPs in their roles as committee convenors and party spokespersons, making for an uneasy relationship with ministers over legislative discussions (*The Herald*, 30 June 1999). The Executive pointed to the fact that Liberal Democrat MSP Margaret Smith resigned as party spokesperson on health on assuming the position of convenor of the Health Committee. The Executive's attempt to place this issue before the Parliament's Procedure Committee was interpreted as an attack on the opposition parties. The issue was batted backwards and forwards between the Procedure Committee and the Convenors' Liaison Group, but was not found to be a problem. Indeed, there was a consensus within the Procedure Committee that the sharing of portfolios between convenors and party spokespersons had caused no difficulties for the independent operation of the committees concerned.[6] The issue disappeared in 2000 when SNP convenors changed after John Swinney became SNP leader.

The initial Parliamentary debate on the committee system threw up a range of potential committee changes. Despite the popularity of the notion of holistic government – problem-based policymaking occurring across departmental boundaries – the Parliament did not propose to establish holistic committees, although it might do so in future. While the designation of particular committees did move across issue areas and departments to some extent – the Social Inclusion, Housing and Voluntary Sector Committee, the Transport and Environment Committee, and the Health and Community Care Committee – this practice was quite limited and followed the allocation of ministerial portfolios in the Scottish Executive. Indeed, some MSPs called for the Social Exclusion Committee to exist as a cross-cutting interdepartmental committee in addition to a special committee on drug misuse which would cover issues relevant to subject committees such as Justice and Home Affairs, Health and Community Care, and Education.[7] Committees embraced the holistic notion to some extent, as was evident in the joint meeting of the Parliament's Finance and Audit Committees on 30 June 1999, but it was left to individual MSPs, the legislative process and cross-party groups to develop the holistic approach. The newness of the system therefore generated a certain caution.

There was also concern over the ability of committees to hold meetings around Scotland as envisaged by the Constitutional Convention and the Consultative Steering Group. There was seen to be a need for the committees to hold inquiries and evidence sessions around Scotland, rather than purely in Edinburgh, for practical purposes as well as for political purposes: to demonstrate that the Parliament belonged to the whole of Scotland not just Edinburgh or the central belt. However, financial limits on the Parliament's budget placed question marks over the ability of committees to convene sessions outside Edinburgh. Some MSPs, such as the SNP's Andrew Wilson, sought to gain Parliamentary support for touring committees during the early weeks of Parliamentary life,[8] but the issue seemed to fall by the wayside as the committees accepted the financial restrictions and became Edinburgh-centric. Following the Parliament's formation, committees met weekly or fortnightly in Edinburgh, which was quite practical given the fact of life of all other Parliamentary business occurring centrally, and they seldom ventured out of Edinburgh. The Enterprise and Lifelong Learning Committee visited Inverness on 20 October 1999 to take evidence on economic development, but few other committees ventured as far, if at all. In fact, that was the only committee to meet outside Edinburgh in 1999: one meeting out of a total of 175. Since then, committees have begun to meet around the country, but such visits remain few and far between. The Local Government and European committees held meetings in Glasgow in January 2000, Stirling was the venue for the Social Inclusion, Local Government and Justice committees in February and March 2000, the Petitions Committee held a meeting in Galashiels in March to consider the Borders rail petition, and the Rural Affairs Committee held a meeting in Melrose in April 2000. In addition, committee investigations frequently involved visits by MSPs to local communities so the Edinburgh-centric nature of the committees was some-what exaggerated and limited to official committee meetings.

Case study 3 The Justice and Home Affairs Committee

The Justice Committee has been one of the busiest in the Parliament, and its fourteen meetings in 1999 and twenty-five meetings in 2000 dealt with a vast number of topics, including five bills: the Abolition of Poindings and Warrant Sales Bill, the Abolition of Feudal Tenure Bill; the Adults with Incapacity Bill; the Regulation of Investigatory Powers Bill; and the Bail, Judicial Appointments etc. Bill. The fact that it was the lead committee responsible for debating five bills was immensely time-consuming. This role involved taking evidence on the proposed legislation and producing large reports on stage one of each bill, in addition to considering detailed amendments at stage two (see Chapter 6). Such work severely limited the committee's ability to deal with non-legislative matters, and consequently the committee only conducted short inquiries into family law, domestic violence, stalking, vulnerable witnesses, freedom of information and the prison system in 1999–2000, rather than the substantial inquiries conducted by other committees such as Enterprise and Lifelong Learning. The committee also dealt with a number of different petitions, subordinate legislation and European documents, but its agenda was predominantly driven by the Executive's legislative programme. Given the importance of Scots law to the Parliament and the fact that many legislative proposals affect the legal system, it is not surprising that this committee was both extremely busy and had a high profile within the Parliament. Future

---

legal reforms such as land reform, divorce and children's rights will ensure a packed legislative agenda for the Justice Committee in the future. Its first convenor, Roseanna Cunningham, had a high profile through this role as well as acting as the SNP's Justice spokesperson in the Parliament. Her former role as an advocate, added to the presence of a number of other solicitors and advocates on the committee, gave it a clear cutting edge in dealing with legislation and scrutinising ministers. The latter was particularly evident when the Justice Minister appeared before the committee to discuss the Noel Ruddle case (see Chapter 6) and prison closures in 1999.

Case study 4 The Education, Culture and Sport Committee
Despite the partisan climate within this committee, it was effective in dealing with legislation and policy issues. Disputes between the SNP, Conservative and Labour MSPs on the committee occurred on several occasions, with votes called along party lines. However, this type of behaviour did not disable the committee in its work. In terms of legislation, the committee's scrutiny role was limited in its 1999 meetings. Most of the committee's legislative work on the Standards in Scotland's Schools Bill was completed in February–May 2000, with a total of fourteen meetings on the subject. Such meetings included evidence sessions with the teaching unions, Scottish School Boards Association, Convention of Scottish Local Authorities (COSLA), the General Teaching Council and a number of individual schools and organisations. While this piece of legislation dominated the committee's agenda, it was also proactive in instituting a range of scrutiny inquiries. The committee adopted the procedure of using reporters (*rapporteurs*) to institute individual inquiries on behalf of the committee rather than relying on the committee as a whole to investigate an issue. This procedure lacked the depth of full-committee inquiries but had the benefit of spreading the committee's investigative capacity around several areas. This goal was particularly important given the committee's wide remit: not just education, but culture and sport. Thus, in its first year of operation the committee was able to begin inquiries into the Scottish film industry, special educational needs, Hampden Park and rural schools. The committee also produced a report on a petition about Roman remains at Cramond in Edinburgh.[9]

– THE INITIAL IMPACT OF THE COMMITTEE SYSTEM –

Like so many other developments associated with devolution, the Parliament's committee system is in its infancy. The workload of the committees was varied in its first year (see Table 5.2), as was the pattern of their activities. Such activities fall into five areas: legislative scrutiny, committee investigations, designing the Parliament, dealing with subordinate legislation, and processing public petitions. In terms of overall workload, some committees were clearly busier than others, and this will be a persistent pattern throughout each Parliamentary year. The number of committee meetings was conditioned by a number of factors. Some committees had no government legislation to consider in 1999 because of the times at which bills were introduced – this was the case with the Transport and Environment Committee. Other committees such as Justice and Home Affairs had to deal with three separate pieces of legislation in 1999 alone and more in subsequent years (see Case study 3). Subordinate legislation and petitions also had a differential impact on committee business across the various policy areas. However, committees themselves had an important influence over their workloads: their agendas were not merely determined by the pace of government legislation or MSPs' bills, but by their own investigative efforts. Some committees sought to institute a number of investigations during their first year – Justice and Home Affairs and Health and Community Care for example – while other committees were less active.

Formal meetings of committees were one indication of how busy each committee was, although they only tell part of the story. They do not detail the informal business of the committees in terms of pre-meetings or visits conducted by MSPs outside meetings. Examples of this phenomenon included:

1. visits by local government committee members to twelve individual local authorities to determine responses to the Commission on Local Government and the Scottish Parliament
2. the work of three subcommittees of the Equal Opportunities Committee dealing with race, gender and sexual orientation issues
3. the work of four different reporters on the Education, Culture and Sport Committee in 1999–2000, dealing with consultation with children and young people, sport in schools, the Scottish film industry, and rural schools
4. Visits by MSPs on the Enterprise and Lifelong Learning Committee to examine the pilot scheme for individual learning accounts in Fife
5. Rural Affairs Committee members held investigation meetings in Dingwall, Newton Stewart and Stornoway and also visited Islay to investigate the closure of the creamery.

Table 5.2 Meetings of committees 1999–2000

Committee	1999	Jan–6 July 2000
Audit	8	11
Education, Culture and Sport	11	23
Enterprise and Lifelong Learning	9	17
Equal Opportunities	9	17
European Union	10	14
Finance	10	19
Health and Community Care	16	18
Justice and Home Affairs	14	25
Local Government	12	23
Procedures	9	8
Public Petitions	6	12
Rural Affairs	11	22
Social Inclusion	12	26
Standards	16	11
Subordinate Legislation	14	23
Transport and Environment	8	18
Total	**175**	**287**

– Legislative scrutiny –

The legislative functions of the committees were extremely varied in 1999–2000. Because of the substance and timing of the government's legislative programme, individual committees had different levels of involvement in considering legislation. For example, the Transport and Environment, Rural Affairs and Enterprise and Lifelong Learning committees had no bills to consider from June 1999 to February 2000 (although the latter did deal with legislation after that date). This situation meant that these committees were free to conduct their own investigations into government policy or specific policy areas. This situation contrasted with that of the Justice and Home Affairs Committee which had a very busy legislative agenda in 1999–2000 (see Case study 3), and the Finance Committee which was responsible for debating stages of all bills proposed in 1999–2000 for their financial implications and was therefore required to scrutinise and report on eleven different bills in addition to subordinate legislation. As bills were often discussed by more than one committee, then almost every committee had some legislative scrutiny in the Parliament's first year, though some was relatively minor. The major players in 1999–2000, with the heaviest workloads, were: Justice, which dealt with five bills in total in 1999–2000; Education, Culture and Sport, which discussed the Standards in Scotland's Schools Bill at fourteen meetings; Local Government, which debated the Ethical Standards in Public Life Bill on fourteen occasions, as well as the Abolition of Poindings and Warrants Sales Bill and the Transport Bill; and the Rural Affairs Committee, which discussed four different bills, including ten meetings on the National Parks Bill, and a vast amount of subordinate legislation.

The legislative scrutiny offered by committees did lead to some changes in legislation and defeats for the Executive. The stand of the Equal Opportunities Committee over the Census Order 2000 was one clear example of the Executive being defeated by a committee. The committee wanted a question on religion to be included in the census, and had considerable support from MSPs of all parties. The Executive was forced to give ground and adopt the committee's position in February 2000. Similarly, several committees supported the Abolition of Poindings and Warrant Sales Bill against the Executive's position, leading to the Executive's defeat at the first-stage vote on the bill in 2000 (see Chapter 6 on MSPs' bills).

– Investigating –

The Parliament's committees had a varied approach to their investigative functions. All committees, barring Procedures and Subordinate Legislation, conducted investigations of some type from 1999–2000. Some were short evidence sessions dealing with particular topics, such as the Justice and Home Affairs Committee's investigation into the prison service, and the Equal Opportunities Committee's evidence on the impact of the European Convention on Human Rights on Scots law in February 2000. Other investigations involved more lengthy inquiries that examined issues in detail and produced reports (see Table 5.3). The form of investigation was attributable to the issue involved, the committee's other workload, and the culture and demands of the committees themselves. For example, the Equal Opportunities Committee monitored a large number of issues but only published one report; the Audit Committee produced a large number of one-off reports and investigations; the Education, Culture and Sport Committee produced short inquiries and reports into areas as diverse as the arts companies, special educational needs in schools, the Scottish film industry, Hampden Park and rural schools, but no major inquiry. By way of contrast, some committees spent a large part of their first year conducting in-depth investigations into single topics. The Enterprise and Lifelong Learning Committee spent eleven meetings investigating local economic development services and produced a major report in May 2000; the Transport and Environment Committee discussed the issue of telecommunications development at five meetings (see Case study 5); the Health and Community Care Committee devoted nine meetings to its community care inquiry in the Parliament's first year; the Social Inclusion, Housing and

Table 5.3 Committee inquiry reports 1999–July 2000

Committee	*Report*
Audit	Fourth Report 2000: Scottish Enterprise: Skillseekers training for young people
	Third Report 2000: The Scottish Ambulance Service
	Second Report 2000: The private finance contract to complete and operate the A74(M)/M74 motorway in Scotland
	First Report 2000: Scottish further education colleges: managing costs
	Second Report 1999: The millennium threat: is Scotland ready?
Education	Fifth Report 2000: Response of the Committee to Petition PE9 on Roman remains at Cramond
	First Report 2000: Report in inquiry into the national arts companies
Enterprise	2000: Inquiry into the delivery of local economic development services in Scotland: Final report 1999: Inquiry into the delivery of local economic development services in Scotland: Interim conclusions phase 1
Equal Opportunities	First Report 1999: The Stephen Lawrence Inquiry – an action plan for Scotland
European	Fourth Report 2000: Report on mainstreaming environmental issues into government policy in Scotland
	Third Report 2000: Report on Objective 2 plans
	Second Report, 2000: Report on European Structural Fund programme management executives and their relationship with the Scottish Executive
	Third Report, 1999: Report on the Objective 3 operational plan
	Second Report 1999: Report on the European Fisheries Council of December 1999
Finance	Twelfth Report 2000: The finance functions of the Scottish Executive
	Sixth Report 1999: Scottish Budget sub programme expenditure plans (Level 2 figures)
Health	Third Report 2000: Report on Stobhill Petition PE 48
	Ninth Report 1999: Report on Stracathro Petition PE 13
	Eighth Report 1999: The Health and Community Care Committee's review of Fair Shares for All – The National Review of Resource Allocation for the NHS in Scotland
Justice	Third Report 2000: Report on Petition PE14 from Carbeth Hutter's Association
Local Government	Eight Report 2000: Non-domestic rates
	Third Report 2000: Issues arising from the McIntosh Report

Procedures	First Report 1999: Draft standing orders of the Scottish Parliament
Rural Affairs	Sixth Report 1999: Interim report on the Agricultural Business Improvement Scheme
	Fifth Report 1999: The impact of the Scottish Adjacent Waters Boundaries Order 1999
	Second Report 1999: Impact of amnesiac shellfish poisoning on the fisheries sector
Social Inclusion	Third Report 2000: Housing stock transfer
Standards	Third Report 2000: Register of Members' staff interests
	Second Report 2000: Register of interests of staff of Members of the Scottish Parliament
	First Report 2000: Code of conduct for Members
	Fourth Report 1999: Report on complaints against Mike Watson MSP
	Third Report 1999: Interim complaints procedure
	Second Report 1999: Regulation of cross-party groups
	First Report 1999: Report of an inquiry into matters brought to the attention of the Committee by The Observer newspaper.
Transport and Environment	Third Report 2000: Report on inquiry into the proposals to introduce new planning procedures for telecommunications developments

Case study 5 The Transport and Environment Committee and the telecommunications inquiry

The planning regulations for mobile telephone masts were one of five major issues of interest identified by the Transport and Environment Committee at its two-day informal briefing session in summer 1999. There was a consensus within the committee to investigate the issue as several MSPs had received representations from constituents on the subject and the Scottish Parliament Information Office had produced a briefing paper on it. The issue arose from local concerns about the ease with which mobile telephone masts could be erected in sensitive areas such as hospitals or in areas of natural beauty with minimal planning procedures. There was also concern about the health risk associated with the masts, in terms of radiation, as well as the multiplicity of masts used by the individual companies. The inquiry was launched on 27 September 1999 with a call for evidence on three distinct questions: the institution of full planning control for telecommunications developments, the identification of health and environmental criteria for the siting of telecommunications developments, and the content of Scottish Executive guidance to telecommunications operators.[11] The committee took evidence on the issue at four different meetings in November and December. These sessions featured oral evidence from mobile phone companies such as Atlantic Telecom, Orange and Vodaphone, environmental agencies such as Scottish Natural Heritage and the Natural Radiological Protection Board, local authorities such as Highland Council, Dumfries and Galloway Council and Edinburgh City Council, and pressure groups such as Friends of the Earth. The process attracted strong lobbying by the telecommunications industry as well as from local campaign groups concerned at the proliferation of mobile phone masts. The committee published its report on 29 March 2000 with recommendations for the development of national planning regulations for telecommunications developments and the ability of local authorities to practise full planning control and the power to direct developments away from sensitive areas such as hospitals, schools and nurseries.[12] Notably, the recommendations conflicted with the positions of the Department of Trade and Industry, the Scottish Executive and telecommunications companies. Also, significantly, the report did not disappear down a black hole, and was the subject of the first committee-sponsored debate in the plenary of the Parliament on 11 May 2000. The debate was attended by the Transport and Environment Minister, Sarah Boyack, who pledged to use the report as the basis for changes to planning procedures, with full planning consent necessary for some types of development, as well as new legislation to deal with telecommunications developments.[13]

Voluntary Sector Committee conducted a major inquiry into housing stock transfer, which took twelve meetings and a major report in July 2000, as well as a second inquiry into drugs, which was discussed at eight meetings in 1999–2000. The stock transfer report was a notable event as it was the product of a divided committee in which SNP MSPs walked out of the final meeting on the report and produced their own minority conclusion as an annexe to the report (The Herald, 13 July 2000).[10] Given that the stock transfer issue was a highly partisan question and a key part of Labour's policy in the Scottish Parliament, such a divison was predictable. It is in contrast to other major inquiries which did not focus on such high-profile and divisive issues and were able to produce reports with an all-party consensus.

– Determining the Parliament's rules –

Several committees were also active in determining the rules and procedures of the Parliament in 1999–2000. The Procedures Committee was extremely busy in debating the Parliament's standing orders during its first year of existence, in addition to discussing the effectiveness of ministerial question time, video-conferencing facilities and the role of the Convenor's Liaison Group. The Standards Committee was active in designing a code of conduct for MSPs, considering the issue of lobbying (including an investigation into 'Lobbygate') and investigating individual complaints against MSPs.

– Subordinate legislation –

Most committees dealt with subordinate legislation as a matter of course. Often they reviewed small pieces of legislation intended to institute and maintain laws and regulations across many aspects of government in Scotland. The Subordinate Legislation Committee was the centre of discussion on such regulations and statutory instruments and its work is extremely legalistic and technical. The committee was responsible for evaluating such riveting pieces of legislation as the Docks and Harbours (Rateable Values) (Scotland) Order 2000 (SSI 2000/draft), Local Authorities' Traffic Orders (Exemption for Disabled Persons) (Scotland) Regulation 2000 (SSI 2000/60), and the Crab Claws (Prohibition of Landing) Revocation (Scotland) Order 2000 (SSI 2000/81). Despite the obscurity of these pieces of legislation, they are necessary to give effect to a vast number of government laws and policies. Moreover, they impact upon a large number of the Parliament's committees by spilling over onto their agendas. For example, in 1999–2000 the Rural Affairs Committee published six reports on subordinate legislation, the Health and Community Care Committee published sixteen reports on subordinate legislation, and the Local Government Committee published nine reports on the subject. All committees had to deal with large amounts of subordinate legislation in the Parliament's first year of existence, a reality which dominated some committee meetings and generated numerous reports as indicated.

– Processing petitions –

Most committees also had to deal with public petitions, referred to them through the Parliament's Public Petitions Committee.[14] The Parliament had designed a specific procedure for public petitions, partly out of dissatisfaction with arrangements at Westminster, where they are largely ignored within Parliamentary processes. Petitions mostly end up, unacknowledged, undebated and placed in a bag behind the Speaker's chair. In the Scottish Parliament, petitions are directed towards the Petitions Committee which was charged with processing them formally. Usually, this involves discussing the form of a petition and determining which institution it should be referred to, and this often brings the Petitions Committee to direct a petition to another Parliamentary committee for discussion and action. The Petitions Committee is bound to process each petition, and has to discuss each one that is lodged, even if it recommends no action in relation to a petition. Moreover, the petition process is outlined on the Parliament's website and in information documents, so that the public or organisations are able to read guidance on the style and format of petitions and submit them electronically. Petitions can be presented by an individual, collection of individuals, group or organisation. The treatment of public petitions varies according to the type of issue involved, although some committees are negative about them as they can dominate their agenda and push the committee away from the issues it is most concerned with. Many petitions merely involve a committee writing to the Scottish Executive to raise the issues outlined, but a number of petitions involve more serious action by Parliamentary committees and demonstrate the utility of the petitions process as an agenda-setting exercise and as a grievance procedure.

A good example of the latter type was the petition from the Strathcathro Hospital Staff Action Committee (PE13) in Brechin, concerned at the hospital's future, which led to an investigation and report by the Parliament's Health and Community Care Committee in December 1999.[15] The report was severely critical of the handling of the hospital's future, especially in relation to the actions of Tayside Health Board, and thus, the committee sought to make a quango accountable for its actions. The Justice and Home Affairs Committee discussed petitions at seven out of its eighteen meetings from June 1999 to 1 February 2000. It also took evidence on a number of petitions, notably that of the Carbeth Hutters in Stirlingshire (PE14) who petitioned about the landowner's rent rise on their properties, and managed to produce a public campaign as well as considerable media coverage. The committee took evidence on the situation at Carbeth and published a report of its evidence in February 2000,[16] and the Scottish Executive subsequently launched a consultation exercise on legal changes to protect the hutters (The Herald, 7 July 2000). The Health and Community Care Committee undertook an inquiry into the public consultation over the proposed secure unit at Stobhill Hospital by Greater Glasgow Health Board in February 2000.[17] The report, conducted by former GP Richard Simpson MSP, was critical of the health board's efforts to involve the public in its decision-making. The appearance of health board officials at an earlier Petitions Committee meeting also demonstrated the level of scrutiny facilitated by the Parliament's existence, compared with previous arrangements. Quangos such as the health boards were no longer able to shelter behind Westminster's remoteness from their decisionmaking, but had to contend with the locality and activism of the Scottish Parliament and new routes for public action.

Table 5.4 Examples of public petitions 1999–2000

Petition from Western Isles Council on Skye Bridge discounting options for Western Isles residents (PE17) (lodged on 1 October 1999)

Petition from Penicuik and District Community Council calling for a concessionary bus fare scheme to be operated nationally by the Scottish Executive (PE21) (lodged on 21 October 1999)

Petition from the Island of Cumbrae Tourist Association outlining concerns in relation to the fare structure of Caledonian MacBrayne for the ferry to Cumbrae Island and calling for more detailed financial information to be made available (PE22) (lodged on 21 October 1999)

Petition from Friends of the Earth Scotland calling for the Scottish Parliament to (1) exercise its powers to ensure that it will not permit the release of genetically-modified crops into the environment by way of trials or commercial planting; and (2) establish a mechanism in Scotland which will address the concerns regarding the impact of such releases on the environment and human health (PE51) (lodged on 21 December 1999)

Petition by Age Concern Scotland calling for the Scottish Parliament to implement all of those recommendations contained in the report of the Royal Commission on Long Term Care for the elderly, which its devolved powers permit (PE77) (lodged on 25 January 2000)

Petition by Steven Birrell calling for the Scottish Parliament to ascertain the feasibility of a permanent webcast facility covering the proceedings of the Chamber and non-private committee meetings once the Parliament returns to Edinburgh (PE206) (lodged on 23 May 2000)

The sources of public petitions were varied. Some came from pressure groups, such as PE2 from Ayrshire Chamber of Commerce, PE24 from the National Farmers Union of Scotland (which launched a number of petitions as an agenda-setting exercise), and PE8 from the Scottish Homing Union for Pigeons. Some came from local community and residents' groups such as PE23 from Save Wemyss Ancient Caves Society and PE30 from Almondell Terrace residents in Livingston. Other petitions emanated from concerned individuals, especially Frank Harvey, a one-man petitioning machine who lodged thirty-five petitions in the Parliament's first year, dealing with everything from banning animal circuses to improving passenger safety on public transport. However, despite the output of this one individual, the most striking thing about the petitions procedure was that it was taken seriously by Parliamentary committees, who processed the petitions in a variety of ways. There were 244 petitions lodged between June 1999 and the close of the Parliamentary year in July 2000, and around half of them made progress in the Parliament during this period. The petitions procedure was both popular with the public and pressure groups and seen as a useful route to press for Parliamentary action and involvement. It also had the effect of keeping the MSPs in touch with lower-profile and local issues of concern to the public.

– Reform of the committee system –

Although the committee system had been in operation for less than a year, the Parliament discussed proposals for reforming the committees in the spring of 2000. The legislative overload of the Justice Committee and the varied workloads of other committees led to questions about reshaping the system. Reviewing the workings of a system which had begun to bed down by 2000 was a natural reaction to the different activities and demands on committees, and underlying such a debate were more fundamental factors relating to the pressure on MSPs to participate fully in committee life. For example, while there are 129 MSPs in the Scottish Parliament, this does not mean that there are 129 people available to fill committee places. Twenty-one MSPs are ministers in the Scottish Executive and therefore do not participate in the Parliament's committee system. The two opposition leaders, John Swinney and David McLetchie, do not serve on any Parliamentary committees, nor are the Presiding Officer, David Steel, and one of his deputies involved in committee work. So, in fact we are looking at only 104 possible committee members. There are, however, 169 committee places, plus a requirement for three members of the Presiding Officer's team, four members of the Scottish Parliamentary Corporate body, and members and deputy members of the Scottish Parlimentary Bureau. The numerical gap between the number of available MSPs and the number of committee places goes a long way to explaining why many MSPs actually serve on two committees on the Mound, including twelve out of sixteen committee convenors. And, among those serving on just one committee, a fair number are also party spokespersons. The workload of individual MSPs in committees is the most important and time-consuming part of their Parliamentary responsibilities, and it is especially time-consuming for those serving on two committees. There is a clear potential for overload and exhaustion when government legislation has to undergo detailed scrutiny in the Parliament's committees, from Parliamentarians who have to scrutinise several bills simultaneously, conduct their own investigations of government policies, examine subordinate legislation and deal with public petitions.

Similarly, the government's proposals to cut the number of Scottish MPs at Westminster in order to address the West Lothian question will seriously impinge on the size of the Scottish Parliament. There is a proportional link between the number of Scottish MPs at Westminster and the size of the new Parliament. A smaller Westminster contingent will bring about a smaller number of MSPs, and John Curtice (1998) calculated that Scotland would see a Parliament of 109 MSPs in operation in 2007. If we subtract the twenty-five MSPs unavailable for committee work now, we can see there will only be eighty-four MSPs left to serve on committees that currently require 169 bodies. That will prove to be crunch time for devolution.

– CONCLUSION –

The first year of the Parliament offered a steep learning curve for the new committee system as each grappled with its agendas and policy areas, in addition to establishing working relationships between a disparate group of committee members. However, the committees increasingly asserted their authority with a series of detailed reports and interventions on government and policy: the economic development and telecommunications reports were two clear cases in point. Moreover, as the committees were intended to generate cumulative policy expertise amongst MSPs, then the longer the committees scrutinise issues with the current committee formats and memberships, the more effective they should become. What might prevent the committees achieving this level of scrutiny and expertise is their overloaded agendas. The experience of the Justice and Home Affairs Committee in its first year was the sole example of a committee dominated by legislation and unable to proceed with other forms of scrutiny, but it was a clear instance of the downside of the multifunctional committee system. Parliamentary debate over the reform of the committee system in 2000 was an indication that the problem of overload was recognised.

The area of policy and administration in which the committees were most effective was the area of quangos. Such public bodies were subject to a range of scrutiny exercises by committees, especially in the case of the health boards. Committees were less effective in scrutinising the work of the Scottish Executive, but then this type of scrutiny stretched across many different bodies and activities, and MSPs were individually active in scrutinising the Executive, as were the opposition parties. The intention of placing committees at the heart of the Parliament's legislative and scrutiny processes was effective both in terms of the level of scrutiny provided by the committees as revising chambers in relation to Executive legislation, and in the work of ministers and government bodies. Finally, party conflicts occurred within the committee system, but not seriously enough to disable the committees concerned.

– Notes –

1. This approach was proposed by the committee convenor, Mike Watson, after a trip to the Yemeni Parliament.
2. Tom McCabe MSP (Minister for Parliament), col. 623, Scottish Parliament, *Official Report*, 17 June 1999, vol. 1, no. 10.
3. Ibid.
4. Motion S1M–37, Scottish Parliament, *Official Report*, 8 June 1999, vol. 1, no. 7.
5. Scottish Parliament Committee Guidance, *Role of Committee Convenor*, 1999.
6. Procedure Committee, *Official Report*, 15 February 2000.
7. Keith Raffan MSP, Scottish Parliament, *Official Report*, 8 June 1999, vol. 1, no. 7, col. 271.
8. Motion S1M–7, Scottish Parliament, *Official Report*, 1999.
9. Education, Culture and Sport Committee, *Fifth Report 2000: Response of the Committee to Petition PE9 on Roman Remains at Cramond*.
10. See Social Inclusion, Housing and Voluntary Sector Committee, *Third Report 2000: Housing Stock Transfer*.
11. Committee news release, 'The Transport and Environment Committee Telecommunications Inquiry', Scottish Parliament, 27 September 1999.
12. Transport and Environment Committee, *Third Report 2000: Report on the Inquiry into Proposals to Introduce New Planning Procedures for Telecommunications Developments*, 29 March 2000.
13. Scottish Parliament, *Official Report*, 12 May 2000, col. 562–8.
14. *Scottish Parliament Standing Orders*, 15.4 to 15.6, pp68–9.
15. Health and Community Care Committee, *Ninth Report 1999: Report on Stracathro Petition PE13*.
16. Justice and Home Affairs Committee, *Official Report*, 16 February 2000.
17. Health and Community Care Committee, *Official Report*, 23 February 2000.

CHAPTER 6

The legislative process of the Scottish Parliament

– INTRODUCTION –

The Scottish Parliament was designed to fulfil an ambitious agenda of participatory politics by the public and pressure groups as well as power-sharing between parties and legislators and the pursuit of consensus politics. The policy process of the Parliament, largely designed by the Consultative Steering Group, sought to give birth to a 'new politics' which relied upon open government, a strong legislature and multiple opportunities for consultation and public access to decisionmaking. Those responsible for designing the Scottish Parliament had high aspirations for its performance as a legislature, often fuelled by highly negative perceptions of Westminster. The Scottish Constitutional Convention sought a Parliament characterised by 'accountability, accessibility, openness, and responsiveness to the people' (Scottish Constitutional Convention, 1995: p. 24). The Consultative Steering Group attempted to design a Parliament which would be 'accessible, open, responsive and develop procedures which make possible a participative approach to the development, consideration and scrutiny of policy and legislation' (Consultative Steering Group, 1999: p. 3).

The legislative process of the Scottish Parliament was intended to embody such goals of openness and accountability. Features such as the process of pre-legislative consultation and the requirement for bills to be accompanied by memoranda which reported on the outcome of consultation were intended to make policymaking more open and participatory. The number of stages of bills, the ability of committees and individual MSPs to make legislation, and the multiple roles of committees were all intended to strengthen the Parliament against the executive. As the Scottish Parliament is a unicameral system, it is the committees which have been given the task of acting as revising chambers for legislation and thus play a key role in the legislative process.

– Understanding the legislative process –

Unlike Westminster, where the executive dominates the legislative process and there are few opportunities for backbenchers to make laws, the Scottish Parliament features a number of legislative processes with the potential to empower backbench MSPs and the Parliament's committees. How such potential becomes a reality remains to be seen, but the Parliament's legislative arrangements do allow political actors other than the Executive to draft legislation. It enables committees to propose legislation as committee recommendations could be easily ignored by government and the committees could have no opportunity to implement their proposals or recommendations – one of the flaws of Westminster's Select Committee system. The legislative process contains other features that are intended to lead to more open policymaking. Each of these features is examined below.

– Pre-legislative scrutiny –

The Parliament's policy process was devised to involve a procedure for pre-legislative scrutiny. Rather than consultation with relevant agencies and pressure groups occurring after a bill is published, pre-legislative scrutiny allows detailed discussion of legislative proposals before they are published in the form of a bill. This development formalises a process often carried out informally and in private. It also facilitates more public discussion of legislative proposals and brings pressure group involvement out into the open, with the effect of contributing to a more competitive pressure group environment. Two additional factors are worth considering in relation to pre-legislative scrutiny. First, the process guarantees access and involvement to pressure groups. They cannot be excluded from the process in its early stages and the Scottish Executive cannot be selective in allowing access to the policy process for certain groups. Second, the fact that the outcome of consultation has to be included in a memorandum to accompany draft bills means that some pressure group preferences and responses become public rather than quietly contained within the Executive. This situation brings into the open opposition to certain proposals as well as specific amendments at a much earlier stage in the legislative process than normal. Given the way in which legislation is made, such early scrutiny wedded to the coalition, multi-party, consensual style under which legislation will be discussed, offers opportunities for legislation to be altered before it becomes a bill, let alone an Act. It also enables the Executive to test out particular policy proposals and amend them according to public and/or pressure group opinion. One example of this practice was the Scottish Executive's decision to drop its proposals for congestion charges on the M8 motorway between Glasgow and

Edinburgh following pre-legislative consultation on the Transport White Paper in 1999. The business community in particular was opposed to congestion charges on such an important communications link in central Scotland, which would push up business costs as well as penalise consumers.

Of course, there is a downside to such inclusive and exhaustive consultation. First, civic Scotland has been consulted to death. Pressure groups involved in some devolved areas have found themselves constantly consulted over policy proposals by both the Scottish Executive and a number of Parliamentary committees at different stages of the policy process. Second, consultation is just that – consultation. And since everyone is consulted, then no group would appear to gain a particular advantage from the process. Also, as Brian Hogwood noted, writing in 1985, 'if consultation is everything, then may be it's nothing'. This situation might obtain here because the Executive is bound to consult, yet is not bound by the results of the consultation; indeed, it can ignore them. Third, the system of pre-legislative scrutiny, when added to the process for Parliamentary scrutiny of legislation, lengthens the time it takes to pass laws. This system meant that the first year of the Parliament was one of seemingly endless consultation and deliberation of legislative proposals, with few proposals actually passed until the latter stages of the first year of the Parliament.

– MEMORANDA TO BILLS –

One innovation which differentiates the legislative process of the Scottish Parliament from Westminster is the requirement for bills to be accompanied by a number of additional explanatory documents, for example, bills must contain accompanying documents outlining the main goals and features of the legislation. In addition, a bill must have two different memoranda to explain aspects of the proposal. A financial memorandum details the costs of the legislative proposal, and outlines where those costs are likely to fall, such as the Scottish government, local government, or other organisations or individuals.[1] The proposal must also contain a policy memorandum setting out the policy objectives of the legislation, and it must provide details of the pre-legislative consultation process, and outline why the particular legislative proposal – as opposed to other proposals – was adopted. The policy memorandum must also include an assessment of the effects of the legislation on equal opportunities, human rights, island communities, local government, sustainable development and any other matters which the Scottish ministers consider to be relevant.[2]

The benefit of such memoranda is that they are written in plain English. Rather than having to wade through the obscure, highly legal format of a bill, MSPs, pressure groups, journalists and individual members of the public can read the policy memorandum in order to determine the aim of a bill, as well as its impact upon different areas of policy. The various options examined by the Scottish Executive and the reasons it chose to pursue a particular set of proposals are all dealt with in the memoranda. Such mechanisms significantly increase the openness of the policy process by increasing the amount of information available to participants in the process. Sure enough, some memoranda are long and complex and leave one with the feeling of being buried under a mountain of paper, but the amount of information available through the policy and financial memoranda versus that which can be gleaned from a bill is radically different.

The Scottish Executive published its policy memorandum on the Abolition of Feudal Tenure (Scotland) Bill, on 6 October 1999. The memorandum contained nine pages of information, outlining the bill's objectives, the details of three alternative approaches to the legislation in the bill, as well as the consultation process for the bill. Consultation was widespread, for a number of reasons. The bill was largely the outcome of earlier consultations by the Scottish Law Commission from 1991 onwards. The Scottish Executive also contacted around 3,000 organisations from 30 June 1999 onwards as part of its pre-legislative consultation: a process which yielded sixty-five replies.[3] The general thrust of these replies was included in the policy memorandum, followed by details of the effects of the bill on sustainable development, human rights, and so on. Moreover, the accompanying document to the bill comprised forty three pages of description of the bill's aims and objectives, as well as a financial memorandum outlining the costs of the legislation to feudal superiors such as individual landowners and local authorities, in addition to the public costs of the changes in relation to administration and compensation.

In contrast to the wealth of detail provided by the Executive to accompany the Abolition of Feudal Tenure (Scotland) Bill, other policy memoranda were less revealing in relation to consultation. Some merely stated that consultation had taken place and provided no detail on the level of substance of responses. The small number of responses to consultation (see Table 6.1) also illustrated that it was mostly a one-way process, and most of the groups and individuals consulted did not respond. The prominent exception involved the Ethical Standards in Public Life Bill. However, the vast majority of responses to this proposal involved the repeal of section 2a/28 of the Local Government Act which prevented local authorities from spending money on promoting homosexuality. Many of the responses in this area also featured pressure groups from across the world, rather than civic Scotland alone.

Table 6.1 Consultations undertaken in pre-legislative scrutiny

Bill	Consultations issued	Consultations received
Ethical Standards in Public Life	approx 6,500	approx 2,300
Adults with Incapacity	N/A	160
Public Finance and Accountability	approx 50	17
Standards in Scotland's Schools	approx 27,000	N/A
GTC paper	approx 5,600	130
Abolition of Feudal Tenure	3,000	65
National Parks	2,500	330
Transport	N/A	102

Source: Policy Memoranda of the Scottish Executive 1999–2000

– Multiple access points –

A third feature of the Scottish Parliament's legislative process is the way in which it provides multiple access points to outside interests such as pressure groups. Such access is provided in two ways and is explained in more detail below. First, the existence of pre-legislative scrutiny, the need for Executive consultation, draft bills, committee scrutiny and amendments, and plenary debates offers multiple opportunities for pressure group access to the policy process. Second, the fact that there are different routes to proposing legislation through Executive, committee and members' bills, which each feature these access points, allows opportunities for pressure groups to promote legislation and suggest amendments. For example, there is scope for pressure groups to campaign for non-Executive bills in a number of areas in conjunction with individual MSPs or groups of MSPs.

Of course, while both the Consultative Steering Group and supporters of the Parliament presented its openness and accountability as positive benefits which will democratise Scottish politics and decisionmaking, other interpretations can be given. Michael Dyer, for example, identified some of the problems that may develop with the Scottish model in practice (1999: p. 22):

> The extenuated legislative process could easily become sclerotic; the specialist committees are likely to attract MSPs representing producer rather than consumer concerns; and the legally-enshrined opportunities for direct participation could be meat and drink for interest groups . . . The bias of participation in favour of the articulate could well prove a balance against the poor, ill-educated and unconnected. Holyrood is closer to Edinburgh New Town than Drumchapel. Scotland's constitution may have escaped the frying pan of Westminster for the fire of Washington.

The involvement of the 'usual suspects' in the policy process – those pressure groups that already had good relations with government pre-devolution – was a notable feature of the Parliament's committee system (Lynch, 2000). The public and less well-resourced groups did not enjoy the same level of access: a reality typical of policymaking processes in most states.

Similarly, despite the design of the Parliament, with committees intended as a counterweight to a potentially dominant executive, party politics will often intrude. It would be a surprise if it were otherwise. The committee structure encourages MSPs to act independently in relation to scrutiny of government activities and legislation, but MSPs represent parties not themselves. The chamber and each committee enjoyed a numerical majority for the coalition government, and MSPs can be viewed as both supporters and opponents of government in relation to their party affiliation. Whether the need for Labour and Liberal Democrat MSPs to sustain their government's legislation and policies emasculates the functioning of the committee system during the four-year session of the Parliament remains to be seen.

THE SCOTTISH EXECUTIVE'S
LEGISLATIVE PROGRAMME 1999–2000

The legislative activity of the Scottish Parliament in its first year had a number of different origins, such as party manifestos, the partnership agreement between the coalition parties, MSP activism and the annual activities of the Parliament. However, some of the policies processed through the Scottish Parliament as Executive bills were not new to devolution. Many of the initial eight bills proposed by the Labour-Liberal Democrat coalition were subject to some part of the policy process before the election on 6 May 1999. They were not new pieces of legislation, but proposals that had already been prepared through the Scottish Office and a number of agencies in the period from 1997–9. For example, the measures for land reform had been considered by the Scottish Office's Land Reform Policy Group, which published two consultation papers in 1998 (Land Reform Policy Group, 1998a, 1998b), as well as a final set of recommendations in 1999 (Land Reform Policy Group, 1999). The proposals to establish national parks in Scotland were subject to a consultation paper by Scottish Natural Heritage on behalf of the Scottish Office in 1998 (Scottish Natural Heritage, 1998) and a set, of recommendations in 1999 (Scottish Natural Heritage, 1999). The Scottish Executive's education proposals were mirrored in Labour's education White Paper in 1999 (Scottish Office, 1999), and the proposals for a bill to improve standards in local government mirrored Labour's consultation paper on local government in 1998 (Scottish Office, 1998).

However, although such bills were part-processed in terms of adminis-trative preparation, discussion and consultation, they would have taken many years to be passed at Westminster given the fact that few Scottish bills were dealt with by Westminster before devolution. However, what was curious about the Executive's first bills was that a number of them had already been subject to widespread consultation and discussion and, follow-ing devolution, this process was then replicated by the Scottish Parliament. After devolution, the Parliament's committees considered these bills for the first time, but the same pressure groups and interests were consulted as before. Thus, despite the obvious repetition, pressure group Scotland had a second bite at some of the bills and was able to attempt to amend legislation through the medium of the Parliament's committee system.

The government's legislative programme for 1999–2000 had a number of distinct parts. On the one hand, there were legislative proposals such as the Public Finance and Accountability Bill and the Budget Bill that were of interest to MSPs alone and not the wider public. But beyond these examples were a range of bills of much broader relevance such as the Adults with Incapacity Bill, the Abolition of Feudal Tenure (Scotland) Bill, the Ethical Standards in Public Life (Scotland) Bill, the National Parks (Scotland) Bill and the Standards in Scotland's Schools Bill. Two bills introduced in 2000 were also intended to make changes in Scots law that conflicted with the European Convention of Human Rights. The Bail, Judicial Appointments etc. (Scotland) Bill and the Regulation of Investigatory Powers (Scotland) Bill both arose from Scotland's need to comply with the European Con-vention over police powers of surveillance and the ability of the Scottish Executive to appoint temporary sheriffs and operate bail procedures. These two pieces of legislation did not originate in party mainfestos or pressure group lobbying and were simply laws required because the European Convention was incorporated into Scots law in the Scotland Act 1998. In addition, these laws were introduced into the Scottish Parliament without pre-legislative consultation, although the Executive did consult with a variety of legal institutions.[4]

There was also an unpredictable element to some aspects of legislation. For example, the decision of the Executive to abolish section 2a/28 of the Local Government Act (1986), which prevented local authorities promot-ing the issue of homosexuality, brought about intense media and public scrutiny. Although the Ethical Standards in Public Life (Scotland) Bill was a fairly uncontroversial measure to institute a new standards regime within Scottish local authorities, the decision to use the bill to repeal section 2a/28 provoked a storm of protest. A number of religious groups protested about the change, leading to the formation of the Keep the Clause campaign funded by Stagecoach owner Brian Soutar. Instead of the Scottish Parliament considering the bill at plenary and committee sessions in relative obscurity, the bill was subject to intense campaigning and lobbying by a variety of pressure groups. Acting through a PR agency, Keep the Clause financed advertising hoardings across Scotland to retain the clause and succeeded in making the topic a prominent issue at the Ayr by-election in March 2000. Stagecoach owner Brian Soutar also financed a postal referendum to the tune of £1 million to retain the clause, which produced 1,094,440 (86.8 per cent) votes in favour of the law being retained, compared to 166,406 (13.2 per cent) in favour of repeal, although only 32 per cent of Scotland's four million voters returned ballot papers at the referendum. Despite such high-profile campaigning and the referendum result, section 2a/28 was abolished by the Parliament on 21 June 2000, by ninety-nine votes to seventeen.

Finally, there was policy changes which originated in coalition negotiations such as the treatment of the issue of student finance. The introduction of tuition fees by Labour at Westminster in advance of devolution significantly altered the position of student finance, requiring the payment of up front tuition fees of £1,000 per year. The issue played a prominent role at the 1999 Scottish election, with the Conservatives, Liberal Democrats and SNP pledged to abolish tuition fees, while Labour was committed to their retention. The post-election coalition agreement established a special committee, chaired by former CBI chief Andrew Cubie, to examine the broad issue of student finance rather than simply tuition fees alone. The issue was highly sensitive as each partner in the coalition was pledged to opposing positions on the issue, and unless resolved to the satisfaction of each party, it had the potential to destroy the coalition and bring down the government. The Cubie committee published its report in December 1999, and the Scottish Executive agreed its own position in January 2000. Then, the coalition presented its own proposals rather than merely adopting the Cubie recommendations, and the coalition, survived. However, as will become clear below, Executive bills were not the only legislative proposals to wind their way through the legislative process. A considerable number of MSPs' bills were also proposed in the Parliament's first year, with a number of them gaining sufficient support to be presented as bills from 1999–2000.

– THE LEGISLATIVE PROCESS –

The Scottish Parliament's legislative process offers five ways in which bills can be proposed, depending on the nature of the legislation and who has proposed the bill. The five routes apply to Executive bills, committee bills, two different procedures for MSPs' bills and a special, emergency procedure for fast-tracking legislation through the Parliament first used with the passage of the Mental Health (Public Safety and Appeals) (Scotland) Act in 1999.

– EXECUTIVE BILLS –

The process through which the Scottish Executive presents legislation to the Scottish Parliament is best understood through three different phases: the pre-legislative phase; the Parliamentary phase when committees and MSPs consider the legislation in principle and in detail (and itself comprises three stages); and the legal phase at which the bill is examined by law officers and the Secretary of State for Scotland. An example of the functioning of this complicated legislative process is provided in Case study 6, which illustrates the progress of the Abolition of Feudal Tenure Bill through each phase of the legislative process.

The first phase – the pre-legislative phase – refers to the process before the bill reaches Parliament. Executive bills are proposed when the Scottish Executive announces its legislative proposals, either individually or through the 'big-bang' approach adopted in the first year of the Parliament when eight bills were presented in a mini-Queen's Speech. The Executive will produce a White Paper on a legislative initiative and it will then be subject to pre-legislative consultations between relevant ministers and committees, followed by a period of Executive consultation with pressure groups which will feed into the preparation of a draft bill. The draft bill will include a statement on its legislative competence which will be examined by the Presiding Officer and responsible minister, to ensure that the proposal falls within the Parliament's powers. Also, the Executive will publish a bill alongside memoranda dealing with a range of related issues such as the aims of the bill, the pre-legislative consultation process and the financial implications of the proposal (see above under 'Memoranda to bills').

The Parliamentary phase of the legislative process has three distinct stages. In the first stage, the bill is handed over to committees for consideration of the general principles of the legislation. For example, the Abolition of Feudal Tenure Bill was published on 6 October 1999; the Justice and Home Affairs Committee considered the general principles of the bill on 9 and 17 November 1999, published its report on 9 December 1999, and the bill was formally introduced into the Parliament by the Executive for its first-stage reading on 15 December 1999. This first stage involved a plenary debate on the general principles of the bill before the bill was sent back to committees for detailed consideration – known as stage two.

In this second stage, the committee undertakes detailed, line-by-line scrutiny of the bill, perhaps with the involvement of other relevant committees, arranges further consultations, takes evidence about the bill and its implications, and produces, amendments to the legislation. At the conclusion of this stage, the committee reports back to the plenary with an explanation of amendments.

In the third stage of the Parliamentary phase, the Plenary debates committee amendments, suggests additional amendments and votes on the final bill. Assuming that the bill is passed at this final plenary, the legislation is then passed to the Parliament's legal officers.

The final phase is the legal phase. Following the pre-legislative and Parliamentary phases of the legislative process, the Parliament's law officers and the Advocate-General at Westminster, currently Lynda Clark MP, have four weeks in which to examine the legality of the proposal to determine whether it is consistent with the division of powers of the Scotland Act: particularly, whether it conflicts with the powers of Westminster outlined in Schedule 5 of the Scotland Act 1998. If a conflict of powers is seen to exist, the legislation may be passed to the Judicial Committee of the Privy Council for adjudication. In addition to this arrangement, there is a four-week period in which the Secretary of State for Scotland can examine legislation under section 35 of the Scotland Act 1998 to assess whether proposals are incompatible with the UK's international obligations, defence or national security or have implications for Westminster's reserved powers. If legislation is in breach of the Scotland Act in these two areas, the Secretary of State for Scotland can make an order under section 35 to prevent the Presiding Officer from submitting a bill for Royal Assent. If these two constitutional processes are not enacted, then the Presiding Officer is able to submit the bill for Royal Assent and the bill then becomes an Act of the Scottish Parliament.

– COMMITTEE BILLS –

The second way in which legislation can be made in the Scottish Parliament is through committee bills. One of the weaknesses of the select committee system at Westminster is that committees lack legislative powers. They can identify policy failings by government and recommend changes, but not implement change. The ability of Scottish committees to propose legislation is intended to remedy this weakness, as the committee can propose a law if the Executive does not respond to some of its recommendations and reports. Committees are able to make legislative proposals within their specific remits, and they are required to make a report to the plenary of the Parliament outlining the need for legislation. At this stage, the plenary

Case study 6 The policy process of the Scottish Parliament and the Abolition of Feudal Tenure Act (2000)

On 30 June 1999, the Scottish Executive announces it will introduce legislation to achieve the abolition of feudal tenure. It does not publish a White Paper but proposes to adopt the report and draft bill already prepared by the Scottish Law Commission and published on 11 February 1999.

Pre-legislative phase

Summer-autumn 1999: the Scottish Executive writes to around 3,000 organisations stating that it will adopt the Scottish Law Commission's proposals for the abolition of feudal tenure, a consultation which elicits sixty-five responses. Previously, the Scottish Law Commission had consulted on its proposals.

Pre-legislative consultation with Justice and Home Affairs Committee.

6 October 1999: Abolition of Feudal Tenure Bill is published by the Scottish Executive along with policy memorandum, financial memorandum and the statements on legislative competence issued by the Justice Minister and Presiding Officer.

Parliamentary phase: stage one

9 and 17 November 1999: The Justice and Home Affairs Committee debates general principles of the bill taking evidence from the Civil Law Division of the Scottish Executive Justice Department, the Solicitor's Office of the Scottish Executive, the Feudal Reform Working Party of the Royal Institution of Chartered Surveyors, Scottish Environment LINK, Land Reform Scotland, the Law Society of Scotland, Shelter, the Scottish Council of Voluntary Organisations and Action of Churches Together in Scotland.

23 and 29 November 1999: The Subordinate Legislation Committee debates the general principles of the bill.

1 and 7 December 1999: The Justice and Home Affairs Committee debates its report on the principles of the bill in private.

9 December 1999: The Justice and Home Affairs Committee publishes its *Third Report, 1999: Stage 1 Report on the Abolition of Feudal Tenure etc. (Scotland) Bill.*

15 December 1999: Plenary debate and vote on general principles. The bill is passed at stage 1 without a vote.

Parliamentary phase: stage two
6, 15, 21, and 29 March 2000: The Justice and Home Affairs Committee discusses the detail of the bill and consider three sets of amendments.

25 April 2000: The Subordinate Legislation Committee discusses the bill.

Parliamentary phase: stage three
3 May 2000: The Subordinate Legislation Committee publishes its sixteenth *Report, 2000: Delegated Powers Scrutiny – Abolition of Feudal Tenure etc. (Scotland) Bill as Amended at Stage 2.*

3 May 2000: Plenary debates the bill for two and a half hours. The bill is passed without a vote, but the debate involves consideration of a number of Executive and opposition amendments and five votes on those amendments.

Legal phase
Legal officers at Scottish Parliament and Westminster and the Secretary of State for Scotland scrutinise the bill in relation to legislative competence, reserved powers and international obligations. Each decides to pass the bill. It then gains Royal Assent to become an Act of the Scottish Parliament on 9 June 2000.

---

can either support or oppose the proposal. If Parliament opposes the committee bill, that is the end of the matter. If Parliament assents, then the Executive might agree to produce the bill itself. at which stage it becomes an Executive bill. If the Executive does not wish to adopt the proposal, the committee becomes responsible for the legislation. In this case, the committee convenor organises the preparation of the bill which is then drafted and introduced, accompanied by the policy and financial memoranda and the Presiding Officer's statement on its legislative competence.

The bill is then be debated in general terms in the plenary of the Parliament and put to a vote (stage one). If the plenary agrees to progress the bill, then the second stage commences with a committee of the whole Parliament undertaking detailed scrutiny of the bill. The bill then enters stage three of the legislative process, at which it is debated in amended form by the plenary, and either passed or rejected. If Parliament passes the bill, it is then be scrutinised by the law officers and the Secretary of State for Scotland to determine whether the bill impinges on Westminster's reserved powers, agreements with the European Union, international obligations, and soon. If acceptable, Royal Assent makes the bill an Act of the Scottish Parliament. However, despite the provision for committees to make their own legislation, no committee bills emerged in 1999–2000.

– MSPs' BILLS –

The process by which individual MSPs can propose legislation is relatively straightforward. It involves two different routes for MSPs to follow: through one of the Parliament's committees or through the plenary session. However, after a legislative proposal is accepted, the bill follows the same system of checks and balances as committee bills or Executive bills. Therefore, although proposing is fairly simple, passage of an MSP's bill is as complicated as other pieces of legislation. MSPs are able to introduce a maximum of two bills in a Parliamentary session and one MSP, Tommy Sheridan, used both his opportunities in the first few months of the Parliament in 1999. Nationally, this fact could lead to 258 MSPs' bills in a four-year Parliamentary session. However, given that government ministers and the Presiding Officer are unlikely to propose such bills, there is actually a much smaller potential number of MSPs' bills. Indeed, the small number of MSPs' bills in the first year of the Parliament indicated the limited nature of backbench activism. Very few MSPs' bills were proposed and most MSPs appeared not to have thought about proposing legislation. This might be related to the fact that it was the Parliament's first year, with MSPs taking time to adapt to the committee and constituency workload.

There are two routes for MSPs' bills in the Scottish Parliament. First, an MSP submits a written proposal for legislation to the Parliamentary Bureau for consideration. The Bureau then passes the proposal to a lead committee of the Parliament which examines the case for legislation. At this stage, the committee either rejects or accepts the proposal for, legislation. If accepted, the proposal becomes the equivalent of a committee bill. The alternative route is for an MSP to gain support from 10–20 per cent of the Parliament to introduce the bill to the plenary of the Parliament if the Presiding Officer agrees that the proposal falls within the Parliament's powers. Thus a proposal requires the support of at least eleven other MSPs to be accepted, and they have to indicate their support for the proposal within one month of its publication in the Parliament's business bulletin. From then on, the bill is treated as an Executive bill and will proceed through the three phases for such legislation. If a bill fails to gain the support of MSPs within one month of its publication, the bill falls and may not be reintroduced by any MSP until six months later.[5]

The types of MSPs' bills proposed within the Parliament in 1999–2000 were varied and individual. The two bills proposed by Scottish Socialist MSP Tommy Sheridan related to legal changes associated with his campaigning against the poll tax in the late 1980s. Sheridan proposed both the Debtors (Amendment) Bill, which was lodged in August 1999, and the Poundings and Warrant Sales Bill in September 1999. Green MSP Robin Harper picked up on an environmental theme with the Organic Food and Farming Targets Bill. Conservative education spokesperson Brian Montieth produced the Tuition Fees Bill, while the Liberal Democrat MSP for Shetland, Tavish Scott, proposed the Sea Fisheries (Shellfish) (Amendment) Bill, an obvious constituency interest. More significantly, a number of MSPs' bills had cross-party support, a fact which said something about the confidence of backbenchers and the consensual nature of the Parliament. Such cross-party support was also indicative of potential legislative success, especially if it involved members of the coalition, for example, Mike Watson's anti-hunting bill was supported by thirteen SNP and eighteen Labour MSPs among others. The Abolition of Poindings and Warrant Sales Bill gained support from fourteen SNP and six Labour MSPs, in addition to the independent MSP Dennis Canavan. Tavish Scott's bill was supported by Labour, SNP and Conservative MSPs, as well as by those of his own party. Alex Neil's Public Appointments (Confirmations) Bill was supported by a number of Liberal Democrat MSPs, in addition to those of the SNP. Such genuinely cross-party bills contrasted with Brian Monteith's Tuition Fees Bill and Alex Johnstone's Meat Labelling Bill which were supported solely by Conservative MSPs.

Of the fourteen bills listed in Table 6.2, five were introduced into the Scottish Parliament in 1999–2000: the Abolition of Poindings and Warrant Sales Bill, the Sea Fisheries (Shellfish) (Amendment) Bill, the Protection of Wild Mammals Bill, the Mortgage Rights Bill and the Family Homes and Homelessness Bill. However, only the Sea Fisheries Bill had been passed when this book was completed. The progress of MSPs' bills produced some key moments in the Parliament's first year of existence: the combination of high drama and backbench rebellion associated with Tommy Sheridan's Abolition of Poindings and Warrant Sales Bill was the most prominent

Table 6.2 MSPs' bills 1999–July 2000

Bill	Sponsor	MSPs' support
Debtors (Amendment) Bill	Tommy Sheridan (SSP)	26
Abolition of Poindings and Warrant Sales Bill	Tommy Sheridan (SSP)	24
Protection of Wild Mammals Bill	Mike Watson (Lab)	35
Leasehold Casualties Bill	Adam Ingram (SNP)	15
Public Appointments (Confirmation) Bill	Alex Neil (SNP)	23
Family Homes and Homelessness Bill	Bob Brown (Lib Dem)	15
Mortgage Rights Bill	Cathy Craigie (Lab)	21
Sea Fisheries (Shellfish) (Amendment) Bill	Tavish Scott (Lib Dem)	11
Tuition Fees Bill	Brian Monteith (Con)	17
Meat Labelling Bill	Alex Johnstone (Con)	19
Organic Food and Farming Targets Bill	Robin Harper (Green)	38
Alzheimer's and Dementia Care Bill	Christine Grahame (SNP)	19
Civil Marriages Bill	Euan Robson (Lib Dem)	13
Bank Arrestment Bill	Alex Neil (SNP)	15

example, but there were others. For example, the issue of MSPs' bills created early problems for the Parliament in relation to the drafting of legislation, which then created difficulties for MSPs and Parliamentary standards. As MSPs began to submit bills in August 1999, they found the Parliament lacked staff for drafting legislation. The Executive had staff for drafting legislation, which meant it could proceed with its own legislation, but the Parliament's lack of staff meant that MSPs' bills were effectively stalled (*The Herald*, 8 September 1999). Thus, one key aspect of the new devolution scheme, intended to facilitate backbench activism, was damaged by the newness of the institution itself and the lack of preparation for MSPs' bills within the Parliament and Executive. There was also the suspicion that the Executive was not unhappy that the lack of drafting personnel would stall progress on MSPs' bills it opposed and prevent such legislation from cutting into the Executive's Parliamentary time.

The drafting problem was resolved in time, but not before MSPs had to resort to outside individuals or organisations to assist them in drafting bills, for example, Mike Watson's Protection of Wild Mammals Bill was drafted with the assistance of anti-hunt groups. Such assistance had the potential to breach the Parliament's code of conduct which prevented MSPs from gaining external financial assistance to promote specific issues. Although Watson's use of external assistance was a pale imitation of the 'cash for questions' issue at Westminster, it did produce some difficulties for the MSP concerned and the Parliament. First, the MSP had not registered his financial support over the issue. This fact itself led to a Parliamentary investigation by the Standards Committee, a committee fresh from the Lobbygate inquiry. Second, this inquiry took place when the Parliament lacked a code of conduct, as it was still being discussed in draft form by the Standards Committee, although it had produced an interim complaints procedure. Third, the people who sought to exploit the issue of paid assistance for Mike Watson's bill were pro-hunting activists. Conservative MSP Ben Wallace made a formal complaint against Mike Watson over the declaration of interests in an attempt to frustrate the progress of the anti-hunt bill. The Committee found in Mike Watson's favour in December 1999.[6] Other opponents of the bill took legal action through the European Convention on Human Rights to try to declare the bill illegal (*The Herald*, 20 October 1999). All of this sprang from a lack of drafting personnel within the Parliament.

The MSPs' bill that had most impact in the Parliament's first year was Tommy Sheridan's Abolition of Poindings and Warrant Sales Bill. It was introduced into the Scottish Parliament on 24 September 1999 and proposed to amend the Debtors (Scotland) Act 1987 to prevent the use of poindings and warrant sales to recover debts.

Such procedures had been used by local authorities in pursuit of poll tax defaulters, and they had continued to use them after the abolition of the poll tax to ensure payment of the council tax.[7] The bill was published, along with its financial and policy memoranda and proceeded to the first stage of the legislative process at a meeting of the Justice and Home Affairs Committee on 17 November 1999. The committee discussed the principles of the bill at that meeting, with a presentation by the sponsor of the bill and questions from MSPs.

Stage one continued on 11 January 2000, with an evidence session by the Justice Committee featuring civil servants from the Justice Department of the Scottish Executive, representatives of the Scottish Consumer Council and the Society of Messengers at Arms and Sheriff's Officers. Tommy Sheridan joined in the committee questioning of witnesses as the bill's sponsor. The bill was discussed at three meetings of the Justice and Home Affairs Committee in total, which was the lead committee in early discussions. The Parliament's Local Government and Social Inclusion Committees also discussed the bill, took evidence and produced reports. The Justice and Home Affairs Committee held one evidence session on the bill, while the Local Government Committee held two sessions and the Social Inclusion Committee held three. Significantly, all three committees came out in favour of abolishing poindings and warrant sales at the end of the evidence sessions,[8] despite the opposition of the Executive and the fact that the committees contained substantial numbers of Labour MSPs.

Of course, while the committees came out in favour of abolition, the Scottish Executive remained opposed to it, especially as there was no alternative mechanisms for debt recovery in the bill. Executive opposition to the bill continued throughout the committee discussions, despite Labour

MSPs on these committees supporting abolition and despite the number of Labour backbenchers who had supported the bill originally in August 1999. The Labour MSPs' group meeting to discuss the issue in advance of the Parliamentary vote on stage one of the bill on 27 April 2000 also indicated that the Executive faced difficulties from its own backbenchers. Despite such Labour backbench support for the Sheridan bill, the Executive proposed a wrecking amendment to defeat the bill. However, this amendment was withdrawn during the debate by the responsible minister, Jim Wallace, amid scenes of confusion within the Executive and among the coalition partners.

Stage one of the Abolition of Poindings and Warrant Sales Bill was therefore passed by seventy-nine votes to fifteen against and thirty abstentions. The seventy-nine supporters of the bill included thirty-nine labour MSPs (meaning all Labour MSPs apart from ministers in the Scottish Executive), as well as two Liberal Democrats and all the SNP MSPs. Significantly, the only MSPs who voted against the bill were the Conservatives. The abstentions included the remaining Liberal Democrats, one Conservative and all fifteen Labour ministers within the Executive, demonstrating that Labour could only deliver the payroll vote on this issue, but even then only deliver an abstention rather than a vote against the bill.[9] This occasion was not one in which the Executive covered itself in glory, and was interpreted as a great victory for the Parliament and its backbenchers. Executive dominance was overturned, despite party pressure and the coalition majority. Sure enough, it was only stage one of the bill, with much more detailed scrutiny to follow, but it was still a highly significant event in the life of the new Parliament.

– THE EMERGENCY LEGISLATIVE PROCESS –

Before the Noel Ruddle case in the summer of 1999, the Parliament's ability to pass emergency legislation was a relatively unexplored aspect of the Consultative Steering Group report and the Parliament's standing orders. Most attention had focused on the Parliament's inclusive legislative procedures and the role of committees as a revising chamber which could challenge the Executive. However, following the Consultative Steering Group's recommendations, the Parliament's standing orders did provide for special procedures to bypass the existing legislative process in special circumstances. Under rule 9.21, a government minister could present a motion to the Parliament proposing that an Executive bill be treated as an emergency bill and follow a more rapid legislative process than normal. If Parliament agreed to the government's motion, the emergency bill would be subject to just two legislative stages with substantial differences from normal procedures. The bill would be immediately referred to the Parliament for consideration of its general principles, thereby avoiding pre-legislative consultation and a committee report on the general principles of the bill. If the Parliament agreed to the bill's general principles, the legislation would be referred to a committee of the whole Parliament for detailed consideration. All stages of the emergency bill were to be taken on the same day, unless the Parliamentary Bureau decided to hold debates over several days, thus suspending the normal procedure in which legislation was subject to two weeks of delays between each of a normal bill's three stages. The normal multiple access points and time for deeper consideration and amendment were therefore excluded from the emergency procedure.

The emergency legislative procedures would have remained an obscure part of Parliament's standing orders without the circumstance of the Noel Ruddle case. Ruddle had murdered a neighbour with a Kalashnikov rifle and was later diagnosed as a paranoid schizophrenic. He had been detained for an unlimited period in the state hospital at Carstairs since 1992, following his incarceration for murder in 1991, and had undergone various treatments at Carstairs. However, medical reports by the Mental Welfare Commission and Carstairs placed doubts over whether Ruddle's illness was actually treatable. He appealed to the local Sheriff's Court in Lanark to be released from Carstairs under section 63(2) of the Mental Health (Scotland) Act 1984 as his personality disorder was untreatable. The Sheriff ruled that since Ruddle's personality order failed the 'treatability test', he should be discharged from Carstairs, a decision which was implemented on 2 August 1999.

The Ruddle case was not merely a legal or mental health issue, it was a highly-charged political issue that caused serious difficulties for the Scottish Executive and led to the passage of emergency legislation on 2 September 1999. For example, the Scottish Executive gave the appearance of having acted very slowly on the issue. While the Justice Minister, Jim Wallace, had known of the background to the Ruddle appeal on 14 July 1999,[10] officials within the Scottish Office had been aware of the potential loophole in the mental health legislation and Ruddle's desire to appeal his confinement since March 1998. This fact cast a shadow over First Minister, Donald Dewar, as he had been Secretary of State for Scotland from 1998–9, and his department had not acted on the legislative loophole in a substantive way beyond opposing Ruddle's discharge. Following the Lanark Sheriff's judgement that Ruddle should be released from Carstairs, it became public that other inmates also intended to use the appeals process to exploit the treatability loophole. There was a public outcry, intense media interest and a general mood that the Scottish Executive had failed to act in the public interest over this issue, especially as it had been foreseen well before the establishment of the Scottish Parliament itself. The opposition parties were particularly scathing about the slowness of the Executive's response to a serious problem that had been known about for over a year.

The Scottish Executive responded to the outcry following Ruddle's discharge, and the threat of other inmates exploiting the legal loophole over treatability, by proposing emergency legislation on 4 August, two days after Ruddle's release. The Justice Minister held a special meeting to discuss the appeals with the SNP's Roseanna Cunningham (the convenor of the Justice and Home Affairs Committee) and Conservative leader David McLetchie, which was to form the basis of an agreement to pass emergency legislation. The legislation proposed to amend the Mental Health (Scotland) Act to allow the question of public safety to be taken into account by the courts when considering appeals for release from the state hospital at Carstairs. In addition, both the government and the individual concerned were to be given a right of appeal over court judgments on application for release, with applicants to be detained for the duration of the Scottish Executive's appeal. The legislation was to be applicable to all mental health appeals that were made from the day after the emergency legislation was passed, making it effective from 9 September 1999.

Jim Wallace introduced the motion to make the Mental Health (Public Safety and Appeals) (Scotland) Bill an emergency bill on 2 September 1999. But while Parliament agreed to consider the proposal under emergency legislative procedures, the bill was not dealt with in one day. Indeed, the passage of the Mental Health Bill was somewhat confused. The bill was introduced one week, and then stages two and three of the legislative process were held the following week on 8 September 1999. Discussion of the bill itself was further delayed by the need to agree the timetable for debate at stages two and three, as well as additions to the bill by the Finance Minister. Stage two involved a committee of the whole Parliament discussing amendments to the bill that included three amendments by the Justice Minister which had been submitted after the deadline for amendments had closed.[11] Muddling through seemed to be the order of the day. Voting on amendments to the bill demonstrated some partisan divisions on the legislation, in addition to the general consensus on large sections of the bill. Only four of the thirty-nine amendments were passed: three from the government and one from the opposition. There were only five votes on amendments, all of which were won by the government in the face of opposition from the SNP and the Conservatives (opposition that was not combined but quite separate). Many amendments were also withdrawn by their proposers as the debate progressed, mostly by the Conservatives and the MSP for Falkirk West, Dennis Canavan. At the end of the day, the bill was passed as the government sought after three hours of debate. Stage three of the bill was completed after ten minutes of debate the same day, with MSPs supporting the bill as amended without a vote. After a good deal of controversy and difficulties with the legislative process, the first piece of Scottish Parliamentary legislation since the Act of 1707 was passed. An historic event, although not exactly an historic piece of legislation.

– CONCLUSION –

After a slow start in 1999, the Scottish Parliament's legislative process came into its own in 2000. A number of bills became Acts as they completed the different stages of the legislative process and they were replaced by new bills as the legislative cycle progressed. The initial slow speed of Parliamentary procedures left the Noel Ruddle case as the only issue which produced an Act of the Scottish Parliament in 1999. By the end of the Parliament's first year in July 2000, the Parliament had passed eight bills in total: Abolition of Feudal Tenure etc. (Scotland) Bill, the Adults with Incapacity (Scotland) Bill, the Budget (Scotland) Bill, the Census (Amendment) (Scotland) Bill, the Mental Health (Public Safety and Appeals) (Scotland) Bill, the Public Finance and Accountability (Scotland) Bill, the Standards in Scotland's Schools etc. Bill, and the National Parks (Scotland) Bill. A further eleven bills were making their way through the Parliament's legislative process. The Parliament was therefore succeeding in what it was designed to do: make Scottish legislation. The large number of bills debated, passed and in progress was dramatically superior to the amount of Scottish legislation dealt with at Westminster over the space of several decades. However, the progression of bills into Acts was only the first part of the policy process, which would await implementation in the future. It would be some time yet before Scottish voters experienced the outcomes of these new pieces of legislation.

– NOTES –

1. *Standing Orders of the Scottish Parliament*, Chapter 9, rule 9.3.2, 1999.
2. Ibid, rule 9.3.3.
3. Abolition of Feudal Tenure etc. (Scotland), *Policy Memorandum*, 6 October 1999.
4. Policy Memorandum, *Regulation of Investigatory Powers (Scotland) Bill*, 25 May 2000, and Policy Memorandum, *The Bail, Judicial Appointments etc (Scotland) Bill*, 25 May 2000.
5. *Standing Orders of the Scottish Parliament*, rule 9.14, Members' Bills, clause 6.
6. Standards Committee, *fourth Report 1999: Report on Complaints Against Mike Watson MSP*, 17 December 1999.

7. Abolition of Poindings and Warrant Sales Bill 1999 (SP Bill 3).
8. Justice and Home Affairs Committee, *first Report, 2000: Stage 1 Report on the Abolition of Poindings and Warrant Sales Bill*, 9 March 2000.
9. Scottish Parliament, *Official Report*, vol. 6, no. 2, 2000, col. 196.
10. Justice and Home Affairs Committee, *Official Report*, 31 August 1999, col. 22.
11. Scottish Parliament, *Official Report, Mental Health (Public Safety and Appeals) (Scotland) Bill: Stage 2*, 8 September 1999, vol. 2, no. 3, col. 209.

CHAPTER 7

Pressure group Scotland

– INTRODUCTION –

Pressure groups are an important facet of the policy process in most countries, and Scotland is no exception to this. Even a brief reading of Scottish newspapers would be sufficient to gain a picture of the existence of significant pressure group activity in Scotland, for example, there was substantial media coverage of the blockade of Faslane nuclear submarine base organised by Scottish CND on 14 February 2000 at which 189 members of the public were arrested. In another typical example, *The Scotsman* of 15 March 2000 revealed that the Communities Minister, Wendy Alexander, had held a meeting with the Scottish Federation of Housing Associations to discuss proposals to extend the right-to-buy to housing association properties.

Similarly, one can find a range of pressure group interactions with the Scottish Parliament. The Scottish National farmers Union petitioned the Parliament on eight separate occasions in 1999 (PE61–68) on issues such as exemptions from the climate change levy, compensation for farmers for the introduction of the Euro, and increased resources for agri-environment measures in Scotland. The meeting of the Parliament's Equal Opportunities Committee on 6 March 2000 took evidence on the Ethical Standards in Local Government Bill from the Roman Catholic Church, the Church of Scotland, the Evangelical Alliance, and Christian Action, Research and Education, with each group seeking to present their views on the sections of the bill that would replace section 2a/28 preventing the promotion of homosexuality in schools. Pressure groups are thus not some obscure phenomenon in Scotland, but have an integral role in policymaking and political debate. This chapter will assess the characteristics of pressure groups in Scotland, the impact that devolution has had on pressure group Scotland, and relations between pressure groups and the new Parliament.

– PRESSURE GROUPS AND POLITICS –

Pressure groups have become one of the more noticeable aspects of Scottish politics in recent years. While the phenomenon has attracted a growing literature within UK politics, there have been few studies of pressure group activity in Scotland. However, devolution is likely to push the activities of a large number of pressure groups into the public sphere, particularly given the openness of the legislative process of the Scottish Parliament and the intention to facilitate pressure group involvement in policymaking. Defining a pressure group has not been without its problems, especially as groups can often resemble political parties, businesses or quangos. Wyn Grant (1989: p. 9) defined a pressure group in an inclusive manner as:

> an organisation which seeks as one of its functions to influence the formulation and implementation of public policy, public policy representing a set of authoritative decisions taken by the executive, the legislature, and the judiciary, and by local government and the European Community.

Pressure groups come in all shapes and sizes, and political scientists have adopted a range of approaches to classify different types of groups. For example, a number of authors differentiate between interest/sectional groups and cause/promotional groups. The former are seen to be characterised by membership restricted to certain socioeconomic groups or backgrounds (Baggot, 1995: p. 14). They exist to protect the interests of their members, although they might have policies on and interests in a broader set of issues. Within Scotland, examples of the interest/sectional group classification would include CBI Scotland, the Scottish Chambers of Commerce, Scottish Financial Enterprise, the Scottish Landowners Federation, the Scottish National Farmers Union and the Scottish Trades Union Congress. Cause/promotional groups enjoy open memberships, with members who share common values or policy goals, and they seek to advance a particular policy or interest rather than their own self-interest (Baggot, 1995: p. 14). Examples include Age Concern Scotland, RSPB Scotland, Scottish CND, Scotland Against Nuclear Dumping and Action for Churches Together in Scotland. Of course, some pressure groups appear to span both types of classification, for example, Age Concern Scotland represents a distinct segment of the population, rather than society as a whole. But most groups can be understood from these two classifications.

A second means of differentiating between pressure groups revolves around their status or strategic role as insider or outsider groups (Grant, 1989). Insider groups are seen to be those which have sought and gained the ear of government, are recognised as legitimate political actors in the policy process and are able to play a role in policymaking. This role involves acceptance of the rules of the game in policymaking, which places constraints on group behaviour. Outsider groups are seen to be those that are excluded from government consultation exercises and policy processes, because of their unorthodox views or tactics. Insider groups seek inclusion in government decisionmaking structures through participation in consultation exercises, advisory committees and bilateral meetings with ministers and civil servants; outsider groups tend towards unconventional political action such as protest actions and demonstrations. However, many outsider groups would seek to become insider groups if it improved their chances of influencing government decisions (Grant, 1989: p. 17). Of course, to some extent, the legislative process of the Scottish Parliament seeks to defy the insider/outsider categories of pressure group. Pre-legislative consultation and the legislative process are designed to be inclusive and ensure that outsider groups have more equal access to consultation exercises and to Parliamentary scrutiny of legislation. However, whether this enables outsider groups to gain access to Scottish Executive ministers and civil servants remains to be seen.

There are four additional points to make about pressure groups. First, although they are independent of government, some are actually funded by government. The Scottish Consumer Council, Scottish Council for Single Homeless and Scottish Association for Mental Health are well known Scottish pressure groups that receive the bulk of their funds from the public purse and seek to promote the interests of particular client groups who would otherwise be too weak and fragmented to organise themselves effectively. Second, many pressure groups have a stakeholding role in policymaking because they are actively involved in policy implementation in their particular area. This fact gives them a role within the policy process as well as making it necessary for them to monitor and influence policy that will directly affect their operations. Examples include the Church of Scotland and Catholic Church, which have an interest in social work and welfare legislation which impacts upon their care homes and counselling services; environmental groups such as the Royal Society for the Protection of Birds (RSPB) Scotland which are landowners implementing aspects of government policy in relation to raptors, corncrakes and other bird species on their land; and the Convention of Scottish Local Authorities (COSLA), whose local authority members are responsible for implementing many different government policies in education, environment, transport and planning.

Third, a number of pressure groups enjoy an advisory role with government and are included on government bodies, either because they have a particular policy expertise or a role in implementing legislation. For example, the Scottish Advisory Committee on Drug Misuse contains a range of representatives from the police, local drugs agencies, medical professionals and local authority staff responsible for education and social work. The board of the Scottish Qualifications Authority includes representatives of the Scottish School Boards Association and CBI Scotland.

Fourth, while it has usually been possible to differentiate between parties and pressure groups through the fact that pressure groups do not contest elections and seek to become the government, there are some exceptions. For example, anti-abortion campaigners have adopted both pressure group and party strategies to publicise their cause. Groups such as the Society for the Protection of the Unborn Child (SPUC) have opted for an orthodox pressure group route, while other anti-abortion campaigners used the electoral route to stand candidates for the Prolife party at the 1997 Westminster elections (Lynch, 1998a), the 1999 Scottish elections and a number of by-elections (albeit with limited success). The Keep the Clause campaign sought to influence the outcome of the Ayr by-election in 2000 through campaign activity and buying up billboard advertising in the constituency. Although it did not contest the election itself by standing a candidate, it has discussed this prospect for future elections. Finally, while this chapter deals primarily with pressure groups, it should be said that Scotland has also seen the development of a number of social movements. Environmental and women's movements have been prominent examples, as have the anti-poll tax groups which later fed into the Scottish Socialist Party. Such broad movements have often had an important impact. For example, the women's movement scored notable successes in Scotland in relation to devolution (Brown, McCrone and Paterson, 1998), with the adoption of gender balance measures for the selection of Labour candidates to the Scottish Parliament, following the electoral contract signed by Labour and the Liberal Democrats in 1995 after the Scottish Constitutional Convention (Scottish Constitutional Convention, 1995). The fact that 37 per cent of MSPs were women in 1999 was a clear example of the representational impact of the women's movement. The adoption of zero-tolerance campaigns over violence towards women by a number of local authorities in Scotland was also a good example of the impact of the women's movement.

– PRESSURE GROUPS IN SCOTLAND –

Pressure groups have been thick on the ground in Scotland for a number of years, and this density is due to two features. First, the continued existence of a distinctive Scottish civil society after the Union of 1707 fed specific organisational interests in Scotland. A separate educational, legal, local government and religious system all contributed to the existence of distinctive Scottish pressure groups. Second, while the growth of government size and functions since the nineteenth century led to the organisation of a large number of groups around an enlarged public sector, this process had particular effects in Scotland because of the existence of the Scottish Office. Basically, as functions were added to the Scottish Office, it encouraged the formation of distinctive pressure groups or the establishment of Scottish branches of UK pressure groups to take account of the Scottish administrative situation. For example, because the Scottish Office was the sponsoring ministry for construction in Scotland, the construction industry formed its own distinctive pressure group, the Scottish Building Employers Federation (Grant, 1989a). Similarly, the different building regulations in Scotland and the role of the Scottish Office in housing and planning led to the existence of a Scottish House Builders Association (Grant, 1989a). The former Scottish Development Agency, now Scottish Enterprise, established by the Scottish Office, was instrumental in establishing Scottish Financial Enterprise in 1986 as a representative of the Scottish financial sector (Moore and Booth, 1989: p. 78).

A vast number of pressure groups and social organisations in Scotland have some interaction with government institutions and the policy process. Many pressure groups are small, voluntary organisations that are run on a shoestring but there is also a range of well-resourced pressure groups that can be considered as major institutions, for example, some pressure groups have extensive memberships that eclipse the political parties. The Educational Institute for Scotland (EIS) has a membership of 51,000 and represents most primary and secondary school teachers in Scotland, and the Royal College of Nursing represents over 32,000 nurses in Scotland. Such organisations compare well with a Labour party of approximately 28,000 members.

Although the actual number of pressure groups active in Scotland is difficult to determine accurately, the size of government consultation exercises affords a fairly clear picture of the size of pressure group Scotland. For example, the Consultative Steering Group's consultation over the operation of the Scottish Parliament in early 1998 was circulated to 799 organisations and received 336 responses. A number of those consulted were public bodies such as health boards, local authorities and NHS trusts or major businesses, but a large number were pressure groups of the UK, Scottish and local varieties. The list of pressure groups consulted included Age Concern Scotland, Alzheimer Scotland, Capability Scotland, Childline Scotland, Children in Scotland, NCH Action for Children Scotland, Royal Society for the Protection of Birds (RSPB) Scotland, Worldwide fund for Nature (Scotland), YMCA Scotland, Youthlink Scotland, Scottish Council for Voluntary Organisations (see Case study 7), the Automobile Association, the Federation of Small Businesses, Scottish Chambers of Commerce and the National Union of Students Scotland. Significantly, the consultation process brought responses from fifty-three business organisations, thirty-two professional organisations and fifty-two voluntary sector bodies among others.[1] The scope of pressure group organisation is therefore both extensive and numerous.

Pressure group Scotland can be understood as being comprised of two sets of organisations: Scottish pressure groups and Scottish divisions of UK pressure groups. Each are affected to varying degrees by devolution, and it cannot be said that the purely Scottish, groups are affected by devolution, while the UK groups are unaffected. Some groups deal solely with Holyrood, some groups solely with Westminster (the Schedule 5 groups), and a number of pressure groups straddle the Holyrood/Westminster policy divide and must carefully distribute their lobbying and monitoring efforts between both institutions.

– SCOTTISH PRESSURE GROUPS –

Scottish pressure groups are those solely organised in Scotland, with their own staff, membership, finance and leadership. Examples include the Convention of Scottish Local Authorities (COSLA) (see Case study 9), the Educational Institute for Scotland (EIS), the Law Society for Scotland, the Scottish Trades Union Congress (STUC), Scottish Financial Enterprise (SFE), the Scotch Whisky Association, the Scottish Crofters Union (see Case study 8) the Scottish Grocers Association and the Scottish Wildlife Trust. Organisationally, devolution is not much of a challenge for these groups as they do not need new structures or functions to adjust to the new Parliament and Executive. However, they are affected by devolution in completely different ways. As education, law and local government are important responsibilities of the Parliament, pressure groups in these areas will become deeply involved with the new devolved institutions. However, the Scotch Whisky Association, for example, may be solely organised in Scotland, but most of its policy concerns such as trade, taxation, exchange rates, alcohol duty and product standards are Westminster functions, and some are also EU responsibilities. Similarly, Scottish Financial Enterprise has some interest in the domestic Scottish economy with which the Parliament and Executive is involved, but its main concerns revolve around an international economy that is covered by Westminster and the EU. The

STUC, meanwhile, has member unions concerned with core Scottish Parliament functions in education, health and local government, but also has a strong Westminster dimension through the fact that employment legislation is a reserved power.

– SCOTTISH DIVISIONS OF BRITISH PRESSURE GROUPS –

The second main type of pressure group in Scotland involves Scottish divisions of larger UK organisations. Such groups are prevalent across a range of policy areas and are particularly strong in areas characterised by centralised economic management, meaning that many business organisations and trade unions are Scottish divisions of UK-wide organisations. Examples include CBI Scotland, the Institute of Directors (Scotland), Unison, the Amalgamated Engineering and Electrical Union, and the Transport and General Workers Union. However, beyond the economic arena, there are many other Scottish divisions of UK pressure groups, such as Age Concern Scotland, NCH Action for Children Scotland, Friends of the Earth (Scotland) and the Worldwide Fund for Nature (Scotland). Some of these groups were able to cope with devolution, as their offices and organisations had sufficiently devolved powers within the UK body to function in the new devolved environment. However, others needed to change their organisations in order to give more powers to the Scottish division. For example, CBI Scotland was given more autonomy within the CBI to facilitate its independent policymaking role in relation to the Scottish Executive and Parliament; thus, devolution to Scotland involved devolution to CBI Scotland (see Case study 10).

Case study 7 The Scottish Council of Voluntary Organisations (SCVO)

The Scottish Council of Voluntary Organisations has existed as the umbrella organisation for the voluntary sector since the 1940s, with offices in Edinburgh, Glasgow and Inverness. While the organisation may have had a modest impact on politics for most of its existence, it has experienced a period of rapid expansion in recent years. Three key developments have raised the status and activity levels of the SCVO. First, the Labour government's social inclusion policy agenda has involved a range of interactions between government and the voluntary sector across Scotland. The government has also sought to develop a partnership with the voluntary sector and taken steps to encourage individuals to undertake volunteering. Second, the SCVO and voluntary sector generally, were the recipients of considerable

---

levels of new funding from the National Lottery Charities Board, the government's social inclusion programme and the European Social Fund. Such funds helped to finance new staff for the SCVO at various levels, in addition to providing the money to run a number of voluntary organisations. Third, devolution raised the status of the SCVO and the voluntary sector in the new Parliament, especially as the SCVO was able to promote its role through its increased staffing and resources and its status as the coordinating body for civic Scotland. Such status was evident in its formative role in the Scottish Civic Forum. The SCVO exists as a pressure group on two distinct levels. First, it is the group that represents Scotland's voluntary sector to the Scottish Executive and Parliament, and engages in lobbying and consultations as the umbrella body of Scottish voluntary organisations. Second, the SCVO is a facilitator and supporter of lobbying by its component members: the voluntary organisations themselves. The SCVO provides a number of support mechanisms and advice for lobbying by its own members, and these can be understood as efforts to plug the gap between resource-rich pressure groups such as the CBI and STUC and small community groups that are resource-poor. For example, the SCVO provides a Parliamentary Information and Advisory Service for its members, offering a general service for member organisations giving policy updates, briefings and guides to the Parliament, alongside a bespoke service for organisations with an annual income in excess of £100,000. It also provides training courses on lobbying and Parliamentary campaigning as well as access to the voluntary sector network generally. More generally, the SCVO's Research Unit and European Unit provide specialist briefings on a broad range of policy issues, in addition to advice on submitting funding bids to the government and the European Union and a wide range of training and information events.

Finally, the SCVO has been a partner in the com.com/holyrood project. This project was launched in January 2000, with the intention of establishing internet access sites in community centres and village halls across Scotland to enable community groups and voluntary organisations to lobby the Executive and Parliament online. The project was jointly funded by SCVO, the National Lottery and BT Scotland to the tune of £417,000, with the intention of hosting the SCVO's Parliamentary Information and Advisory Service and acting as a mechanism for linking MSPs to the local community.[2]

Case study 8 The Scottish Crofters Union (SCU)

The Scottish Crofties Union is one of Scotland's more recent pressure groups. Despite the existence of crofting as a political issue since the nineteenth century, with five crofters' MPs elected in the Highlands in 1885 and the passage of the Crofting Act 1886, the SCU was only founded in 1986. In 2000, the organisation had nearly 4,000 members in fifty-eight branches across the Highlands and Islands, organised into eleven areas that elect the SCU Council, President and Vice-Presidents. Although the SCU appears as a trade union for crofters, it actually operates as a pressure group. Its objectives involve the protection and promotion of the agricultural and other interests of crofting and the crofting community; encouraging the development of crofting and the crofting community; and protecting and furthering the interests of SCU members.[3] The range of issues that the SCU lobbies on is varied: issues of concern include the EU's Agenda 2000 measures for the environment, agricultural grants and support mechanisms for numerous products and livestock, land ownership and reform, and the work of quangos such as the Crofters Commission and Scottish Natural Heritage.

Devolution has substantially altered the SCU's political environment in a number of highly significant ways. First, the Scottish Executive includes a Minister for Rural Affairs and a Deputy Minister for the Highlands and Islands, giving the SCU two dedicated Ministers at which to aim its attentions. Second, the SCU can also direct its lobbying efforts to the Parliament's Rural Affairs Committee and to the large number of MSPs that now represent the Highlands and Islands: seven constituency and seven list MSPs in total. Third, key issues of concern to the SCU such as land reform became key legislative proposals for the Scottish Executive in its first legislative programme. Therefore, both the institutions and policy agenda of devolution can be seen to have moved in the SCU's direction. The SCU utilised the new arrangements by giving evidence to the Rural Affairs Committee on issues such as the sheep industry, meeting with the Rural Affairs Minister on a number of occasions, and supporting petitions to the Parliament related to the tolls on the Skye Bridge. Such access and involvement would point to the SCU existing as an insider group within Scottish policymaking, with close links to ministers and civil servants in agriculture and rural affairs.

Case study 9 The Convention of
Scottish Local Authorities (COSLA)

The Convention of Scottish Local Authorities was established in April 1975 as the sole representative organisation of Scotland's district and regional councils. Prior to COSLA's formation, Scottish local government was represented by four different associations, a clear reflection of the different types of councils and their various functional, regional and political divisions that existed before local government reorganisation. Despite a second reorganisation into unitary authorities in 1995, COSLA remains prone to divisions between its member authorities, a natural outcome of the diverse nature of Scottish local government (see Chapter 11). All Scottish councils are members of COSLA and the organisation exists 'to promote and protect the interests of councils in Scotland by providing a forum for discussion of matters of common concern'.[4] The organisation operates as a lobbyist on behalf of its member councils and provides research and briefings for local authorities. In addition, it acts as an employers' representative in certain areas such as teachers' pay and local authority conditions of service. COSLA contains a central office, responsible for policy development, administration of its various policy groups, publicity and Parliamentary monitoring. Most of its decisions and policy debates are undertaken through the leaders' forum of council leaders and chief executives as well as the COSLA Convention that meets four times a year. These structures were steamlined following devolution, along with the appointment of a group of twenty-two spokespersons from the council membership, to represent COSLA across its various concerns. COSLA is an example of a resource-rich pressure group, with fifty staff and a budget of approximately £2.3 million funded through membership subscriptions from local authorities.[5]

Politically, COSLA has always been divided on party lines with voting within the Convention, the election of office-bearers and the adoption of policy all influenced by parties (Craig, 1980). As Labour dominates Scottish local government, COSLA has traditionally been viewed as a Labour-dominated organisation, although it has always taken to steps to involve and represent other parties. For example, one of its Vice-Presidents is usually an independent councillor, currently Hugh Halcro-Johnston of Orkney. Politically, COSLA faces the difficulty of existing as a representative of Labour local authorities in a period in which Scottish and UK government are Labour-controlled. Thus, the financial restrictions on councils and the 2000 financial settlement were inflicted upon Labour councils by members of their own party.

Case study 10 CBI Scotland

CBI Scotland is one of the longstanding business organisations in Scotland. It represents over 26,000 businesses and has organised its membership into around sixty distinct trade associations. The organisation is active in multi-level governance through lobbying the Scottish Executive, UK government and the European Union on a variety of different issues.

The organisation's office in Glasgow was transformed into a Scottish national office following the CBI's 1998 decision to devolve powers to its regional offices in Scotland, Wales and Northern Ireland. Since the establishment of the Parliament, CBI Scotland has been responsible for autonomous policy development in relation to devolved areas, meaning it is free to have different policies to the CBI's UK organisation. In addition, CBI Scotland became responsible for developing a lobbying strategy of its own in relation to the new Parliament. However, CBI Scotland is still an example of a Scottish branch of a UK pressure group, with an issue agenda that involves several different levels of government. CBI Scotland's activities are therefore not solely directed at Scottish issues such as transport, environment, business rates, education and industry, but at UK issues such as taxation, interest rates, sterling and exports, as well as EU issues such as the single market and international trade. Significantly, CBI Scotland has both its own organisation and the main CBI office in London to pursue many of these non-devolved issues.

In recent years, in anticipation of devolution – a policy it previously opposed (Lynch, 1998) – CBI Scotland has adopted an increasingly prominent profile in public policy. It developed an agenda-setting role in the 1990s through the publication of reports such as *Manufacturing Matters* (1994), *The Scottish Business Agenda* (1994) and *Business and Parliament: Partners for Prosperity* (1998). Since devolution it has revamped and expanded its organisation and developed a more-focused approach to lobbying the Parliament, with special briefings for MSPs, meeting with ministers and civil servants, and participation in the various consultation exercises on transport congestion, education and many other issues. Politically, CBI Scotland can be considered as a sectional group which is also an insider group in relation to ministers and civil servants: a result of the fact that all parties have adopted pro-business agendas that view business as a legitimate partner of government. It also has the resources to make an impact on the Mound. However, the organisation also has a weakness in that it is a 'peak' association representing a disparate group of businesses with their own conflicting policy interests (Grant and Marsh, 1977).

– THE IMPACT OF DEVOLUTION –

Devolution has impacted upon pressure group Scotland in a variety of ways, especially when compared to the political environment for pressure groups in Scotland pre-devolution. Before devolution, pressure group politics was a relatively closed environment. The main focus of pressure group attention was Scottish Office ministers and civil servants. Westminster offered limited opportunities for pressure group action because of the closed nature of its procedures and the small extent of Scottish business. Scottish groups faced a highly competitive situation at Westminster, given its locus as an institution for pressure groups across the UK, although this did allow Scottish organisations to form broad alliances with other UK groups. However, the relative lack of Scottish business at Westminster, the limited role of the Scottish Affairs Select Committee and Scottish Grand Committee, and the small amount of Scottish legislation did not make for participatory politics by pressure groups. All of this changed with the Scottish Parliament and its committees.

Devolution introduced a much more promising political environment for pressure group Scotland. It offered an open Parliamentary system, with commitments to open government and participatory democracy. It produced a lengthy legislative process of guaranteed pre-legislative consultation, multiple-access points for discussing legislation with MSPs in committees and in plenary, and opportunities for further consultation with committees. The Scottish Executive's report on consultation, published in the form of the policy memoranda attached to bills, offers a further opportunity for pressure groups to assess their impact on the policy process. Besides the legislative process, devolution has also brought about a range of opportunities for pressure group involvement. The designation of a number of subject committees created a direct forum for pressure group access, in addition to the 129 MSPs and twenty-two ministers in the Scottish

Executive. Similarly, MSPs' ability to present motions for debate and propose members' bills offered some scope for single issue politics, as did the ability to use the process of public petitions to set the political agenda or spur the Parliament into action. Put simply, under the old system, the executive in the shape of the Scottish Office was the dominant force within the policy process; under devolution, the Parliament itself offers an important alternative arena for influence over policy that Westminster was never able to achieve. The pressure groups are also able to combine with the Parliament to challenge the hegemony of the civil service in relation to ministers. Pressure groups do not merely seek to influence ministers through lobbying, they also offer an alternative source of expertise, information and policy analysis for ministers and civil servants alike, and can therefore break the civil service stranglehold on advice to ministers. Finally, the establishment of a Scottish Civic Forum attached to the Parliament offers an institutionalised mechanism for dialogue between pressure groups and the new devolved institutions.

– DEVOLUTION AND PRESSURE GROUP EXPANSION –

One of the outcomes of the devolution process was an expansion in three ways of pressure group activity in relation to the Parliament. First, this expansion involved the appointment of new staff to deal with the Scottish Parliament or with the agenda of issues associated with the creation of an autonomous sphere of Scottish decisionmaking (see Table 7.1). Second, a number of pressure groups established offices in Scotland for the first time. Third, a number of pressure groups altered their internal structures to devolve more powers to their Scottish arms.

Devolution also brought new pressure groups to Scotland. The Scottish Retail Consortium was established in 1998 as the Scottish office of the existing British Retail Consortium; the National Association of Homecare Workers established a Scottish office and organisation in 1999, as did the Association of the British Pharmaceutical Industry. Also, as a mirror of the devolution process, a number of pressure groups underwent organisational changes in order to adjust to the Scottish Parliament. CBI Scotland gained new staff and more powers from the UK organisation of the CBI in London so that it could determine its own policy on all devolved subjects independently – therefore it could decide its own policies on local taxation, Scottish Enterprise, transport, the environment, and so on (*Scotland on Sunday*, 21 June 1998). It also gained the ability to direct its lobbying and information campaigns at MSPs and Parliamentary committees, in addition to seeking to monitor and influence Scottish legislative proposals on behalf of its 26,000 member firms. Other pressure groups made similar adjustments to devolution, for example, the British Diabetic Association's Scottish office took on national status and expanded its staff, as did the Scottish Council of the Royal College of General Practitioners.

Table 7.1 Pressure group appointments resulting from devolution 1998–2000

Organisation	Job type	Date
Church of Scotland	Parliamentary officer	1998
British Medical Association	Parliamentary officer	June 1998
NCH Action for Children	Public policy officer	August 1998
Shelter	Campaigns coordinator	August 1998
Roman Catholic Church	Parliamentary liaison officer	September 1998
Scottish Retail Consortium	Parliamentary officer	October 1998
CBI Scotland	Head of media and public affairs	November 1998
CBI Scotland	Head of policy	November 1998
British Airports Authority	Parliamentary officer	December 1998
Scottish Council of Voluntary Organisations (SCVO)	Media officer	January 1999
SCVO	Two policy/information officers	January 1999
SCVO	Research assistant	January 1999
Carers National Association	Director	January 1999
Association of Scottish Colleges	Policy officer	January 1999
Royal Incorporation of Architects in Scotland	Parliamentary officer	January 1999
National Pharmaceutical Association	Scottish public affairs executive	April 1999
British Diabetic Association	Policy/communications officer	May 1999
Royal College of GPs	Information/policy officer	May 1999
Shelter	Parliamentary and public affairs officer	June 1999
Association of the British Pharmaceutical Industry	Scottish office manager	August 1999
Tarmac	Scottish Parliamentary officer	August 1999
Oxfam	Media and public affairs manager	September 1999
	Executive secretary	September 1999
Friends of the Earth	Parliamentary officer	October 1999
Chartered Society of Physiotherapy	Policy officer	December 1999
Leonard Chesire Scotland	Parliamentary officer	May 2000
Scottish Society for Autism	Parliamentary and policy officer	June 2000

Source: The weekly jobs sections of *The Scotsman*, *Scotland on Sunday*, *Sunday Herald* and *The Herald* newspapers

– PRESSURE GROUPS AND THE POLITICAL PARTIES –

Political parties – both in and out of government – are often the object of pressure group attention. Groups frequently seek to influence the policies of the main political parties through briefing papers, meetings with party spokepersons and functions at party conferences. The reason for such activity is not merely to influence the influential, with groups seeking to press their views on parties, but it can be seen as a process that assists the political parties in a number of ways. Arguably, political parties are weak in terms of policy expertise. Before the rapid expansion in party staff that accompanied devolution, all of Scotland's political parties were resource-poor in terms of policymaking, and party research staffs were small aspects of each party's organisation. Often, one or two researchers would need to juggle vast numbers of issues and policy areas. This situation changed markedly with devolution as parties and MSPs employed significant numbers of researchers and Parliamentary assistants. However, many of these remained policy generalists as opposed to the policy experts resident in many Scottish pressure groups. When parties sought information on technical or specialised topics, pressure groups were often a welcome port of call with briefing papers on legislation and government proposals. Indeed, to some extent pressure groups can be thought of as organisations able to generate policy ideas that can be adopted by the political parties.

In advance of the 1999 Scottish election, a number of pressure groups published their own manifestos and engaged in discussions with the political parties. Some of these discussions fed into party policy: the British Medical Association Scotland's *Partners in Care: The BMA and the New Scottish Parliament* included the idea of creating a Minister for Public Health within the Scottish Executive, while children in Scotland's *Manifesto for Scotland's Children, Young People and Families – What the Parties Say* argued for the creation of a Minister for Children. Both of these proposals were adopted by the SNP in its Scottish election manifesto. In addition, a number of pressure groups were involved in supporting Mike Watson's MSP's bill to abolish fox hunting: groups such as Advocates for Animals, the League Against Cruel Sports and the International Fund for Animal Welfare were responsible for financing a researcher to assist him in drafting the fox-hunting bill,[6] an issue later examined by the Parliament's Standards Committee.

Pressure groups are often conspicuous through their attendance at Scottish party conferences. Groups will have an information stall at conferences, hold fringe meetings and debates, and seek to contact party spokespersons and specialist policy groups. Pressure group activity at some party conferences increased as the party appeared close to power, for example, the Labour conference at Inverness in 1996 brought a larger-than-usual turnout of pressure groups and companies, so much so that they had to be accommodated in a special marquee attached to the conference hall. The prospect of power was also responsible for a similar phenomenon at the SNP's 1998 conference in Inverness, with a vastly inflated attendance by pressure groups, businesses and lobbyists. Devolution, and the potential of government status for at least three of Scotland's four main parties, is likely to permanently increase pressure group activity at party conferences, especially in advance of elections.

Pressure groups have developed a number of different strands to their relationships with political parties, with some group activity targeted directly at the electoral cycle. For instance, pressure groups produced a number of manifestos and policy documents in advance of the Scottish election in 1999. Such documents were intended as an agenda-setting exercise for pressure groups to get their issues across to the public and the parties through the media, by focusing directly on the election itself. Thus, CBI Scotland published *The Key to Scotland's Prosperity*, which followed earlier lobbying on manufacturing and devolution (Lynch, 1998); the Scottish Wildlife Trust produced *Scotland's Manifesto for Wildlife*; the Automobile Association published an *Agenda for Scotland: AA Priorities for the New Scottish Parliament*; the British Medical Association outlined its vision for healthcare in Scotland with *Partners in Care: The BMA and the New Scottish Parliament*, as did the Royal College of Nursing with *Scotland's Parliament, Scotland's Health*. Such efforts were a fairly common activity before elections, but were more important in 1999 because of openness of the Scottish election and the legislative system that would result. There was no point in attempting to influence one political party because the electoral system was likely to produce a coalition administration; because three of the four main parties appeared to be contenders for government; and because the policy process of the Parliament involved a cross-party dimension through the committee system rather than a simple government-opposition decisionmaking process.

– THE SCOTTISH CIVIC FORUM –

Supporters of devolution associated with the Scottish Constitutional Convention had argued for the establishment of a civic assembly to shadow the Parliament for a number of years. A Scottish Civic Assembly was established prior to 1999 chaired by the former STUC leader Campbell Christie, with a variety of pressure groups and civic organisations involved in developing a formalised mechanism to facilitate an exchange of views between Parliament and civic Scotland. There was support for the idea of a civic forum before the Scottish elections from a range of groups and from the SNP, which had itself piloted a number of civic assemblies in advance of the election in order to debate its manifesto contents and key themes. Support for the idea of a civic forum was also expressed in the Consultative Steering Group's report *Shaping Scotland's Parliament* (1999: p. 7). The Scottish Civic Forum was formally launched on 20 March 1999, although its exact relationship with the future Scottish Parliament and Executive was difficult to discern at that stage.

The Labour government also expressed support for the notion of a civic forum before the election, with two Scottish Office civil servants seconded to the forum in March 1999, with the objective of providing organisational support for the development of the new body. Civil service support for the forum was to last for three years, along with a funding package of £100,000 over that period. Of course, government support for a civic forum sounds rather suspicious. On the one hand, it pointed to the clear weakness of civic Scotland. On the other hand, it opened the door to the potential for government influence through the Forum's financial and organisational dependency on the Scottish Executive. Of course, government itself funds all sorts of organisations and pressure groups which are able to act independently of their funders – such as the Scottish Consumer Council – however, it did leave the Scottish Civic Forum in a slightly uncomfortable position in terms of its organisational autonomy.

The Scottish Civic Forum was established with the aim of bringing the people of Scotland closer to the Parliament, by allowing civic organisations to participate in the policy process and scrutiny of legislation alongside MSPs. In doing so, it was intended to facilitate involvement in the numerous access points in the Parliament's policy process such as pre-legislative consultation, hearings on proposed legislation, and evidence before Parliamentary committees. The forum gave itself seven specific functions:

1. to take forward consultations on issues of public policy in an inclusive and participative way
2. to explore problems and possible solutions; clarify feasible options for the Parliament and the Executive and analyse differences and disagreements where they exist
3. to undertake formal consultation exercises for the Parliament and the Executive; assemble inclusive lists of interested parties to involve on particular issues, and provide feedback to contributors on any impact their views make
4. to help get otherwise excluded voices heard in the public policy debate
5. to explore new forms of participation in public policy debate, including the use of IT, the internet, policy forums, conventions and so on
6. to act as a signpost and information centre which will enable civic interests and the Parliament to work more closely together for the benefit of Scotland
7. to foster dialogue across civic society on matters of priority interest.[7]

By the end of 1999, over 650 groups had registered an interest in the Scottish Civic Forum, with 240 formal members by March 2000. Members included a broad mix of groups such as Amnesty International Scotland, the Association of Scottish Community Councils, the Baha'i Council for Scotland, Childline Scotland, Citizens Advice Scotland, Grampian Autistic Society, Land Reform Scotland, Pilton Elderly Forum, RSPB Scotland, Scottish Federation of Housing Associations and Victim Support Scotland. Significantly, the initial membership was largely comprised of cause and promotional groups rather than sectional interest organisations. Small, local and voluntary organisations were prominent, while producer interests such as business and trades unions did not join the forum. Indeed, some of the stronger pressure groups – those with substantial finances, staff and organisational resources – may have viewed the Scottish Civic Forum as an inappropriate body compared to their normal lobbying efforts. The forum may therefore operate as a support mechanism for resource-weak pressure groups and those that might otherwise struggle to involve themselves in the policy process.

Of course, one has to ask whether a civic forum can actually operate as a mini-Parliament for civic Scotland? Certainly, it can be seen to work effectively as an institutional support for pressure groups, alongside the Scottish Council for Voluntary Organisations, but can it actually aggregate interests and opinions from within its membership and advance them within the policy process? The answer so far has been yes. The Scottish Civic Forum sponsored three policy forums from October 1999 to February 2000 to examine its members' responses to the Scottish Executive's Education Bill, the Ethical Standards in Public Life Bill and the National Parks Bill. These involved participation by relevant civil servants within the Scottish Executive and resulted in the submission of consultation papers on behalf of the Scottish Civic Forum. Twenty-three groups were involved in the consultation on the Education Bill while fourteen groups were involved in the discussion over the Ethical Standards in Public Life Bill. Of course, the value of these submissions is difficult to determine, when added to the wide range of individual consultation documents submitted on each bill. However, the Scottish Civic Forum may have a promotional role in galvanising pressure groups to participate in the consultation exercise and involve themselves in the Parliament's policy process.

Despite such activities, the exact relationship between the Scottish Civic Forum and the Scottish Parliament remains unclear. The Scottish Civic Forum discussed the notion of a concordat to guide relations with the Parliament and Executive, but the nature of the relationship could be problematic. For example, although the Civic Forum may wish to present itself as the authentic voice of pressure group Scotland which deserves privileged access to the Parliament, it only represents a fraction of Scottish pressure groups. Its views may therefore be quite unrepresentative of pressure group Scotland and also unrepresentative of public opinion (Paterson, 1999).

– CONCLUSION –

To a certain degree, the campaigns for devolution made a fetish of civic society. Support for constitutional change was seen to come from civic society and the various components of civic Scotland were interpreted as important checks on the power of government. Pressure groups were seen as legitimate participants in democratic politics – and occasionally as the embodiment of the democracy itself – and the Parliament was designed to ensure that decisionmaking was open and accessible to pressure groups and public alike (Consultative Steering Group, 1999). However, this classic pluralist interpretation of pressure groups and democracy is open to challenge. Rather than seeing pressure groups as equal participants in policymaking, it is often the case that some pressure groups are more equal than others when it comes to access to decisionmakers. The ability of a resource-rich CBI Scotland to lobby ministers and MSPs is very different to that of local community groups and resource-poor pressure groups across Scotland. Whether the combined efforts of the Scottish Council of Voluntary Organisations, the Scottish Civic Forum and com.com/holyrood can redress this imbalance between pressure groups remains to be seen. However, at least group disparities were clearly recognised and some efforts made to support the weaker pressure groups in their interactions with the new Parliament. Although devolution does not have an equal impact upon all pressure groups, it has at least produced a more open and competitive means for elite interaction and involvement in policymaking than existed under the *ancien régime*. For all its flaws, the Scottish Parliament has provided a more accessible legislative process, pre-legislative consultation and a large number of opportunities for pressure group Scotland to exert an influence.

– NOTES –

1. Report of the Consultative Steering Group on the Scottish Parliament, *Analysis of Responses to the CSG Consultation Exercise Received by 31 July 1998*.
2. SCVO press release, 'Local groups get virtual foot in Holyrood's door', 24 January 2000.
3. http://www.scu.co.uk
4. http://www.cosla.gov.uk
5. COSLA, COSLA, *Local Government and the Scottish Parliament: A Consultation Paper*, Edinburgh: COSLA, 1999, p. 2.
6. *The Scotsman*, 11 November 1999.
7. http://www.civicforum.org.uk/role/

CHAPTER 8

The Scottish Secretary, the Scotland Office and Scotland at Westminster

– INTRODUCTION –

Although the establishment of a Scottish Parliament fundamentally altered the focus and nature of Scottish politics, Westminster and Whitehall remain important parts of the Scottish political scene. Devolution only devolved some government functions to the Scottish Parliament. Westminster's reserved powers are substantial (see Chapter 2) and the extent of UK government in Scotland remains impressive whether in relation to policy, public expenditure or employment. The range of UK government functions in Scotland required both administrative and political oversight that could not be provided by the Scottish Parliament. Consequently, there remained a role for the Secretary of State for Scotland and the Scotland Office as well as for Scottish committees and MPs at Westminster. Similarly, while Scottish business at Westminster was reduced by devolution it was not eradicated; there remained a need for specifically Scottish arrangements within UK governmental and Parliamentary structures in spite of devolution. This chapter will examine the role and future of the Secretary of State for Scotland and the Scotland Office as well as the treatment of Scottish issues at Westminster since devolution.

THE SECRETARY OF STATE FOR SCOTLAND AND THE SCOTLAND OFFICE

The position of Secretary of State for Scotland was established in 1885, following a campaign by Scottish MPs and peers to establish a special ministerial post for Scotland. The post was partly intended to ensure Parliamentary control over a range of Scottish administrative boards (quangos) which had developed in the nineteenth century such as the Scotch Education Department. Politically, the post was seen as promoting

Scotland within the UK, with both Conservatives and Liberals north of the border competing to establish the post as a symbol of their Scottishness (Mitchell, 1990). The Scottish Secretary became a cabinet member from 1892 onwards, and became eligible for an equal salary from 1926 after the post was made a Secretary of State (Kellas, 1984: 31). While the Scottish Secretary was initially responsible for administering a small office, the growth of government in the twentieth century rapidly increased the size of the Scottish Office from a staff of twenty-two in 1900 (Mitchell, 1990: p. 19) to 13,724 in 1998 (Parry, 1999a: p. 66).

The Scottish Secretary's functions before devolution included acting as Scotland's representative within the cabinet and UK government, with key lobbying functions on behalf of Scottish interests; functioning as the chief executive of Scottish administration in areas such as education, the legal system and local government; and operating as a territorial manager for Westminster in Scotland. The post itself involved a number of anomalies, for example, the Scottish Secretary was not really Scottish at all, but a UK appointment made by the Prime Minister of the day from the party with a majority at Westminster (rather than in Scotland). Sure enough, the Scottish Secretary was always a Scottish MP or peer, but there was no requirement that he or she had to be. Also, the Scottish Secretary was viewed as the chief spokesperson for Scottish interests, yet from 1979–97, the Secretary of State represented a political minority that had been rejected decisively at elections in Scotland in this period. Moreover, the political importance of the Scottish Secretary has always been questionable: at Westminster and in cabinet, the Scottish Secretary was usually regarded as a fairly junior post and thus a relatively minor figure (Rose, 1987). However, in Scotland, the Scottish Secretary was the key government figure, in spite of the limited functions of the Scottish Office. Willie Ross, Secretary of State in 1964–70 and 1974–6, referred to public expectations of the post as 'approaching the archangelic' in Scotland (Ross, 1978) and there was a tendency for the post to create exaggerated expectations among politicians and the public. Such high expectations were transferred to the Scottish Parliament with devolution (Brown, McCrone, Paterson and Surridge, 1999).

As a result of devolution, the existence of the Scottish Secretary became debatable. The role of chief executive of Scottish administration was lost to the First Minister, along with control of the Scottish Office civil service machinery – the post therefore had nothing left to administer, with no legislative power or uniquely Scottish policy functions. The Scottish Secretary did have a role in ensuring that Scottish legislation did not conflict with Westminster's reserved powers (see Chapter 2), but this role did not necessarily require a Scottish Secretary or a cabinet minister: it could be dealt with by a junior minister. The Scottish Secretary's ability to represent Scottish interests was fundamentally changed through the direct election of a Scottish Parliament, which could represent Scotland much more effectively than a post appointed by the Prime Minister. Where the Scottish Secretary did retain a role was as a representative of Scottish interests in central government. The First Minister and Scottish Executive ministers did not enjoy such direct access to Westminster and Whitehall despite the complex inter-governmental arrangements of concordats and Joint Ministerial Committees (see Chapter 9). There was also seen to be a need to retain the post to act as a political representative of the UK Government in Scotland.

More practically, the post was retained because the Scottish Secretary still had certain government functions through the Scotland Act 1998 and there was a need to oversee Westminster's reserved powers in Scotland. For example, the Labour Government's legislative programme at Westminster in 1999–2000 contained a number of policy areas which were reserved powers concerning Scotland: the Child Benefit, Pensions and Social Security Bill, the Transport Bill, the Utilities Bill, the Political Parties, Elections and Referendums Bill, the Sexual Offences (Amendment) Bill, the Electronic Communications Bill and the Prevention of Terrorism Bill in that session were all applicable to Scotland. Indeed, despite devolution, seven of the eleven bills at Westminster in 1999–2000 affected Scotland. Such legislation provided a clear role for the Scottish Secretary, although this reality did not mean that the post had to retain its cabinet status. It was clearly something that aided Scotland and fed English suspicions of devolution as Scots gained an autonomous Parliament and yet retained a post in the cabinet as well as control of a large number of other cabinet positions.

The Scottish Secretary's ministerial team grew throughout the twentieth century and changed again with devolution. The Scottish Secretary was joined by a Parliamentary Under-Secretary for Health in 1919; two Under-Secretaries of State in 1940 and 1951; a Minister of State in 1951; and a third Under-Secretary in 1979 (Kellas, 1984: 33). By 1998, the Scottish Office contained a Secretary of State (Donald Dewar), a Minister of State (Henry McLeish), and five Under-Secretaries of State (Helen Liddell, Sam Galbraith, Calum MacDonald, Lord Sewell and Lord MacDonald), plus the Lord Advocate and Solicitor-General. This ministerial team was reduced to two after devolution, with John Reid as Secretary of State and Brian Wilson as Minister of State, alongside the Advocate-General (Lynda Clark), and Baroness Ramsey, the Scotland Office's official spokesperson in the House of Lords.

After the Scottish Parliament assumed its powers on 1 July 1999, the Secretary of State for Scotland found himself living in reduced circumstances. The transfer of the Scottish Office to become the civil service of the Scottish Executive left the Scottish Secretary bereft of staff and an office. The Secretary of State renamed his administrative machinery as the 'Scotland Office' and sought to carve a role as the representative of Scottish interests in reserved matters within UK government. Indeed, with a continued role as a cabinet minister bringing involvement in Cabinet committees and Whitehall negotiations, the Scottish Secretary and Scotland Office retained a capacity for participation in central government that is not available to the Scottish Executive or Parliament. The Scottish Secretary and the Scotland Office have five functions post-devolution:

1. to represent Scottish interests within the UK government in matters that are reserved to the UK Parliament under the terms of the Scotland Act 1998
2. to promote the devolution settlement by encouraging cooperation between Edinburgh and London at the executive and legislative levels
3. to be responsible for payment of the block grant from Westminster to the Scottish Parliament through its funding of the Scottish Consolidated Fund
4. to conduct certain functions reserved to the Secretary of State for Scotland under the Scotland Act 1998, such as the conduct of elections.[1]
5. to ensure that Acts of the Scottish Parliament do not impinge on Westminster's reserved powers nor are incompatible with the UK's international obligations.[2]

The staff of the Scotland Office shrank with devolution in 1999. Indeed, the office was left with around 100 staff upon the establishment of the Scottish Executive and Parliament, and most of its staff are involved in monitoring policy and legislation in Westminster, Whitehall and Scotland (see Table 8.1). Initially, the Scotland Office had been expected to operate on a budget of £2,455,000 in 1999–2000, which was to increase to £4,215,000 in 2000–1. However, because of increased staff numbers and the transfer of civil servants from the Scottish Executive to the Scotland Office, the estimated cost rose to £5.7 million (*The Herald*, 5 October 1999). More money for the Scotland Office meant less money for the Scottish Executive's public services, a fact that the SNP and Conservatives in the Scottish Parliament were quick to assert. The increase in spending also laid the Scottish Secretary open to accusations of empire-building, although it would seem that UK government had underestimated the level of post-devolution activity required by the Scottish Secretary and Scotland Office. One of the reasons for this situation was that the majority of the pre-devolution ministerial team within the Scottish Office – Donald Dewar, Henry

McLeish, Sam Galbraith and Lord Sewell – were preoccupied with becoming members of the Scottish Parliament. Similarly, Scottish Office civil servants were concerned with establishing the new Parliament and executive rather than ensuring a continued role for the Scottish Secretary.

Table 8.1 Scotland Office staff by administrative group, June 2000

Administrative group	Staff numbers
Senior management	2
Parliamentary and Constitutional Division	17
Economy and Industry Division	6
Home and Social Division	7
Ministerial private offices	13
Special advisers	2
Finance and administration	7
Information services	4
Legal secretariat to the Advocate General	5
Office of the Solicitor to the Advocate General	19
Private Legislation Procedure Office	3
UK Parliamentary draftsman	1

Source: Scotland Office (2000), *The Government's Expenditure Plans 2000–1 to 2001–2*. Cmnd 4619

To a significant extent, the Scottish Secretary had to be reinvented post-devolution, a process that was far from complete when this book was written, and the Scottish Secretary, John Reid, adopted a rather muscular approach to the post after devolution. Rather than accept the diminished position of the Scottish Secretary and the Scotland Office, Reid and his ministers sought to ensure a high-profile role. The Scottish Secretary's intervention over the closure of the Kvaerner shipyard at Govan in the summer of 1999; the decision to reconvene the Scottish Grand Committee; and the political attacks on the 'Scottish Six' by Minister of State, Brian Wilson, were all attempts to reassert the role of the UK government in Scotland post-devolution. Unfortunately, such efforts appeared to generate 'turf wars' between the Scottish Secretary and the First Minister, as the Scotland Office was seen to be trying to challenge the role of the Scottish Executive as the leading political authority in Scotland. Without careful management, the resuscitation of the Scottish Secretary was always likely to ruffle the feathers of the Scottish Executive and this was exactly what occurred in 1999 as the two institutions jockeyed for position under the new devolved arrangements. However, such efforts did breathe life into the post of Secretary of State for Scotland in the immediate post-devolution period.

The survival of the Secretary of State for Scotland as a cabinet minister is not guaranteed, and the subject was discussed within the UK government in 2000. The reality of devolution placed question marks over all of the territorial ministers, especially with the English backlash over Scotland's ability to have its own government, Parliament and cabinet representation in London. However, it is difficult to see all three Scottish, Welsh and Northern Irish cabinet ministers being abolished. Devolution has been so unstable in Northern Ireland that removing the Secretary of State for Northern Ireland would be an unwise move. Similarly, the fact that the National Assembly for Wales does not have primary legislative powers presents difficulties as there remains a need for a Welsh Secretary to present legislation to the House of Commons. The three territories are also so different, with such distinctive traditions and devolution arrangements, that it is difficult to see them served at Westminster by just one Territorial Secretary of State or Minister for Intergovernmental Affairs.

– SCOTLAND AT WESTMINSTER –

The establishment of a Scottish Parliament also impacted upon the treatment of Scottish issues at Westminster – the point of devolution itself. Devolution meant changing roles for Scottish MPs and Westminster committees, and some were uncomfortable with this. Other developments associated with attempts to resolve the West Lothian question and find a means for involving the regions in the work of a reformed House of Lords brought further potential changes to life at Westminster. Each of these developments is examined below.

– SCOTTISH MPs –

Scotland currently elects seventy-two MPs to the Westminster Parliament. However, this number is set to decline to around sixty in 2005–6 when the Boundary Commission reduces the number of Scottish MPs in order to address the West Lothian question in line with section 86 of the Scotland Act 1998. This change will not only reduce Scottish representation at Westminster, but will also reduce the size of the Scottish Parliament by cutting the number of FPTP constituencies, and causing a knock-on effect on the number of additional members in the Parliament (Curtice, 1998).

Scottish MPs traditionally occupied two worlds at Westminster. In the Scottish world of Westminster, they were MPs with their own bills, committees, question times and ministers, pursuing Scottish affairs in areas of Scottish Office responsibility such as local government, education or health. In the British world of Westminster, they were MPs pursuing UK-wide issues that affected Scotland or government generally, such as social security, pensions or foreign affairs. Devolution brought considerable change to this situation. While leaving the British world of Westminster largely untouched, the creation of a Scottish Parliament considerably disturbed the Scottish world of Westminster; indeed, it was largely intended to replace it. What need was there for a Select Committee on Scottish Affairs or a Scottish Grand Committee when devolution had involved the transfer of so many government functions to the Edinburgh Parliament? What role was there for Scottish MPs at Westminster given that many of their core policy interests and constituency concerns were no longer the responsibility of Parliament in London?

Of course, the fact that Scottish MPs were shorn of half their policy concerns was not necessarily a problem for them, since many Scottish MPs could be seen as preferring UK issues to involvement in purely Scottish affairs. Michael Keating (1975) had classified Scottish MPs holding Scottish or UK preferences. Those MPs holding UK preferences, such as those interested in defence, social security, Europe and foreign affairs, were little affected by the establishment of a Scottish Parliament, since their main policy concerns remained part of the Westminster world. Similarly, MPs keen to pursue UK political careers, with its broader range of ministerial opportunities would find devolution did not affect their prospects, although there was the suspicion that the post-1997 Labour government operated its own informal answer to the West Lothian question in cabinet posts by keeping Scots in the 'federal' ministerial posts such as the Treasury, Defence, the Foreign Office and Social Security rather than those affected by devolution.

In contrast, devolution did offer substantial challenges to Scottish MPs at Westminster. First, it led to a considerable reduction in their workloads. This reduction related both to their constituency activities and mailbags but also to their Parliamentary responsibilities. Simply put, devolution halved their workload as they were no longer responsible for health, education, housing, environment, agriculture, and so on. They were no longer active in the House, pursuing these issues in terms of debates and oral and written questions following the Speaker's ruling in July 1999 that 'where matters have been clearly devolved to the Scottish Parliament or Welsh Assembly, questions on the details of policy or expenditure would not be in order.'[3] This ruling frustrated Scottish MPs, who were quick to point out that there were no similar restrictions on MSPs in the Scottish Parliament. However, while MSPs are able to debate any issue – devolved or reserved – Scottish Executive ministers have refrained from answering questions on reserved matters.

In addition, there were no more Scottish bills requiring the attention of

Scottish MPs at Westminster and limited roles for both the Select Committee on Scottish Affairs and the Scottish Grand Committee. Scottish MPs at Westminster therefore felt themselves marginalised in relation to Scottish affairs and eclipsed by the new Parliament. This reality was especially evident in Scottish media coverage of the two Parliaments: coverage of the Scottish Parliament and its MSPs rocketed while Westminster affairs slipped down the media headlines; indeed, Scottish MPs largely disappeared from the press and broadcasting. This situation created a good deal of bad blood at Westminster, with briefings by MPs against MSPs and Scottish Executive ministers. Some Scots MPs also clearly relished the difficulties that the Scottish Parliament experienced during its first six months of existence.

Scottish MPs had two ways of responding to their anomalous position, as second-class MPs in the House. First, they could seek to emerge more clearly as 'Schedule 5' MPs for Scotland and Scottish interests. Schedule 5 of the Scotland Act 1998 contained a vast number of UK government functions that affect Scotland. Since such policies required scrutiny, Scottish MPs now had a range of defined areas on which to focus their attention. They could become more effective Scottish MPs by scrutinising UK government in Scotland and questioning UK ministers as well as the Scottish Secretary. Second, they could seek to become more effective UK MPs through their involvement in UK issues. For example, it can be argued that devolution did not really involve a reduction in Scottish MPs' workloads. It might have lessened their constituency mailbag but it also provided opportunities to take a more focused approach to Westminster life. Rather than seeking to juggle a large number of policy issues and constituency interests, devolution offered them the chance to become policy experts rather than generalists in the House, especially through the select committee system.

One area of controversy for Scottish MPs at Westminster post-devolution involved the activities of MPs who had also become MSPs in 1999: Donald Dewar, Henry McLeish, Sam Galbraith, John McAllion, John Home-Robertson and Malcolm Chisholm from Labour, the SNP's Alex Salmond, John Swinney, Margaret Ewing, Roseanna Cunningham, Alasdair Morgan and Andrew Welsh, the independent Dennis Canavan and Liberal Democrat MPs Jim Wallace and Donald Gorrie. The parties had agreed that the new MSPs would remain as Westminster MPs but would retire at the next UK general election, thus avoiding the need for a series of by-elections. However, two developments cast doubts over this arrangement. First, the media investigated the activity levels of the dual-mandate members at Westminster and cast doubts on their continued involvement – *The Times* (4 January 2000), for example, unearthed the low number of occasions in which dual-mandate members had voted in the division lobbies at Westminster from October to December 1999. Second, Cynog Dafis, the Plaid Cymru dual member for Ceredigion and for the West Wales list, resigned his Westminster seat in order to concentrate on his work in the Welsh Assembly. This decision overturned the cross-party agreement on retaining the dual mandates until the general election, and forced a by-election in his Ceredigion constitiuency on 3 February 2000. However, none of Scotland's dual-mandate MSPs followed suit and resigned their Westminster seats.

– THE SCOTTISH COMMITTEES –

Devolution did not merely raise questions about the workload of Scottish MPs, it also challenged the continued existence of Scottish business at Westminster. For example, both the Select Committee on Scottish Affairs, and the Scottish Grand Committee existed as substitutes for devolution. The Select Committee was established after the 1979 general election and portrayed as a mechanism to promote Scottish Parliamentary accountability instead of a devolved Parliament; indeed it was presented as a concession to Scotland by the Conservatives (Dewar, 1981). From 1992 to 1997, the Conservative government reformed the Scottish Grand Committee on two occasions. First, following the 'Taking Stock' exercise in 1992–3, the committee was able to debate the second stage of legislation and the opposition were allowed expanded opportunities to hold debates at the committee (HMSO, 1993). Second, Michael Forsyth's reforms in 1995 enabled UK ministerial question times at the Scottish Grand Committee in addition to taking it on tour around Scotland. With the coming of 'real' devolution in 1999, the continued existence of these two Parliamentary committees was open to question. For example, Labour MP John Maxton, who chaired the Scottish Grand Committee after the 1997 general election, expressed scepticism about the continuation of the Scottish committees:

> The Scottish Parliament with its extensive legislative and executive powers ensures that the wishes of the Scottish people are met but, with its establishment, the need for specific Scottish bodies in the British Parliament is reduced if not totally removed . . . The Scottish Parliament will establish its own scrutiny system which will investigate much more thoroughly the activities of the executive in Scotland. Therefore the need for a Scottish Select Committee disappears . . . Equally the Scottish Grand Committee becomes redundant. Its remit is to debate matters relating to the work of the Scottish Office. That work now becomes the responsibility of the Scottish Parliament where issues will not only be debated but resolved unlike the Grand Committee.[4]

The future of each committee was a key aspect of the Select Committee on Procedure's investigation into the procedural consequences of devolution in 1998–9. Both the Procedure Committee and the UK government argued for the retention of the Select Committee on Scottish Affairs (Select Committee on Procedure, 1999). Although the Select, Committee no longer had any role in scrutinising Scottish administration, as the old Scottish Office had been transferred from central government to the Scottish Parliament, there was still useful work to be done scrutinising the work of the Scottish Secretary and UK government departments operational in Scotland. Thus, the Select Committee on Scottish Affairs would be able to examine Schedule 5 reserved powers, such as the implementation of social security policy in Scotland, the provision of air transport services, Scottish coastguard services, oil and gas, nuclear energy and broadcasting. The chair of the Select Committee on Scottish Affairs, David Marshall MP, argued that there were some reserved powers that had a specifically Scottish dimension to them that could not be dealt with by other committees of the House, such as excise duty on whisky, petrol prices in the Highlands and the impact of air-passenger duty on the Scottish economy.[5]

While there was consensus over the role of the Select Committee on Scottish Affairs the Procedure Committee and the government parted company when it came to consideration of the role of the Scottish Grand Committee. The Procedure Committee argued for the suspension of the committee when devolution was in place. It supported the notion of establishing a forum within Westminster to debate territorial matters, but was concerned that the Scottish Grand Committee might be seen as a forum through which MPs sought to recover some power and influence over devolved policies (Select Committee on Procedure, 1999). Also, with Scottish devolution, there was no longer any requirement for the Scottish Grand Committee to handle stages of Scottish legislation as it had since 1992. However, the government argued for the continuation of the Scottish Grand Committee and the other grand committees in a somewhat rein-vented format, and Margaret Beckett, Leader of the House, said of the grand committees:

> They may, for instance, be the appropriate forum for debate on the block grants made each year to the devolved administrations. The Northern Ireland Grand committee, for instance, will be asked to consider the Comprehensive Spending Review at its first meeting in the 1999–2000 session. A regular pattern of meetings could be established to debate reserved matters. The Government expects that, in the light of experience, there will be a need to adjust the procedures of the grand committees, but it would prefer not to make any changes at this stage.[6]

Thus, the two sets of committees that were originally intended to be substitutes for a Scottish Parliament actually survived devolution. The Select Committee on Scottish Affairs was able to busy itself with inquiries into issues such as poverty in Scotland and the operation of the BBC and Broadcasting Council for Scotland in the 1999–2000 Parliamentary session. However, the future of the Scottish Grand Committee was more uncertain. The Scottish Secretary, John Reid, made arrangements for it to be reconvened for a number of sessions in 2000 to examine issues such as the New Deal and Employment and Fairness at Work, but its exact nature post-devolution was questionable. It provided a forum for MPs to debate the operation of reserved policy areas in Scotland and for ministers to make announcements and political speeches, but was essentially just an add-on to Scottish questions and the efforts of the Scottish Affairs Select Committee. However, the political intent of reconvening the Grand Committee was relatively clear. The fact that the media profile of Scottish MPs and Westminster generally had slipped off the radar screen necessitated efforts to reassert the role of the UK dimension to Scottish politics. Thus, the relaunch of the Scottish Grand Committee was not purely an exercise in additional scrutiny of Schedule 5 issues but a political strategy to raise Westminster's profile in Scotland as part of Labour's strategy for the 2001/2 UK general election. It was also a convenient forum for the Secretary of State to indulge in Nat-bashing.

– SCOTTISH QUESTIONS IN THE HOUSE –

Devolution led to the reduction of Scottish questions in the House of Commons rather than their eradication. The question time was reduced from forty-five minutes to thirty minutes and following the Speaker's ruling, MP's questions – both written and oral – had to avoid devolved issues and concentrate on reserved matters. Often, this led to pretty thin question times, although some did occasionally stray into devolved matters – indeed, there were a number of occasions on which questions should have been ruled out of order. For example, on 22 February 2000, questions on student finance in Scotland were ruled to be just in order because they dealt with the English dimension to the changes to student tuition fees in Scotland, and questions that dealt with section 28 were allowed even though the matter was devolved. Similarly, questions about the Lockerbie trial were clearly out of order, but they were permitted by the Speaker on 9 November 1999. Tam Dalyell was allowed two oral questions to the Advocate General for Scotland, Lynda Clark, over the Lockerbie issue, and each elicited the same response: 'My right honourable friend the Secretary of State has no responsibility for legal or other matters relating to Lockerbie.'[7] Despite the fact that Lockerbie was clearly the responsibility of the Scottish Executive, the Speaker allowed a portion of Scottish questions to be wasted on an issue that should have been ruled out of order. As Parliamentary conventions are often observed when they are breached rather than followed, this should come as no surprise. But it was certainly the case that Westminster MPs were allowed to stray and indeed deliberately trespass into devolved issues in breach of the Speaker's own ruling. However, in most other cases, oral questions either dealt with policy areas that were clearly reserved, such as rail transport and the minimum wage, or with devolution issues that affected the Scottish Secretary and Scotland Office (see Table 8.2).

Table 8.2 Scottish questions topics, July 1999–June 2000

Date	Topic
27 June 2000	Ferry services
	Assisted areas map
	Special advisers
	Economy
	NHS policy coordination
23 May 2000	Youth unemployment
	Working families tax credit
	Electricity
	Tax-raising powers
18 April 2000	Referenda
	Digital transmission
	One Pilot project
	Pensioners
	Electronic Communications Bill
21 March 2000	Scottish economy
	Petrol prices
	Parliament building
	Winter fuel payments
22 February 2000	Student finance
	Section 28
	National minimum wage
	Strategic Rail Authority
	Scottish legislation
	European Convention on Human Rights
25 January 2000	Pensioners fuel bills
	Working families tax credit
	National minimum wage
	Student finance
	Devolution
14 December 1999	Rail services
	Poverty alleviation

	European elections
	EU rebate
	European Convention on Human Rights
9 November 1999	Scotland Office (funding)
	Anti-drugs strategy
	Rail safety
	Lockerbie trial
	Beef on the bone
	Manufacturing industry
	Single currency
27 July 1999	Liaison arrangements
	Reserved powers
	Regional air services
	Economy
	Regional aid
	Websites
	Ministerial responsibilities

The fact that Scottish questions post-devolution were stripped of so many policy issues had a negative effect on the quality of questions and interventions. Devolution reduced the cut and thrust of Scottish question time, but so did the fact that the Conservative opposition frontbenchers were not Scottish MPs and had no real experience of Scottish affairs. Indeed, Scottish questions declined markedly with devolution and offered a rather inferior alternative to Scottish Executive questions on the Mound.

– THE DEVOLUTION DIVIDEND –

One traditional argument for devolution was that it would lead to more time at Westminster to debate key issues. In the nineteenth century, this argument meant there would be more time for imperial affairs rather than interminable debates on Ireland and the Irish question. By the end of the twentieth century, territorial arrangements at Westminster for Scotland, Wales and Northern Ireland occupied Parliamentary time through ministerial question times, select committee business and debates on legislation. Devolution altered this timetable to some extent, although not as much as might have been expected. For example, Conservative shadow ministers such as Sir George Young often referred to the removal of territorial politics to devolved administration as a 'devolution dividend' for the Westminster timetable, especially for English MPs. However, the divided turned out to be a limited one. Certainly, devolution brought an end to Scottish legislation at Westminster, with more space for UK or English bills, but the Parliamentary session of 1999–2000 featured a legislative logjam of bills towards the end of the session that belied the existence of any devolution dividend. Similarly, although the Scottish ministerial team was slimmed down at Westminster and its administrative burden shrank with devolution, Scottish questions remained part of the Parliamentary timetable (albeit reduced from forty-five to thirty minutes) and were still held every four weeks. Similarly, the Select Committee on Scottish Affairs remained active, with its complement of English Conservative MPs to ensure party balance on the committee to reflect the overall balance in the House – not much of a dividend for them.

One striking feature of the impact of Scottish devolution at Westminster was its marginal nature in terms of Parliamentary business. There are two reasons for this situation. First, the Labour government sought to proceed cautiously with post-devolution arrangements. It avoided calls from, for example, the Select Committee on Procedure to institute more radical changes to Westminster's operation after devolution, and made limited changes. Indeed, what was obvious about post-devolution Westminster was how much remained of pre-devolution Westminster: the Secretary of State for Scotland in the cabinet, Scottish ministerial question times, the Select Committee on Scottish Affairs and the Scottish Grand Committee. Second, the retention of so many Scottish arrangements at Westminster was directly related to the fact that devolution is just devolution. Enoch Powell's observation that 'Power devolved is power retained' became a mantra for opponents of devolution over the years, yet it is directly relevant to Westminster's significance for post-devolution Scotland. The Scotland Act 1998 did not merely institute a scheme of devolution for Scotland, it also detailed the policy areas and responsibilities of Westminster and UK government in Scotland. Such responsibilities are widespread. Schedule 5 of the Scotland Act, which dealt with Westminster's reserved powers, effectively demonstrated the extent of UK government in Scotland and the limits of devolution, thus providing work for both Scottish ministers and MPs at Westminster.

– The West Lothian question –

Devolution in 1999 also gave rise to the West Lothian question (WLQ). This issue was raised in the 1970s by the MP for West Lothian (now Linlithgow), Tam Dalyell. His question, which was also that of Dicey in relation to Irish Home Rule in the 1880s, concerned the anomalous role of Scottish MPs at Westminster after devolution. The Scottish Parliament would allow a whole range of issues to be determined in Scotland, without the involvement of MPs from other parts of the UK. Nevertheless, Scottish MPs would continue to vote on issues affecting England at Westminster.

The WLQ was frequently employed by opponents of devolution in the 1970s and 1990s, especially as it was seen to be unanswerable under the current devolution arrangements. Labour sought to address the issue by stating its intention to reduce the number of Scottish MPs at Westminster to around sixty through a Boundary Commission review to be completed between 2003–7. However, this proposal would merely reduce the numerical impact of the WLQ rather than eradicate it.

The Conservatives sought to exploit the WLQ in debates over devolution in 1997–8 and then at Westminster after 1999 as part of an effort to raise the issue of English nationalism. The party was keen to exploit the anomalies of devolution and to seek to prevent Scottish MPs from voting on legislation only applicable to England. Of course, in numerical terms, such a course of action – known as the in-out arrangements – would merely have led to a reduction in Labour's overwhelming Westminster majority, rather than to any Conservative majority in the House based on English seats. Additionally, the adoption of such a strategy did not assist the electoral recovery of the Scottish Conservatives who were confronted with a British Conservative Party that was seeking to reduce Scottish participation at Westminster (a counter-Unionist strategy), while making the Conservatives appear as a party of English nationalists. However, the issue also gained currency on the Labour backbenches, and former minister Frank Field sought to introduce a private members' bill to deal with the West Lothian question. Field's House of Commons (Reserved Matters) Bill sought:

> to prescribe which Members of the House of Commons may participate only in proceedings on reserved matters under the Scotland and Northern Ireland Acts 1998 or may be appointed only to a ministerial office having responsibility for such matters.

The bill sought to institute in-out arrangements for Scottish and Northern Irish MPs, but was defeated by 190 votes to 131.[8] However, that was unlikely to be the end of the debate over Scottish representation and voting at Westminster.

– HOUSE OF LORDS REFORM –

Devolution across the UK from 1998–2000 also coincided with discussion of reform of the House of Lords. While these might be seen as separate issues that were solely related to each other by the modernising instincts of the New Labour administration, they were in fact linked. Most of the Lords reforms were concerned with the role of heridatary peers and the democratisation of the House. However, devolution brought a distinctly territorial aspect to the reform programme. The Royal Commission on the Reform of the House of Lords proposed that a number of seats in the Lords be allocated to the nations and regions through the provision of 'regional members'. The Royal Commission offered three options for selecting regional members of the Lords.[9]

1. Model A – sixty-five regional members selected by 'reading off' the general election results to determine what proportion of seats each party should gain in the Lords. One third of the regions would select their regional members at each general election, meaning members would serve for a maximum of fifteen years.
2. Model B – Eighty-seven regional members directly elected at each European Parliament election using the regional list system of proportional representation. One third of the regions would select their regional members at each European election. Scotland would therefore have eight regional members, identical to its European Parliament allocation.
3. Model C – 195 regional members directly elected using the regional list system of proportional representation. Again, one third of the regions would select their regional members at each European election.

Although, these were merely proposals, they did have a number of common themes. First, they involved the representation of populations rather than governments. Thus, Scottish voters rather than the Scottish Parliament would be represented in the reformed Lords. In some ways, this aspect of the reforms could be considered as a missed opportunity: rather than use Scottish Parliamentary representation in the second chamber as a mechanism to create a more coherent and transparent framework for intergovernmental and inter-Parliamentary relations, each of the proposals ignored governmental representation in favour of popular representation. Similarly, the proposals could create a disjointed system in which the second chamber and the Scottish Parliament have no coherent links and engage in a series of turf wars and territorial conflicts, Of course, among European states, only Germany has a second chamber comprised of regional governments, a system that involves dual mandates for members. It acts to represent institutions rather than people and lacks a popular mandate compared to a directly elected second chamber. So there are some downsides to the role of the second chamber as a governmental chamber (Russell, 1999).

Second, and contrary to the latter point about a second chamber of governments, each of the proposals involved direct representation of some type. Models B and C also involved direct election and would effectively democratise the second chamber, although one could be sceptical about the legitimacy of the results given the low turnout for European Parliamentary elections. Also, there must be questions about the exact representative role of regional members. How do they represent their nations and regions compared to the MSPs in the Scottish Parliament or elected members of other devolved bodies in Belfast, Cardiff and London? How do they relate to these bodies and indeed, how does a reformed Lords with regional members relate to the devolved Parliaments and assemblies? Unfortunately, none of these issues was adequately addressed by the Royal Commission.

Thus, while second chamber reform to include regional members was firmly placed on the political agenda after the Royal Commission, its exact impact on Scottish devolution was difficult to determine as a result of the vague intentions of the proposals. The Royal Commission seems to have sought to produce regional members to make the second chamber more representative and give a voice to the nations and regions, but how those members would actually function remains unclear. Finally, they would only operate as one component of the second chamber and their numerical representation within that chamber might be relatively minor, especially as it would remain a predominantly non-territorial second chamber.

– CONCLUSION –

Scottish business at Westminster was only marginally affected by devolution. Sure enough, no more Scottish bills will feature as Commons business, unless Westminster implements section 28 of the Scotland Act 1998 to pass any legislation affecting Scotland that it chooses, but little else has changed. All other Scottish institutions at Westminster remain largely intact. The Select Committee of Scottish Affairs still meets, as does the Scottish Grand Committee, and Scottish ministers still have their own question time. Moreover, Scotland retains a Secretary of State in the UK cabinet, although this may disappear in time as the devolution arrangements bed down and there is a need to assuage the English backlash against devolution. All of these Westminster institutions have been in a post-devolution transitition but, with the exception of the Scottish Affairs Select Committee, their ultimate destination is unknown. Of course, institutions that appear somewhat unnecessary now, may appear necessary in the future. The Secretary of State's role in checking Scottish Parliament bills is politically redundant under the current Scottish Executive, but would not remain so were an SNP administration running a future Scottish Executive. Finally, the issues of the West Lothian question and House of Lords reform bring potential changes to key UK Parliamentary institutions. Changing the voting arrangements at Westminster either through rational change or in response to pressure in England will alter the nature of the Commons and future government abilities to pass legislation within a majority of English MPs. Transforming the Lords in the direction of a quasi-federal territorial chamber will also involve a radical departure from Westminster traditions and engage the Scottish Parliament in Westminster's affairs in an entirely different way.

– Notes –

1. Scotland Act 1998, section 12, p. 6.
2. Scotland Act 1998, section 35, p. 16.
3. *The Herald*, 13 July 1999.
4. Select Committee on Procedure, *Minutes of Evidence*, 5 March 1999.
5. Select Committee on Procedure, *Minutes of Evidence*, 23 February 1999.
6. Select Committee on Procedure, *Memorandum to the Procedure Committee from the President of the Council and Leader of the House of Commons*, First Report, HC148, 24 November 1998.
7. House of Commons Debates, *Hansard*, 9 November 1999, col 870.
8. House of Commons Debates, *Hansard*, 28 June 2000, col. 922–5.
9. Royal Commission on the Reform of the House of Lords, *A House for the Future*, Cmnd 4534 (London, HMSO, 2000).

CHAPTER 9

Devolution and multi-level governance: Scotland, the UK and the EU

– INTRODUCTION –

Devolution did not create a Scottish Parliament in isolation from other government bodies. Indeed, it requires a degree of formalised consultation and cooperation with the UK government rather than institutional separation, because of the concurrent powers of both institutions (Cornes, 1999). Rather than seeing devolution as establishing a strict separation of powers between the Scottish Parliament and Westminster, it is important to realise that it actually created a situation in which powers are shared between the two levels of government. This reality is part of a broader phenomenon associated with devolved and regional government in Europe, namely multi-level governance (Marks, 1996). This concept refers to the fact that so much of government involves overlapping functions by regional, central and European layers of government – in essence, the sharing of functions between the Scottish Parliament, the UK government and the European Union. To take the example of environmental policy, the Scottish Parliament is responsible for determining and implementing environmental policy in Scotland, but many of those policies are actually determined by European Union legislation, and the UK government is responsible for EU matters through the reserved powers of the Scotland Act 1998. Thus, Environmental policy is not decided by one level of government – regional, national or European – but by all three, necessitating cooperation and discussions between all three sides of this policy triangle. However, the different sides of the triangle are not equal actors in the political process, and this brings problems for the operation of multi-level governance and the role of the Scottish Executive and Parliament on account of their subordinate status.

It should also be pointed out that policy made under devolution does not occur in a vacuum. The UK has an integrated economy and society in which decisions made in one part of the UK can spill over into another. For example, the ban on exports of British beef and on the sale of beef on the bone within the UK were both issues governed by devolution arrangements with a need for UK coordination. Such coordination related to the uniform implementation of EU legislation and the need to retain similar arrangements across the UK. The crossborder effect of allowing beef on the bone to be sold in one part of the UK was likely to be considerable, generating inter-regional grievances between farmers, butchers, supermarkets, hotels, and so on. Maintaining uniform arrangements in such an area, despite pressures to do otherwise, was seen to be advisable. Similarly, the Scottish Executive's decision to abandon student tuition fees in January 2000 had considerable spillover effects on UK education policy generally, with many Scottish students studying in England and English students studying in Scotland. New financial arrangements had to recognise such crossborder traffic, and they increased pressures on the UK/English Education Minister to introduce measures for students in England and Wales to match those in Scotland: a case of the devolved tail wagging the UK dog.

THE SCOTTISH EXECUTIVE AND CENTRAL GOVERNMENT RELATIONS

Prior to devolution, Scottish-UK relations were mediated by the Secretary of State for Scotland and the Scottish Office through cabinet and civil service linkages – they were intragovernmental relations. Devolution created a new environment in which Scottish-UK relations occurred between separate institutions – they were now intergovernmental relations. This environment required new mechanisms to facilitate intergovernmental relations and dialogue, most directly, between the Scottish Executive and the UK ministries in Whitehall. Such relations are governed by a Memor-andum of Understanding and a series of 'concordats', published by the Scottish Executive and the UK government in October and November 1999. These documents covered a vast number of areas of cooperation between Scotland and the UK and they contain a number of significant features.

First, there are a large number of concordats: twenty-three in total, if the five concordats attached to the initial Memorandum of Understanding are counted separately (see Table 9.1). Second, the concordats cover a wide range of policy areas from inward investment to defence to the National Lottery. Some concordats – such as those dealing with statistics or the Health and Safety Executive are relatively mundane. Others – such as the concordats on fisheries, agriculture and EU policy issues in which Scottish-

UK policy differences could lead to conflicts – are much more important. Third, the concordats can be understood as mechanisms to ensure and deliver formalised cooperation between Scotland and the UK government as well as the formal institutions of multi-level governance in Scotland, through the establishment of Joint Ministerial Committees (JMCs). Finally, the concordats are not simply Scottish-UK agreements, but also apply in many cases to Wales and to Northern Ireland. A new territorial politics has been born through such arrangements, both supplementing and replacing the traditional institutions of territorial politics such as the secretaries of state in the UK cabinet and the Scottish, Welsh and Northern Irish offices. These new arrangements were also a substantial departure from earlier devolution proposals such as the Scotland Act 1978 and even the Government of Ireland Act 1920, although the Labour government had suggested the potential of Joint Councils for Scotland and Wales and UK government in 1977 (Constitution Unit, 1996: p. 117). The JMCs can be seen as part of an evolving quasi-federal structure within the UK alongside institutions such as the British-Irish Council, House of Lords reform and the establishment of a regional assembly for London.

Table 9.1 Concordats between Scottish ministers, the UK government and the Cabinet of the National Assembly of Wales

1. Memorandum of Understanding and supplementary agreements between Scottish ministers, UK government and the Cabinet of the National Assembly of Wales
   A. Agreement on the Joint Ministerial Committee
   B. Concordat on coordination of European Union policy issues
   C. Concordat on financial assistance to industry
   D. Concordat on international relations
   E. Concordat on statistics
2. Concordat between Scottish ministers and the Secretary of State for Defence
3. Subject specific concordat between the Ministry of Agriculture, Fisheries and Food and the Scottish Executive on Fisheries
4. Concordat between the Department of Environment, Transport and the Regions and the Scottish Executive
5. Concordat between the Scottish Executive and the Lord Chancellor's Department
6. Concordat on health and social care
7. Concordat between the Scottish Executive and the Home Office
8. Concordat between the Department of Social Security and the Scottish Executive
9. Concordat on European Structural Funds
10. Concordat between HM Treasury and the Scottish Executive

11. Concordat on coordination of EU, international and policy issues on public procurement
12. Concordat between the Health and Safety Executive and the Scottish Executive
13. Concordat between the Department for Culture, Media and Sport and the Scottish Executive
14. Concordat between the Cabinet Office and the Scottish Executive
15. Concordat between the Department for Education and Employment and the Scottish Executive
16. Concordat between the General Registry Office and the Scottish Executive
17. Concordat between the Ministry of Agriculture, Fisheries and Food and the Scottish Executive
18. Concordat between the Department of Trade and Industry and the Scottish Executive

– THE CONCORDATS –

The process through which the concordats were devised was not without its difficulties, especially as discussions were held in secret. The fact that there would be agreements between devolved institutions and central government, specifically called 'concordats', had been public knowledge since the publication of the White Paper, *Scotland's Parliament*, in 1997. The topic of concordats had arisen in debates on both the Scotland and Wales bills and the Conservative opposition at Westminster had sought to amend the Scotland Bill to require the concordats to be formally registered so that MPs at Westminster could approve their content.[1] However, debate over the issue was obscured by the lack of detail over the nature and substance of the concordats and the time it took to publish them. For example, the former Secretary of State for Scotland, Donald Dewar, had sought to provide guidance on the issue of concordats in February 1998, but such guidance was vague. Dewar referred to the concordats as non-statutory agreements 'to ensure that the business of government in Scotland and at the UK level is conducted smoothly, by setting the ground rules for administrative cooperation and exchange of information.'[2] The concordats were intended to be completely administrative, rather than related to policy, and were to be agreed between the Scottish Executive and UK government, rather than between the two parliaments.

The secrecy surrounding the nature and substance of the concordats fed suspicions about their aim and contents. For instance, while they could be viewed as purely administrative devices to ensure intergovernmental co-operation in line with the tenets of multi-level governance, they also contained a highly political element. The concordats can be interpreted as political mechanisms to bind the Scottish Executive into UK government structures. UK government drafted the concordats – led by the Lord Chancellor, Lord Irvine, who chaired the cabinet's devolution policy committee – not the Scottish Executive. The Scottish Executive was able to suggest amendments to the concordats, although neither the initial drafts nor the amendments were made public. Therefore, there was no indication of whether the Executive was an equal in discussions on concordats or purely a subordinate partner in the process.

Parliaments were also entirely absent from the drafting process. The drafts were determined by UK civil servants in Scotland and London, with common interests in secrecy and control. Politically, the content of the concordats was determined by a Labour government at Westminster, a Labour-led coalition in Edinburgh, and a minority Labour administration in the Welsh Assembly. Had they been negotiated between governments of different political hues, the process through which the concordats were drawn up, as well as their contents, might have been quite different. Finally, the fact that the contents of the concordats were kept secret until publication in the autumn of 1999 did not help the process either. Secrecy, combined with the length of time it took to make the concordats public, was largely responsible for raising suspicions about their nature and substance.

The concordats covered a variety of issues of government such as the provision of information and statistics between Whitehall and the devolved administrations; mechanisms for consultation between the two sets of governments; and the means of resolving disputes between the different levels of government. This latter aspect was particularly important since it heralded the establishment of Joint Ministerial Committees as mechanisms to resolve conflicts between the Scottish Executive and UK government departments that could not be solved by bilateral negotiations between civil servants or ministers.

– THE JOINT MINISTERIAL COMMITTEES –

The Joint Ministerial Committees (JMCs) are intended to operate as management devices in fairly specific circumstances, namely when intergovernmental negotiations fail to lead to the resolution of a dispute. They also have other uses, which are discussed below. The Memorandum of Understanding stated that:

> The UK Government and the devolved administrations commit themselves, wherever possible, to conduct business through normal administrative channels, either at official or Ministerial level . . . Where a dispute cannot be resolved bilaterally or through the good offices of the relevant territorial Secretary of State the matter may be formally referred to the JMC Secretariat . . .[3]

This conflict resolution role is not the only aspect of the work of the JMCs: indeed, the bodies were given four specific functions:

a. to consider non-devolved matters which impinge on devolved responsibilities, and devolved responsibilities which impinge on non-devolved responsibilities;
b. where the UK Government and the devolved administrations so agree, to consider devolved matters if it is beneficial to discuss their respective treatment in the different parts of the United Kingdom;
c. to keep the arrangements for liaison between the UK Government and the devolved administrations under review;
d. to consider disputes between the administrations.[4]

The JMCs therefore gained a monitoring and coordination role, in addition to a role as a mechanism for resolving intergovernmental disputes. If there is a great deal of friction between the two sets of governments, then it can be expected that the relevant subject-specific JMC will be frequently convened. If there is less friction, as in the case of same-party control in Scotland and London, then the JMCs may seldom meet as disputes will be handled through the normal channels outlined above. Indeed, the institution of weekly meetings between the First Minister and the Scottish Secretary, John Reid, could be viewed as an exercise to minimise disputes and prevent Scottish-UK tensions and turf wars. However, the wider usage of the JMCs was obscured by secrecy and limited parliamentary involvement. At Scottish Executive question time, ministers stressed that they were constantly in contact with UK government, meaning through civil servants, rather than reveal much about the JMC. This fact tended to suggest that the JMCs were not functioning, especially as a mechanism for resolving intergovernmental disputes. Despite this, it can be argued that quasi-JMCs were operating in areas such as agriculture before the publication of the concordats, with joint meetings of the UK, Scottish and Welsh agriculture ministers to discuss the ban on British beef, aid packages for sheep farmers and the lifting of the UK's internal ban on beef on the bone. The Memorandum of Understanding formalised this practice by establishing terms of reference for JMCs, which resemble the operation of the Council of Ministers of the European Union.

The JMCs meet in three sets of formats. First, they meet in plenary at least once a year in a format comprising the Prime Minister, Deputy Prime Minister, Scottish First Minister, an additional Scottish minister, the First Secretary of the Welsh Assembly and another Welsh Assembly secretary, the Northern Irish First Minister and Deputy First Minister and the Secretaries of State for the three regions. The participation of two ministers from devolved administrations enables the main JMC to reflect potential coalition arrangements in Scotland and Wales as well as the permanent coalition in the Northern Irish Assembly envisaged by the Belfast Agreement. The plenary format of the JMC affords a range of opportunities for government ministers to discuss common policy and the prospect for cooperation, to negotiate over conflicts with their fellow government leaders or even to play a grandstanding role through announcing policy initiatives (Cornes, 1999). Second, the JMCs meet in functional formats, through meetings of education, health or transport ministers from UK and devolved governments. These JMCs may also see the involvement of the Secretaries of State for Scotland, Wales and Northern Ireland. Third, two special JMCs were created as a mechanism for consultation on EU policy issues and on inward investment between the UK and devolved governments, chaired by the Foreign Secretary and by the Cabinet Office. The fact that the JMC on inward investment was to be chaired by a representative of the Cabinet Office rather than the Secretary of State for Trade and Industry was seen as a clear victory for the Scottish Executive, as the involvement of the latter would have been seen to advantage the English regions (*The Scotsman*, 1 October 1999). However, it was envisaged that much of these committees' work would proceed via correspondence rather than formal meetings.

The Labour government at Westminster identified the principle of the JMCs as applicable to policy areas beyond those envisaged in the formal concordats. Labour Chancellor Gordon Brown was instrumental in establishing three additional JMCs in the areas of child poverty, pensioner poverty and the digital revolution. These committees were inspired by central government, with the intention of coordinating policy across the devolved administrations in key New Labour policy areas. At a practical level, the fact that both devolved and UK governments are jointly responsible for welfare and economic policies was a justification for the JMCs in these areas and they met several times in 2000. However, these bodies were also intended to demonstrate the importance of cooperation rather than conflict between institutions as well as the continued relevance of UK government after devolution, a move calculated to assist Labour's prospects at the forthcoming UK general election in Scotland. In addition, Prime Minister Tony Blair took the lead in chairing the JMC on health in order to give an impetus to reforms of the UK health service. This particular JMC met on a number of occasions in 2000, and comprised the health ministers of the UK and devolved governments.

The Liberal Democrats within the Scottish coalition appeared to have been largely excluded from discussion over these additional JMCs, which was surprising given the importance of these policy areas to the devolution arrangements, and this exclusion reinforced the perception that they was a UK Labour initiative. In addition, these policy areas are key issues for New Labour at the UK and devolved levels, rather than areas the Liberal Democrats would have chosen. The initiatives also demonstrated the important role of external actors in the operation of the devolution settlement. The Labour Chancellor (and Scottish MP), Gordon Brown, made a number of interventions in Scottish politics in spite of devolution, from his involvement in guiding Labour's 1999 Scottish election campaign to the establishment of the additional JMCs. One commentator remarked that Brown was the UK minister who 'pulls the levers to make devolution work' (MacLeod, 2000: p. 119). Indeed, arguably the Chancellor has had more impact on devolved Scotland than any MSP or minister of the Scottish Executive through his political interventions, and his role in controlling the UK economy and the Treasury's financing of the Scottish Parliament.

– COORDINATION OR CONTROL? –

The difficulty with the concordats and the JMC structure is in interpreting their function and effect in political terms. They can be viewed in a positive light as useful mechanisms to facilitate intergovernmental cooperation and the resolution of conflicts between layers of government: recognition of the reality of multi-level governance. Alternatively, they can be seen in a more negative light as devices to ensure policy uniformity between the different parts of the UK and an attempt by central government to use mechanisms to control the autonomy of the devolved governments. For example, aspects of the concordats could be interpreted as enforcing the supremacy of UK government and its role as a gatekeeper in EU and international relations, through seeking to ensure a unified UK line on policy.[5] The JMCs are chaired by UK ministers who are responsible for convening meetings. It remains to be seen whether the UK minister plays a dominant role within the JMCs or the devolved administrations develop as equal partners capable of using the structures to pursue their own interests. The centralised nature of decisionmaking by New Labour also fuelled suspicions that UK ministers would seek to act as a controlling device within the JMCs in order to limit the autonomy of the devolved institutions.

The proceedings of the JMCs are confidential, minutes of meetings remain private, and they fall outside the Scottish Parliament's desire for open and accountable government. Confidentiality will assist discussion of sensitive topics, but will also feed negative interpretations of the JMCs as devices for central control. Secrecy will enable the SNP and a media suspicious of New Labour's 'control freakery' to argue that the concordats and JMCs were intended to produce uniformity in policy rather than diversity. Finally, as SNP MSPs pointed out in the debate on the Memorandum of Understanding in the Scottish Parliament, the JMCs make no distinction between UK and English ministers.[6] Indeed, the Memorandum of Understanding stated that 'UK Ministers and their Departments represent the interests of England in all matters.'[7] This anomaly undermines one central aspect of the operation of the JMCs as quasi-federal bodies: the UK minister is not a neutral arbiter sitting above the devolved administrations, because England remains governed by Westminster. This conflation of representation could present difficulties, as the UK minister is open to accusations of working in the interests of the largest part of the UK against the interests of Scotland, Wales and/or Northern Ireland. It contrasts clearly with intergovernmental arrangements in federal states such as Canada and Australia where the federal government represents the whole federation rather than individual regions (Cornes, 1999).

Of course, there are a number of counterpoints to this picture of the concordats as a control device to limit the autonomy of the Scottish Executive. First, the concordats exist between governments not parliaments. When the party in government changes, so can the content of the concordats, although existing concordats will prove important precedents. Second, the concordats are non-statutory agreements. As the initial Memorandum of Understanding pointed out: 'The memorandum is a statement of political intent, and should not be interpreted as a binding agreement. It does not create legal obligations between the parties. It is intended to be binding in honour only.'[8] Third, the Memorandum of Understanding made it clear that the JMCs involved agreements rather than decisions. The committees were designed as consultative rather than executive bodies, and agreements are not binding on the participating institutions, although it was expected that joint agreements would be supported by each administration.[9] This particular aspect of the JMCs remains to be tested. Finally, functional meetings of the JMCs can be requested by devolved administrations rather than just the UK government, so that the institution is not solely operated by central government.

Despite this more equable view of the concordats and JMCs, they do involve significant problems when it comes to scrutinising the content and operation of the different concordats and ensuring the parliamentary accountability of ministers active within the committees. The concordats are clearly agreements between executives rather than legislatures, but even so there has been little scope for parliamentary scrutiny. Neither the Scottish Parliament nor Westminster was involved in discussions on the concordats prior to their publication. After publication of the Memorandum of Understanding and the first five concordats in October 1999, the Scottish Parliament held a debate on the issue, but the remaining concordats published later were not debated on the Mound.[10] Consideration of the concordats at Westminster was minimal and solely confined to a few minutes of parliamentary time during the three-hour debate on the Select Committee on Procedure's report on the procedural consequences of devolution.[11]

The First Minister suggested that Scottish Parliamentary committees could scrutinise the operation of individual concordats or allocate time at plenary sessions of the Parliament to discuss the functioning of the concordats,[12] but such proposals appeared as an afterthought in a predominantly administrative process. The prospect of future scrutiny was not taken up by the Parliament in committee or plenary. Indeed, there is no Scottish Parliamentary committee responsible for scrutinising the concordats or intergovernmental relations in general, an ironic fact given the burgeoning nature of such relations with devolution. It would seem that executives will dominate these particular structures at the expense of legislatures. In addition, the Parliament lacks a mechanism for scrutinising the functioning of Scottish ministerial involvement in the JMCs beyond Executive question time.

– SCOTLAND AND THE EUROPEAN UNION –

Devolved governments such as Scotland's have two possible strategies to influence the European Union: intra-state strategies and extra-state strategies (Jeffrey, 1996). Before devolution, intra-state activity was the dominant practice with a Scottish Office largely dependent on the UK Government and the UK's Permanent Representation in Brussels (UKRep) to seek to influence EU policy. While the Scottish Office had developed an extra-state strategy of sorts with the establishment in 1991 of Scotland Europa as a lobbying organisation in Brussels and a number of Scottish local authorities were involved in discussions with the European Commission, these were fairly minor political actors. Instead, it was the Secretary of State for Scotland and the Scottish Office that were the main actors in Scottish-EU relations, both of them UK government institutions. Graham Leicester and James Mitchell (1999) identified two principal ways in which the Scottish Office was able to pursue Scottish interests within the EU before devolution. First, it developed a range of civil service secondments to UK and EU government institutions. Second, the role of the Scottish Secretary in cabinet and the Scottish Office in Whitehall were seen as key factors in Scotland's attempts to influence EU institutions and policy. Devolution significantly changed the institutional environment for Scotland-EU relations and created the potential for greater extra-state relations between the Scottish Executive, the Scottish Parliament and the EU. However, in spite of this development, intra-state mechanisms remain important, and perhaps even more important than the limited avenues for influence available to regional governments in the EU. Much of Scotland's role in the EU is therefore not about Scotland in Europe so much as 'Scotland in the UK in Europe' (Burrows, 2000: p. 125).

The manner in which EU issues were dealt with in the Scotland Act 1998 presented something of a political conundrum for the Scottish Parliament and Westminster, and even more so for the two sets of government. On the one hand, devolution ceded responsibility for major EU policy areas such as agriculture, fisheries and the environment to the Scottish Parliament. On the other hand, the EU itself was a matter reserved to Westminster and firmly ensconced within Schedule 5 of the Scotland Act. Scottish Executive ministers would therefore be functionally and politically responsible for policies involving significant Scottish-EU overlaps and interactions, but it would be UK government that had primacy in relations with the EU. Of course, the EU is a union of states, best exemplified through the fact that it is states that sign and amend the various EU treaties and are the main representatives within the Council of Ministers. However, such states are not always responsible for the policy areas they discuss within the Council itself. This anomaly was most pressing in the case of Belgium and Germany, where federal governments were able to make decisions on behalf of their regional governments in direct contradiction to the constitutional division of powers and policy competences. Such problems led to changes within the EU and its member states to enable regions to play a role within the Council of Ministers and replace central government as the national representative on regional policy issues within the Council (Keating, 1998: p. 167). Article, 146 of the Maastricht Treaty enabled regional governments to represent their state within the Council, with detailed arrangements for the types of issues that regions can act upon as well as for the manner in which regions agree upon EU policy in the Council. However, such developments are largely academic as far as Scotland is concerned, as it must continue to rely upon intra-state mechanisms such as the Secretary of State for Scotland, UKRep and the JMC on European Union affairs.

Of course, participation in EU affairs was one aspect of devolution that had been heavily promoted by the Labour government in advance of the Scottish elections of 1999. A Scottish Executive Minister for Europe and Scottish ministers leading the UK delegation in the Council of Ministers had both been touted as means of trumping the SNP's policy of independence in Europe. However, after the election there was no Minister for Europe, as EU policy was delegated to the Finance Minister, Jack McConnell, and Scottish Executive ministers barely attended Council of Minister meetings, let alone led them. For example, from May to 11 November 1999, Scottish minister only attended one out of thirty Council of Ministers meetings.[13] Where the Scottish Executive had made progress was in the area of paradiplomacy, with the establishment of Scotland House and Scottish Executive Office in Brussels in 1999 (see below).

– THE SCOTTISH EXECUTIVE, CONCORDATS AND THE EU –

The Scottish Executive's role in EU affairs is governed by a specific concordat, which deals with the Executive's role in the formulation of UK policy towards the EU, attendance at meetings of the Council of Ministers, and so on. As discussed above, much of the contact between the Scottish Executive and UK government over EU policy is conducted through the 'usual channels' of routine interdepartmental and ministerial correspondence and civil service links. The concordat on EU policy stated that:

> participation will be subject to mutual respect for the confidentiality of discussions and adherence by the Scottish Executive to the resulting UK line, without which it would be impossible to maintain such close working relationships. This line will reflect the interests of the UK as a whole.[14]

This situation is very much a double-edged sword. On the positive side, the Scottish Executive has guaranteed involvement in the process to determine UK policy on EU issues. But, under such arrangements it will be perfectly possible for the UK government to adopt a policy that is directly opposed to the policy of the Scottish Executive, which then binds the hands of the Scottish Executive to argue against such a policy in the EU. Of course, where the Executive can successfully influence the UK government and help to determine policy, it will enjoy a level of influence far superior to that of a region using Scotland Europa or the Scottish Executive European office. But such a strength is dependent on a level of agreement that might not be forthcoming on all issues.

In a similar way to the other concordats, the EU concordat set out a procedure for inter-institutional consultation and discussion over policy. Some discussions were intended to be dealt with by a special subcommittee of civil servants attached to the JMC on EU affairs. Policy differences that could not be resolved bilaterally or by correspondence would be dealt with by the JMC, acting in similar fashion to the other JMCs outlined above, chaired by the Foreign Secretary and involving UK and devolved ministers. The concordat also dealt with arrangements for attendance at the Council of Ministers. Here, the ability of Scottish Executive ministers to attend Council meetings was to be determined by the lead UK minister on a case-by-case basis: therefore there was no right of attendance. Also, in some cases, the UK minister might allow a minister from a devolved administration to speak for the UK in the Council.[15] Finally, the concordats made it clear that the primacy of UKRep would remain unchallenged by devolution and any regional offices established by the devolved administrations would be subordinate to UKRep. The scope for autonomous Scottish Executive action within the EU is therefore highly limited.

– PARADIPLOMACY IN ACTION: SCOTLAND HOUSE –

Paradiplomacy refers to the efforts of regional governments to play a part in international affairs through diplomatic activity. Such practices developed both through the increase in transnational regimes such as the EU and NAFTA and the restructuring of centralised states into federal and regionalised states (Keating, 1999: p. 1). Regions involve themselves in paradiplomacy for a variety of reasons. In part, they respond to the internationalisation of the economy by using it as a device to encourage inward investment, export promotion and market competitiveness. Many regions have used paradiplomacy for such ends and Scotland is no exception, with Locate in Scotland seeking to attract inward investors to Scotland, and Scottish Trade International promoting Scottish products abroad.

However, paradiplomacy also has more directly political ends in two distinct ways. First, it can be used as a nation-building strategy to raise the profile of the region in preparation for a bid for statehood. Quebec was an example of this phenomenon, with the provincial government of the Parti Quebecois using its presence in the international arena to promote Quebec's national status and bid for sovereignty; this is often referred to as proto-diplomacy (Balthazar, 1999). Such goals can also be found in the external affairs strategy of the SNP, through its proposals to utilise the Scottish Executive and Parliament in European and international affairs.[16] Second, paradiplomacy is a political defence mechanism for regional governments and political parties that wish to resist secession and statehood, and they use it to demonstrate the extent to which the region can play an effective role in international politics without secession. Such goals were evident in Scotland, with the establishment of Scotland Europa in 1991 following the popularity of the SNP's policy of independence in Europe in the late 1980s, and efforts to project Scotland into Europe post-devolution with Scotland House and the role of Scottish ministers in the Council of Ministers. Both initiatives were intended to demonstrate the extent and effectiveness of Scottish-European engagement without tearing Scotland out of the UK. There is, of course, economic and functional logic behind such paradiplomacy too, but political motives are not far away either on this issue.

The bulk of the paradiplomacy associated with Scottish government institutions before and after devolution revolves around the institutions and policies of the European Union. Indeed, the EU has become a prominent arena for paradiplomatic activity since the late 1980s. Such activity grew as the EU expanded into policy areas that were the preserve of regional governments, attempted to engage regional and local government in partnership agreements through the European Regional Development Fund and European Social Fund, and sought to institutionalise paradiplomatic activity in the Committee of the Regions (Hooghe, 1996; Jones and Keating, 1995). Several hundred regions and local authorities also established regional information offices in Brussels to monitor the EU's work and represent their areas in EU policymaking (Jeffrey, 1996a). The involvement of, some regional governments in the Council of Ministers (see above) was the most prominent indicator of the regions' successful paradiplomacy in EU affairs.

Scotland House was established in 1999 as the host body of both Scotland Europa and the Scottish Executive's European Office. Scotland Europa was created as a lobbying forum with a range of public and private organisations operating from its premises (Mazey and Mitchell, 1993). Such lobbying efforts continued post-devolution, with member organisations such as the Committee of Scottish Clearing Bankers, Scottish Enterprise, and the Royal College of Surgeons using Scotland Europa's services. Scotland House was also designed to act as the Scottish Executive's office in Brussels, not the Parliament's, although it was intended to play a role in assisting the Parliament in EU affairs (Sloat, 2000). The Scottish Executive office was given a number of distinct roles and functions. It was intended as a mechanism to promote direct Scottish links with EU institutions, to support the Executive and Parliament in European affairs, and to work 'in an open and cooperative way' with UKRep.[17] Thus, the office combines an extra-state strategy of direct representation with intra-state efforts through UKRep. However, balancing these two strategies will prove problematic. On the one hand, the Scottish Executive European office is intended to pursue distinct Scottish interests within the EU. On the other hand, it is supposed to participate in the work of UKRep, which retains a monopoly in arguing UK policy in Brussels (Leicester and Mitchell, 1999). When these two roles coincide on agreeing an EU policy, the system will prove effective, but when they conflict and a Scottish interest is pursued through lobbying separate from UKRep, then problems will arise.

– THE SCOTTISH PARLIAMENT AND EU AFFAIRS –

Devolution may have partially empowered the Scottish Executive in EU policymaking, but it has had a much lesser effect on the Scottish Parliament despite the creation of a European Committee of the Parliament in May 1999. The European Committee was a mandatory committee designated by the cross-party Consultative Steering Group (1999). The committee has thirteen members, reflecting the broad scope of its functions and the likely pace of European legislation, which it is required to consider. The European Committee exists to sift through EU legislative proposals on behalf of the Parliament, to undertake discussion and analysis of proposals on its own or through referral to subject committees, and to debate a range of EU-related topics. Thus, the committee exists as a forum to consider the impact of EU legislation on the work of the Scottish Parliament but also as a means of discussing and reporting on a range of EU issues. It therefore has an investigative function that involves adopting a proactive role towards Scottish-EU affairs (Consultative Steering Group, 1999).

The membership of the European Committee was intended to operate as a composite of other subject committees (Consultative Steering Group, 1999: p. 29). Thus, individual MSPs could bring their specialist knowledge to bear in the work of the committee, and the work of relevant subject committees in relation to the EU would not occur in isolation. The initial membership of the European Committee from 1999 to 2000 contained three MSPs who were also members of the Committee for Health and Community Care, two MSPs from the Enterprise and Lifelong Learning Committee, two members from the Transport and the Environment Committee, one MSP from the Local Government Committee, and one from the Justice and Home Affairs Committee. The European Committee also contained members with experience of European affairs: Winnie Ewing, who had been MEP for the Highlands and Islands since 1979; committee convenor, Hugh Henry, who had been COSLA spokesperson on European Affairs and a member of the Committee of the Regions; and Irene Old-father, who had chaired COSLA's committee on EMU.

The work of the European Committee is very different to its counterparts in the Scottish Parliament for two reasons. First, it is dealing with legislation from a completely different institution within a tight time frame – a minimum of six weeks under the agreement for national scrutiny of EU legislation agreed under the Treaty of Amsterdam (1998). The pace of EU legislation in any given year – roughly 800 documents – is such that no parliament can be expected to scrutinise all the documents. As a result, the European Committee required a special sifting mechanism to cope with the most important issues to the Parliament. Second, the European Committee has a secondhand representative role in its scrutiny of European legislation. The committee does not exist to represent Scotland in Europe, although it will doubtless attempt to fulfil this role to some extent. Rather, under the devolution legislation, its role is to assist the Scottish Parliament in making recommendations to the UK government, which is represented in the Council of Ministers of the European Union (Scottish Office, 1997: p. 17).

The European Committee was not among the busiest of parliamentary committees in 1999, with only ten meetings, yet it still processed a good deal of business. Scrutiny of EU legislative proposals accounted for approximately half of its workload in its first year, with a considerable amount of time allocated to investigations into the EU Fisheries Council, Objective 3 of the European Social Fund, and the management of the structural funds. The Fisheries Council investigation involved Tavish Scott, the MSP for Shetland, acting as an observer at the Council and preparing a report on the conduct of fisheries policy on behalf of the European Committee. The report recommended that Scottish Executive should lead in EU fisheries negotiations on Scottish interests within the Council and pressurise the European Commission to take more note of Scottish fishing interests in negotiations with Norway, a non-member of the EU.[18]

The European Committee also used key institutions and pressure groups to determine the types of issues it should investigate as a committee. Its consultation heralded seventy-five responses from organisations such as local authorities, the Scottish Council of Voluntary Organisations, the Scottish Crofters Union, the National Farmers Union of Scotland, Scottish Power, the Scottish Chambers of Commerce and the Scottish Enterprise Network.[19] The consultation exercise contributed to the committee's forward work programme for 2000–1, which involved twelve separate investigations and each MSP, except the convenor, acting as a reporter (see Table 9.2).

However, whether the committee or indeed the Parliament can actually have an influence over all of the issues in Table 9.2 is questionable. The committee focused on some issues that affect Scotland that are outside the Parliament's powers, such as the single currency and enlargement. Reports in these areas may assist awareness of EU policy issues and their impact on Scotland, but it is difficult to see how Parliament can influence them. However, the bulk of the investigations dealt with issues that directly affected the Parliament and on which it would like to have some influence. In many ways, investigation of such issues will be the most important aspect of the committee's work, and that which takes it into the public eye. Merely considering and processing EU documents is an important, but low-profile task compared to seeking to set the agenda on EU issues through committee investigations.

Table 9.2 The forward work programme of the European Committee 2000–1

1. Policy implications of the European Commission's Sixth Environmental Action Plan
2. Preparation for, and policy implications of, the single currency
3. Implementation of European legislation in the agricultural sector in Scotland
4. A review of the List 1 designated diseases infectious salmon anaemia and viral haemorrhagic septicaemia in Scotland
5. European education and training initiatives: the policy implications, take-up of programmes and future changes
6. Community economic development and the role of the EU
7. A review of European initiatives in the field of tourism, culture and sport
8. Promoting links through European networks
9. The proposed European Charter on Fundamental Rights: development of a Scottish perspective
10. Enlargement of the EU and the challenges facing Scotland
11. Improving the provision of information on EU issues in Scotland
12. European law and the implications for Scottish justice

– CONCLUSION –

The institutions of multi-level governance in the new Scotland concern governments rather than parliaments. This reality places limits on the new Parliament's ability to participate in relations with the UK and EU institutions: not only do governments dominate the process, but parliaments are largely excluded. Indeed, intergovernmental relations appears as one of the areas in which open, accessible government has fallen short. Much of the work in this area involves civil servants operating in secret, although a large part of their activities are probably rather mundane exchanges of information and documents. Where intergovernmental relations will become important is in the arena of intergovernmental conflict, when the Scottish Executive and the UK government fail to agree a common approach to a particular policy. In that circumstance, the JMCs will be utilised as conflict resolution mechanisms. If they succeed, it will be through compromise, although a tendency to see government disputes as a zero-sum game may lead to accusations of one side of government caving in. If compromise within the JMCs fail and the Executive persists with its own policy in opposition to UK government, then devolution will have been shown to work *in extremis*. However, the give and take of intergovernmental relations and the goodwill between the Scottish Executive and UK government may prevent damaging disputes.

The area of EU relations also presents some difficulties for Scottish devolution and intergovernmental relations. The ability of the Executive and Parliament to operate as autonomous actors within the EU is severely limited by the Scotland Act 1998 and the nature of the concordats. This situation may not be problematic with a Labour-Liberal Democrat coalition in Edinburgh but would be severely tested with an SNP-led administration that sought a more assertive role for the Scottish Executive within EU policymaking. In the meantime, the Scottish Executive must largely rely upon intra-state efforts to influence the EU. Same-party control and Scottish Executive ministerial and civil service links to UK government will facilitate this particular process, although how it will deal with a major policy disagreement remains to be seen.

– NOTES –

1. House of Commons Debates, *Hansard*, 31 March 1998, col. 1149.
2. Scottish Office news release, 'Devolution – Dewar issues guidance On "concordats" between Scottish Executive and UK departments', 27 February 1998.
3. Scottish Executive, *Memorandum of Understanding and Supplementary Agreements*, Agreement on the Joint Ministerial Committee, clauses 24–5, October 1999.
4. Scottish Executive, *Memorandum of Understanding and Supplementary Agreements*, Agreement on the Joint Ministerial Committee, clause A1.2, October 1999.
5. Scottish Executive, *Memorandum of Understanding and Supplementary Agreements*, Agreement on the Joint Ministerial Committee, clause 19, October 1999.
6. Alex Neil MSP, Scottish Parliament, *Official Report*, 7 October 1999, col. 1117.
7. Scottish Executive, *Memorandum of Understanding and Supplementary Agreements*, Agreement on the Joint Ministerial Committee, clause 1, October 1999.
8. Scottish Executive, *Memorandum of Understanding and Supplementary Agreements*, Agreement on the Joint Ministerial Committee, clause 2, p. 1, October 1999.
9. Scottish Executive, *Memorandum of Understanding and Supplementary Agreements*, Agreement on the Joint Ministerial Committee, clause A1.10, October 1999.
10. Scottish Parliament, *Official Report*, 7 October 1999.
11. House of Commons Debates, *Hansard*, 21 October 1999, col. 606–771.
12. Donald Dewar MSP, Scottish Parliament, *Official Report*, 7 October 1999, col. 1102.
13. *The Scotsman*, 11 November 1999.
14. HMSO, *Concordat on Co-ordination of European Union Policy Issues*, 1999, clause B1.4.
15. HMSO, *Concordat on Co-ordination of European Union Policy Issues*, 1999, clause B3.12 and B3.14.

16. Scottish National Party, *Rejoining the World: External Affairs and the Scottish Parliament*, SNP, Edinburgh, 1999.
17. Scottish Office news release, 9 February 1999.
18. European Committee, *Second Report 1999: Report on the European Fisheries Council of December 1999*, 9 December 1999.
19. European Committee, *The European Committee's Forward Work Programme for January 2000 to June 2001*, 26 January 2000, annex 1, pp. 7–8.

CHAPTER 10

Parties, elections and electoral behaviour

– INTRODUCTION –

Electoral behaviour and changes in party support are two developments that have made Scotland distinctive as a political entity since the 1960s. Parties and electoral politics in Scotland exhibit both differences and similarities with UK norms. Three of the four main parties in Scotland are British parties, yet they have all sought to appeal to voters as Scottish parties with Scottish policies. Electoral behaviour in Scotland is influenced by class and issue-voting, yet it has been distinctive in UK terms because of the historical influence of religion on voting and the more contemporary impact of national identity on Scottish voters. Two factors certainly make Scotland's recent electoral history stand out from other parts of the UK: first, the demise of the Conservatives as an electoral force from the party's previous heights in the 1950s; second, the rise of the SNP as a force for change in Scottish politics, to the extent that it has become the main opposition party in the Scottish Parliament with the prospect of a permanent position as the main competitor to Labour. Each of these developments is discussed below in addition to an examination of the impact of class and national identity on voting in Scotland.

– THE POLITICAL PARTIES –

The current range of political parties have been organised in Scotland for several decades and, indeed, three of the four main parties trace their roots back to the nineteenth century. The intervening decades saw both change and stability in the Scottish party system as the Liberal electoral hegemony of the nineteenth century gave way to Labour hegemony in the latter half of the twentieth century. Competition between Liberals and Conservatives gave way to a three-way split with an increasingly popular Labour party, as the Liberals declined. The interwar period saw the emergence of a more pronounced two-party system which ran until the 1960s, and during that period, the Liberals were completely marginalised as an electoral force. From the mid-1960s onwards, however, the Liberals began a slow recovery much overshadowed by the rapid rise of the SNP. Over the past twenty years, the Scottish party system was characterised by a dominant Labour Party accompanied by the three other parties fighting it out as the main challenger. The most recent challenger has been the SNP, particularly in opinion polls and at the Scottish elections of 1999, but whether this situation becomes a persistent trend remains to be seen.

Table 10.1 UK general election results in Scotland, 1945–97

Year	Conservative		Labour		Liberal Democrat		SNP	
	Votes (%)	Seats	Votes (%)	Seats	Votes (%)	Seats	Votes (%)	Seats
1945	41.1	27	49.4	40	5	0	1.2	0
1950	44.8	32	46.2	32	6.6	2	0.4	0
1951	48.6	35	47.9	35	2.7	1	0.3	0
1955	50.1	36	46.7	34	1.9	1	0.5	0
1959	47.2	31	46.7	38	4.1	1	0.5	0
1964	40.6	24	48.7	43	7.6	4	2.4	0
1966	37.7	20	49.9	46	6.8	5	5	0
1970	38	23	44.5	44	5.5	3	11.4	1
1974	32.9	21	36.6	41	8	3	21.9	7
1974	24.7	16	36.3	41	8.3	3	30.4	11
1979	31.4	22	41.5	44	9	3	17.3	2
1983	28.4	21	35.1	41	24.5	8	11.7	2
1987	24	10	42.4	50	19.2	9	14	3
1992	25.7	11	39	49	13.1	9	21.5	3
1997	17.5	0	45.6	56	13	10	22.1	6

Political parties in Scotland exhibit a dual identity as both Scottish and British (Kellas, 1984: p. 114). With the exception of the SNP, the main political parties exist as Scottish branches of British parties, despite their names, policies and constitutions. This Scottish-British duality can have a positive and a negative effect on the parties. For instance, Labour clearly benefited from its dual status and political appeal as a British and Scottish party. It was able to appeal to Scottish voters through its support for devolution, its Scottish identity and the issues it promoted, while benefiting from aspects of its British status such as delivering the welfare state. Balancing its Scottish-British contradictions was often difficult, especially with the challenge of the SNP, but it was mostly successful. Conversely, the

Conservatives were perceived as a predominantly British party which was anti-Scottish in the 1980s and had lost the balance between its Scottish and British sides. Ironically, it was the British aspect of the party's appeal that was so successful in the 1950s but the Tories found this appeal eclipsed from the 1970s onwards by the rise in Scottish national identity, to which they had no effective response.

With devolution, the dual identity of the parties brought particular challenges. The British parties need to compete at Scottish and UK elections against a nationalist opposition, and they need sufficient policy and organisational autonomy to operate within the new devolved system. At the time of devolution, the federal nature of the Liberal Democrats allowed the Scottish Liberal Democrats to emerge instantly as a decentralised organisation which required no adjustments to cope with the new Parliament (Lynch, 1998a). By contrast, both Labour and the Conservatives had to reform their organisational and policymaking structures to adjust to devolution, increasing the powers and autonomy of their Scottish party organisations and electing their party leaders in Scotland. Despite such changes, tensions remain between the Scottish and British party organisations, especially within Labour. Devolution coincided with New Labour's organisational centralisation, giving rise to suspicions that Millbank was running Scottish Labour and curtailing the autonomy of the devolved Parliament.

– SCOTTISH CONSERVATIVE AND UNIONIST PARTY –

Scottish Conservatism has experienced a rapid decline in its fortunes since the 1950s. Nevertheless, the nature and extent of that decline was greatly exaggerated by the party's success in that decade. Because the Scottish Conservatives gained over 50 per cent of the vote in the 1955 general election, it made all that followed appear disastrous. However, the result was very much an exception for a party which had traditionally struggled in Scotland against the Liberals and then Labour. Scottish Conservatism had performed best in circumstances when the Liberals were afflicted by internal divisions and organisational decline. Thus, the Conservatives prospered in Scotland after the formation of the Liberal Unionists, and from 1912 to 1965 when these two parties merged to form the Scottish Unionist Party. Similarly, the Conservatives' ability to attract former Liberal votes in the postwar period through standing as National Liberals and garnering votes as part of an anti-Socialist alliance gave the Tories electoral success in Scotland (Hutchinson, 1998). As Scottish Liberalism made its recovery from the 1960s onwards, it is notable that the Conservatives were the main victims, particularly at the 1983 and 1987 general elections when constituencies with historic Liberal support and active local parties managed to regain seats lost to the Conservatives decades earlier.

Most of the academic attention on Scottish Conservatism has revolved around the party's spectacular decline and its contrast with a healthy Tory party in England. The Conservative decline in Scotland was impressively multi-faceted, with devolution, national identity, a more left-wing working-class Scottish electorate, the decline of the Unionist-voting Protestant middle class, organisational failure, Thatcherism and a middle-class public sector all cited as reasons for the downturn in Conservative electoral fortunes (McCrone, 1992; Bennie and Mitchell, 1995; Seawright, 1999). All these factors certainly contributed to Conservative failure in Scotland, and made the obstacles to party recovery all the more challenging. Electoral recovery was not easy after the 1997 election, with the party's support in 1999 2 per cent lower despite gaining eighteen seats through the regional list system. Indeed, support for the Tories at the 1999 election demonstrated the deep-seated nature of the party's problems. It won no FPTP seats and saw its vote rise in very few constituencies, especially constituencies in which it was a serious challenger.

The party has often proved ill-equipped to respond to its electoral demise. For example, although the Scottish Tories made major changes to their organisation and policymaking after the 1997 general election wipeout, they failed to take action to address their failings in the 1980s. The substantial reforms associated with the Strathclyde Commission Report in 1998, which provided Scottish Conservatives with an elected leader and executive and policy autonomy over devolved areas, contrasted with the minimal reforms after the 1987 election reversal. Indeed, it is striking that the Tories were so ineffective in addressing their electoral decline before the 1997 election, perhaps because they were able to shelter behind the electoral victories achieved by the party in England from 1979–92. However, the 1998 reforms were impressive because they sought to recreate the Scottish Tories as a new autonomous party. The changes were also given credibility by the efforts of Conservative MSPs and the Scottish party leader, David McLetchie, who actively sought to demonstrate the political autonomy of Scottish Conservatives from their British counterparts. Finally, William Hague's willingness to allow Scottish Conservatives to go their own way and differ from the party line at Westminster afforded them some credibility, particularly in comparison to New Labour's alleged 'control freakery'. However, despite the space given to the Scottish Conservatives by the UK leadership, the party remains highly factionalised and prone to suffering from self-inflicted wounds such as the deputy leadership contest in June 2000. It has also continued to suffer from the long-term legacy of Thatcherism and an anti-Scottish image which will take years to reverse.

– Scottish Labour Party –

Labour in Scotland has been consistently successful since the Second World War. The party has maintained its position as the largest party at all elections since 1964, assisted by the FPTP electoral system used at Westminster and local elections. Of course, such representational hegemony was partly terminated by the adoption of the Additional Member System for elections to the Scottish Parliament, and may also be undermined by the use of proportional representation (PR) for local elections in future. However, overall, strong levels of voter support, combined with the structure of the electoral system, consistently made Labour the largest party in Scotland and gave Scotland the appearance of being a Labour country. This appearance was attributable to Labour's mass ranks of MPs and councillors and its ability to control large swathes of local government. It therefore had a strong institutional identity as Scotland's establishment party.

Nevertheless, this position was often achieved on fairly low proportions of the vote. For example, Labour has never received over 50 per cent of the vote as the Conservatives did in 1955. Its recent levels of electoral success were the 39 per cent and 33 per cent achieved at the Scottish election in 1999, the 36.6 per cent at the local council election and 29 per cent at the European election in 1999. It may have gained 46 per cent and 56 seats in the 1997 general election, but it then nearly lost Hamilton South in 1998 and did lose Ayr in 1999 at by-elections. Finally, the electoral system for the Scottish Parliament made the prospects of a Labour majority extremely unlikely. From now on, it must rule in coalition with another party, a sobering long-term thought for a party used to years of unbroken electoral dominance in Scotland. Electoral reform in local government will have a similar effect on the party's ability to dominate representation in the councils of West Central Scotland, undermining Labour's fiefdoms in Glasgow and Lanarkshire in particular.

Labour's electoral success has a number of reasons. First, the party was successful in combining its position as a Scottish party with that of a British one. Whereas the Scottish-British linkage among Conservatives was unbalanced under Margaret Thatcher, Labour consistently managed to appear as a pro-Scottish party as well as a British one. It could portray a Scottish identity through support for devolution and Scottish values, while also showing itself able to deliver economic benefits for Scotland through its UK status. Its Britishness also enabled it to reflect positive attributes such as the NHS, welfare state, full employment, and so on, which were popular in

Scotland. Second, Labour's success was achieved through the party's ability to move from existing as a class-based party to broadening its support into the middle class, especially from the 1980s onwards. Labour was able to move out from the West of Scotland to build a cross-class coalition of voters that enabled it to win in such formerly unlikely constituencies as Strathkelvin and Bearsden and Edinburgh South in 1987 to Dumfries and Inverness East in 1997.

Labour's main contemporary challenger is the SNP. Labour's vote is vulnerable to the nationalists, just as the SNP vote is vulnerable to Labour. The social composition of support for these two parties became increasingly similar in the 1990s (Brand, Mitchell and Surridge, 1994), particularly as the SNP became more accepted as a centre-left party within the eyes of the electorate and a close competitor to Labour (Bennie, Brand and Mitchell, 1997). However, the SNP is a distant challenger to Labour in most constituencies and it is difficult to see Labour's FPTP advantage at Scottish and Westminster elections coming under serious challenge. If Labour successfully manages its Scottish-British coalition, and Scottish Labour is able to cooperate effectively with British Labour through constructive intergovernmental relations between the Scottish Executive and Westminster, then Labour's position will remain strong.

– SCOTTISH LIBERAL DEMOCRATS –

The Scottish Liberal Democrats (SLD) have only existed since 1988, but are the heirs of both of the Scottish Liberal Party and the Scottish Social Democratic Party (SDP). The party therefore has a long history in Scotland, although it was often a dormant organisation in many parts of Scotland. Liberalism was the dominant electoral force in nineteenth-century Scotland, but coped badly with the class politics of the twentieth century. Following multiple splits in the Liberal Party over Irish Home Rule, Asquith versus Lloyd George, and the National coalition in the 1930s, the Scottish Liberals were a minor force by 1945 (Lynch, 1998). Organisationally, the party was too weak to field candidates in many areas and witnessed the Conservatives winning a number of formerly Liberal seats by standing as Conservative and National Liberal. The Scottish Liberals' weak capacity to contest elections contributed to a leakage of support to other parties, particularly the Conservatives and the SNP, with long-term consequences. For example, in 1951, the Liberals contested only nine Scottish constituencies, followed by only five in 1955, at a time when six MPs were elected as Conservative and National Liberal on 8.6 per cent of the vote (Kellas, 1994: p. 676). Even in the 1970s, Liberal organisation was insufficient to give the party a national presence in Scotland. In 1970, the year in which the SNP contested all Scottish seats for the first time, the Liberals contested only twenty-seven seats. It was only in 1983, with the appearance of the SDP Alliance, that the Liberals contested all Scottish seats.

The longer-term impact of the organisational and electoral wasting-away of the Liberal Party was a lack of competitiveness in many parts of Scotland. Sure enough, the Liberal Democrats became a force in parts of Scotland in which there was a strong Liberal tradition, but did so almost exclusively against an unpopular Conservative Party in areas of SNP weakness. Outside the Highlands, the Northeast and the Borders, Liberal Democrat successes were minimal. The party's only central Scotland seat is Edinburgh West in 1997 and 1999, although the party had local council success across Edinburgh and in Inverclyde and East Dunbartonshire councils in 1999. These factors explain why the Liberal Democrats became viewed as the party of the rural fringes in Scotland over the years – these were their sole areas of electoral success.

Despite the Liberal Democrats' modest electoral success in Scotland, the party's position consolidated in the 1990s with fairly consistent levels of electoral support and representation. Indeed, support for the party was fairly static at recent elections. Nonetheless, as a result of the Additional Member System at the Scottish election of 1999, the party now finds itself in government in Scotland, with two Cabinet ministers and influence over a range of policy areas. There is some irony in this situation. First, here are the Liberal Democrats benefitting from the electoral system they helped to design. Second, here is Scotland's fourth party in 1999 holding government office on what could be a permanent basis given its position as the moderate swing party between Labour and the SNP in the Scottish party system. The Liberal Democrats' role in the Scottish Executive still awaits the verdict of the electorate however, and the judgement of Liberal Democrat voters in the party's heartland seats may help to determine the party's future governmental status.

– SCOTTISH NATIONAL PARTY –

The SNP was formed in 1934. It contested a small number of elections and seats until the 1960s and was of little electoral importance until its breakthrough at the West Lothian by-election in 1961. From then until the late 1970s, the party's rise was steady and then meteoric. Slow growth in support in the 1960s, but rapid growth in party membership was followed by the party's emergence on the electoral scene at the two general elections of 1974 (see Table 10.1). The party's victories in 1974 were notable not for the number of seats won, which was modest, but because of the number of marginals created with Labour and the SNP's potential to wreak serious damage to Labour's position within Scotland. This situation was crucial in convincing Labour to support the establishment of a Scottish Assembly and to proceed with devolution legislation in the 1974–9 parliament. However, this electoral high point did not lead to devolution, rather to the fractious and failed referendum of 1979, an event which spurred serious factional divisions within the SNP in the early 1980s. The SNP only began to recover from the combined impact of the referendum and 1979 election losses in the mid-1980s, with progress at local elections. Even then, any 1974-style breakthrough was not forthcoming. Indeed, with the exception of strong showings at European Parliamentary elections and the Govan by-election in 1988, SNP performances were modest until 1999. Even when support for the party increased, such as in the 1992 general election, it found it hard to make progress in the FPTP electoral system.

Two features of the SNP are central to a contemporary understanding of its role and performance. First, the consistent adoption of a centre-left profile from the mid-1980s onwards made the SNP a more effective alternative to Labour and lay behind the SNP's electoral success in 1999. Second, although the SNP has experienced historic divisions between gradualists and fundamentalists over attitudes to devolution and independence, those divisions were largely managed by the party over the last decade despite some outbursts of discontent. Indeed, the fundamentalists' message was blunted to some extent by the fact that most of their leading figures were elected as MSPs in 1999. Since then, there has been a fair degree of pragmatism amongst fundamentalists regarding the role of the Scottish Parliament and the contribution of devolution to the final goal of independence, although differences of opinion were amplified during the SNP leadership contest in 2000. The gradualist-fundamentalist divide will emerge more seriously when the SNP enters the Scottish Executive and needs to compromise on independence and the independence referendum.

Support for the SNP has seen significant fluctuations, especially in the 1970s and in opinion polls between the devolution referendum of 1997 and the Scottish election of 1999. While support for the party stabilised above 20 per cent from 1992 onwards, opinion poll support has failed to be translated into real gains. The SNP has some distance to go before it can turn itself from a party of opposition into one of government. Indeed, Labour's strength has been such that it would take the SNP several elections to challenge for power on a more equal basis. In terms of both policy and organisation, the party requires a good deal of root-and-branch reform before it will be able to compete on FPTP terms with Labour rather than depend on the regional list system to deliver seats in the Scottish Parliament. Support for the party at Westminster elections also appears problematic.

– The new parties –

In recent times, Scottish politics has seen the emergence of new parties, and the most successful were the Scottish Green Party and the Scottish Socialist Party, each of which managed to elect MSPs through the regional lists at the 1999 Scottish election. The SSP succeeded through the popularity of its leader, Tommy Sheridan, who had contested a number of elections in Glasgow. He stood in Pollok at the general election in 1992, despite his incarceration in Saughton Prison, gained 19.3 per cent of the vote and experienced futher growth in support at local elections and the 1994 European election in the city (Milligan, 1999). Such support and the personal popularity of Sheridan were crucial to winning a list seat in Glasgow in 1999. However, despite this success, the position of the SSP was extremely weak, and faced with the electoral obstacle of another leftist party at the 1999 elections – the Socialist Labour Party – its overall performance was limited. It contested only eighteen seats out of seventy-three and its list vote was derisory in most regions. The Greens faced a similar situation, with a strong vote in one region – Lothians – but limited success elsewhere. Indeed, the Greens contested no FPTP seats and concentrated solely on attracting second votes on the list, a sensible strategy given the likelihood of expensive lost deposits. Of course, while the new parties had a limited impact on the election individually, it was significant that the 'others' picked up 11.3 per cent of the vote in 1999. The prospects of PR for local elections must give these parties some hope of gaining greater representation and the opportunity of building up a local base of support in some areas.

– The Scottish election 1999 –

The first Scottish election was held on 6 May 1999. Although turnout was a disappointing 58.8 per cent, it should be remembered that this was not a Westminster election determining the government of the UK. The year leading up to the May election saw considerable political excitement as the SNP rose in opinion polls to run neck and neck with Labour, but Labour had reasserted its lead by the election itself. Soft supporters of the SNP returned to Labour as the election approached and Labour's negative campaign against the Nationalists bore fruit. Labour promoted itself with a number of Scottish and British themes and policies, while attacking the SNP with the slogan 'Divorce is an expensive business'. Similarly the SNP's decision to retain the 1p income tax cut – the 'penny for Scotland' – was seen to play into Labour's hands as the latter projected itself as a tax-cutting party. The SNP was also damaged by Alex Salmond's speech on Kosovo, in which he attacked the NATO bombing of Serbia. Fighting a khaki election was never going to be easy for the SNP but the party fared extremely badly in the 1999 campaign. It appeared to lack the organisational and campaigning ability to cope with an intense onslaught from Labour, which was assisted by the partisan nature of the Scottish press (see Chapter 11).

Table 10.2 Result of the Scottish election 1999

Party	Constituencies Votes (%)	Seats	Regional lists Votes (%)	Seats	Total Seats
Conservative	15.5	0	15.4	18	18
Labour	38.8	53	33.6	3	56
Liberal Democrat	14.2	12	12.4	5	17
SNP	28.7	7	27.3	28	35
Others	2.7	1	11.3	2	3

Note: The Presiding Officer, David Steel, resigned from the Liberal Democrat group so the party really has sixteen MSPs, whilst the loss of Ayr by Labour to the Tories at the by-election means that Labour now has fifty-five seats to the Conservatives' nineteen.

The result of the 1999 election had positive aspects for all of the parties involved. Labour convincingly retained its position as the leading party, dominating the FPTP section of the poll. The SNP did not live up to the opinion poll expectations of 1998 or its goal of gaining forty seats, but it did become the second largest party and the official opposition in the Scottish Parliament, a substantial change for the nationalists. Support for the Liberal Democrats was marginally higher in 1999 than previously and the party did well in both FPTP and regional list contests. Significantly, the Liberal Democrats retained all of the seats they held at Westminster and even added Aberdeen South, which was held by Labour. The Liberal Democrats' elevation into government also gave them satisfaction. The Conservatives, performance was double-edged. On the one hand, the party's vote was 2 per cent less than at the 1997 general election, but, on the other hand, it gained national-level representation in Scotland for the first time since 1997. Thus, an electoral disaster in terms of electoral support was avoided because the party gained eighteen list seats. Finally, the election was notable for the victory of Dennis Canavan, standing as an independent in his Westminster constituency of Falkirk West, as well as the success of Greens' Robin Harper on the Lothians list and the SSP's Tommy Sheridan in Glasgow. These three results meant it was not just the big four parties that had something to celebrate at the election.

– ELECTORAL BEHAVIOUR –

In the period since the Second World War, Scottish electoral politics has had three prominent features: the persistence of Labour, the decline of the Conservatives, and the rise of the SNP. Underlying such electoral developments were changes in Scottish society and in political attitudes which differentiated Scotland from the rest of the UK. However, those changes were not detected within studies of electoral behaviour for some time. Studies of UK voting tended to assume the homogeniety of electoral behaviour across the country, with Scottish voters influenced by the same factors as those in England and Wales. The role of religion in structuring the vote in Scotland was one early challenge to the view of homogeneous UK voting (Bochel and Denver, 1970), although this factor faded over time. Subsequently, the rise of the SNP and decline of the Conservatives made Scotland stand out significantly from other parts of the UK, and in the 1970s, election surveys began to analyse the reasons for the SNP's success and the divergence in Scottish and British electoral behaviour (Miller, 1981). Although studies of Scottish electoral behaviour were neglected after the 1979 election, recent studies in 1992, 1997 and 1999 helped to construct substantial analytical evidence about the Scottish voter in terms of political attitudes, party affiliation, the influence of class and national identity, and the issue of a Scottish Parliament.

Much of the recent debate about Scottish voters has centred around their ideological outlook, which was seen to be central to explaining the unpopularity of the Conservatives and the popularity of the three other centre-left parties. The question of whether Scots were more left-wing than the rest of the UK was a clear issue to address. However, conclusive answers to this question were hard to find. For example, Scottish voters appeared slightly more left-wing than voters in the South of England, but not the North of England or Wales (Brown, McCrone and Paterson, 1998: p. 165). When compared with British voters generally, Scottish voters were slightly more leftist, but their voting patterns were seen to be a result of linkages between Scottish national identity and collectivist political values (Brown, McCrone, Paterson and Surridge, 1999: p. 112). Academic observers were therefore left to examine other reasons for Conservative decline such as the importance of class, particularly subjective working class identity, as well as national identity.

– NATIONAL IDENTITY –

National identities are complex social phenomena which co-exist and interact with other forms of social identity such as class or gender. Moreover, in Scotland, national identity is not an exclusively held identity but, rather, it involves the dual identities of Scottishness and Britishness (see Table 10.3). This finding should not be surprising given the existence of Scotland in Britain for several centuries and the generally harmonious relations between Scotland and its British neighbours in recent times. However, Scottish national identity is significant for two reasons. First, it involves a substantial differentiation with the rest of the UK and is one aspect of Scottish society and voting behaviour that is distinctive. Second, the existence of Scottish national identity acts as a potential for nationalism and therefore for nationalist political mobilisation.

Table 10.3 National identity and voting in Scotland

| | Support for parties (%) | | | | |
Identity	Conservative	Labour	Liberal Democrat	SNP	Number
Scottish not British	5	48	7	22	191
Scottish more than British	8	44	13	18	323
Equally Scottish and British	19	41	11	10	223
More British than Scottish	19	35	16	8	35
British not Scottish	21	38	14	7	30

Source: Brown, McCrone, Paterson and Surridge (1999), *The Scottish Electorate*, p. 67

The dual national identity of Scottish society is a key characteristic of the Scottish electorate. If Scottish national identity was exclusive and also politically mobilised, then SNP support would be of a different magnitude than today. Conversely, if British identity was exclusive, then SNP support would not have arisen to any significant degree and the main UK parties, particularly the Conservatives, could be expected to perform as well in Scotland as in other parts of the UK. However, the reality of dual identity presents parties with a balancing act in relation to their images and appeals. The Britishness of the Conservatives in Scotland in the 1980s and 1990s was problematic because the electorate increasingly saw themselves as Scottish, with the majority viewing themselves as predominantly Scottish or equally Scottish and British: identity groups that were not attracted to the Conservatives. The identity groups in which the Tories did best, the British-more-than-Scottish groups, were the smallest part of the Scottish electorate and therefore an extremely small constituency of supporters for the Tories (see sample size in Table 10.3).

The SNP suffered the reverse problem with national identity. It did best among the more excusively Scottish identity groups, where most of the voters were, but not as well as Labour. Indeed, Labour was the predominant party across all identity groups in 1997. It was able to appeal to Scottish and British identifiers across all identity categories. This successful balancing act remains a central part of Labour's appeal as both a Scottish and British party, able to generate a strong Scottish profile through support for devolution for example, whilst also able to gain support for its commitment to UK policies such as the welfare state and full employment. It also explains how Labour has held off the SNP, as voters see Labour as a Scottish party, despite SNP attempts to cast it as 'London' Labour. Of course, the balance of identities can change over time. Were Labour to become perceived as too British or were there some growth in the more exclusively Scottish categories of national identity, then an increase in support for the SNP would be the likely result. Labour's challenge is to maintain the balance of its dual identity in line with the Scottish electorate, which requires careful image and policy management in the Scottish Parliament and Westminster.

– CLASS VOTING –

Class voting remains an important influence on electoral behaviour in Scotland, despite the extent of social change in the past twenty years. Indeed, class remains a relevant factor even though objectively, class voting appears to have broken down. Class voting refers to the simple reality of two groups of voters – middle and working class – supporting their class parties, Conservative and Labour. Classic studies of voting in Britain (Butler and Stokes, 1969) were able to explain voting along class lines with most middle-class voters supporting the Conservatives and most working-class voters supporting Labour. Since then, class has become a more fluid concept, particularly with social change and the rise of a new upwardly-mobile working class and a new public-sector middle class. Scotland is a good example of these phenomena. First, the notion of a working class comprising unionised, manual workers who are council house tenants has declined rapidly. This socioeconomic picture was dented by the decline of trades union member-ship, the fall in manual employment and rise of the service sector, and the growth of home ownership to make it the dominant tenure in Scotland. For example, public-sector tenancies comprised 43.9 per cent of housing in 1988 compared to 46.7 per cent owner-occupied. By 1998, these figures had changed markedly so that only 26.6 per cent of housing was in the public sector, whilst 61.3 per cent was owner-occupied.[1] Second, the middle class in

Scotland has grown, with the expansion of higher education, occupational changes in the labour market and home ownership. Objectively, Scotland is not as working class as it once was and has become an increasingly middle-class society (Brand, Mitchell and Surridge, 1994).

Despite Scotland becoming more middle class, support for the Conservatives has fallen dramatically. Similar social changes in England aided the Conservatives in the 1980s, but in Scotland Conservatism failed to benefit from a more middle-class society, and support for parties with more working-class images – Labour and the SNP – increased (Bennie, Brand and Mitchell, 1997). This reality presents something of a paradox in terms of Scottish electoral behaviour. The reason behind it relates to the difference between objective and subjective class identities in Scotland. While Scotland became objectively more middle class in terms of housing, employment, income, and soon, Scottish voters saw themselves as working class and identified with working-class parties (Brand, Mitchell and Surridge, 1994). At the 1997 election, 71 per cent of Scots identified themselves as working class (Brown, McCrone, Paterson and Surridge, 1999: p. 64), a view which differed markedly from the objective reality of social groups outlined in Table 10.4.

Table 10.4 Social class and party support 1997

Social group	Conservative (%)	Labour (%)	SNP (%)	Liberal Democrat (%)	Didn't vote(%)
Salariat	22	28	14	19	14
Routine non-manual	9	47	17	12	14
Petty bourgeoisie	18	30	12	12	28
Manual, foremen, technicians	7	51	17	7	17
Working class	2	54	18	7	18

Source: Brown, McCrone, Paterson and Surridge (1999), *The Scottish Electorate*, p. 54

This situation explains part of the reason for Labour's ability to retain its position as Scotland's leading party – it was capable of appealing across different class groups and building a substantial middle-class electorate. At the 1992 general election, Labour attracted the support of 35 per cent of the private-sector middle class (Bennie, Brand and Mitchell, 1997: p. 99), so its success was not purely attributable to public-sector middle-class voters in Scotland. By 1997, Labour was able to attract levels of middle-class support which was far superior to the Conservatives across all social categories (see

Table 10.4). It also attracted the support of 39 per cent of owner-occupiers compared to the Conservatives' 15 per cent (Brown, McCrone, Paterson and Surridge, 1999: p. 55). This development reflected Labour's success in attracting support from those who had purchased council houses as well as those who had voted for the Conservatives in 1992, a central part of New Labour's strategy. Indeed, 18 per cent of Tory supporters in 1992 switched to Labour in 1997 (Brown, McCrone, Paterson and Surridge, 1999: p. 48). However, such changes illustrated Labour's general cross-class appeal in Scotland and its ability to construct an impressive electoral coalition.

Nevertheless, Labour's middle-class appeal and move to the right under New Labour generated problems that were evident at the Scottish elections in 1999: namely, the loss of support among core voters. Not only did Labour suffer from low turnout amongst its core electorate in 1999, but it also saw a decline in its share of the vote within the middle and working classes. Labour attracted the support of 51 per cent of the working class in 1997 but only 35 per cent in 1999. Similarly, the party's share of support in the middle class fell from 29 per cent to 25 per cent.[2] The cross-class aspect to Labour's support remained strong, but its core vote declined, largely to the benefit of the SNP. Appealing to middle England therefore had an electoral downside, although not a critical one in 1999. The fact that only 51 per cent of voters thought that Labour looked after the interests of working-class people compared to 63 per cent for the SNP was obviously a matter of concern. The challenge for Labour is to restore confidence among its working-class base without scaring off its middle-class electorate. Such efforts will need to carefully balance potential losses of support to the SNP on the left and the Conservatives on the right, the classic problem of catch-all centre parties who find their support eroded on each end of the ideological spectrum. However, the persistence of subjective working-class identity may continue to assist Labour in future elections.

– CONSTITUTIONAL OPTIONS AND CHANGE –

The devolution referendum of 1997 gave a clear indication of attitudes to constitutional change in Scotland, although such attitudes have evolved in the years since the referendum itself. The referendum result itself was attributable to a range of factors. National identity was one factor seen to generate support for devolution in 1997 (Denver, Mitchell, Pattie and Bochel, 2000) along with the 'welfare rationalism' of voters who expected that devolution would increase the welfare of Scottish society through use of the Parliament's tax powers (Brown, McCrone, Paterson and Surridge, 1999: p. 121). Rejection of the Conservatives following the experience of 1979–97 was also influential. However, the extent to which the current devolution arrangements represent the 'settled will' of the Scottish people is questionable. A variety of election surveys and opinion polls point to the fluidity of public opinion on Scotland's constitutional future, for example, the 1997 Scottish referendum survey determined that Scottish voters had great expectations of the new devolved Parliament both in its own policy areas and in reserved policy areas. Thus, Scots expected the Parliament could improve the Scottish economy, welfare state and unemployment (Brown, McCrone, Paterson and Surridge, 1999: p. 118) even though these were UK government responsibilities. Similarly, there was an expectation among voters that the devolved Parliament could lead to independence; this was demonstrative of an extremely 'unsettled' will.

Table 10.5 Constitutional options and support for independence

The Herald	Independence (%)	Devolution (%)	Don't know (%)
May 1998	34	58	8
December 1998	34	61	5

Sunday Herald	Independence (%)	Devolution (%)	No Scottish Parliament (%)
February 1998	36	43	14

Scotland on Sunday			
September 1997	28	38	30
February 1998	28	48	21
May 1998	33	48	17

The Scotsman
Q: In a referendum, would you vote for independence for Scotland?

Date	Yes (%)	No (%)	Don't know (%)
5 June 1998	52	41	7
1 July 1998	56	35	9
31 July 1998	49	44	7
5 September 1998	51	38	10
25 September 1998	48	37	15
25 November 1998	49	43	8
12 January 1999	49	42	9
4 February 1999	44	47	9
18 March 1999	42	47	11
4 April 1999	47	44	9

Note: These type of polls were largely discontinued after the establishment of the Scottish Parliament. Contemporary polls seek to judge voter attitudes to independence at a referendum on a Yes/No basis.

Attitudes towards Scottish independence in polls and surveys vary according to the nature of the question. For example, voters asked whether they support devolution, independence or no constitutional change, tend to place independence firmly behind devolution in terms of popular support (see Table 10.5). However, other types of polls reveal the fluidity of support for independence in terms of preferences in a referendum, attitudes to the costs/benefits of independence, and expectations that devolution would lead to independence in the medium term. Thus, voters asked about support for independence in an independence referendum have frequently shown majority support for independence. When the newspaper *Scotland on Sunday* asked voters whether they would vote Yes or No at an independence referendum in January 2000, 47 per cent said 'Yes' compared to 43 per cent 'No' (see Table 10.5).[3] In the same poll, people were asked about the impact of independence on the Scottish economy. The poll discovered that 20 per cent thought Scotland would be better off economically with independence, compared to 39 per cent who thought it would be worse off economically, and 37 per cent who thought independence would make no difference. Finally, there was some expectation among voters that devolution would lead to independence. The Scottish referendum survey of 1997 found that 60 per cent of the survey though it was quite or very likely that Scotland would become independent in the next twenty years (Brown, McCrone, Paterson and Surridge, 1999: p. 147). Other polls reinforced this finding. A Mori Scotland poll for the *Mail on Sunday* in March 1998 found that 62 per cent of Scots believed Scotland would be an independent state within fifteen years, 75 per cent thought it would be independent within fifty years and 25 per cent thought it would happen within five years. Such polls gave heart to the SNP's attempts to portray devolution as a process leading to independence rather than an end in itself.

There is an additional dimension to such polls supporting more constitutional change, namely public support for increasing the powers of the Scottish Parliament. First, there is a public expectation that the Scottish Parliament will become a more important institution than Westminster. Polls in *The Economist* in 1999 found that 46 per cent of Scots thought the Scottish Parliament was the most important government institution, compared to 31 per cent for the EU and only 8 per cent for Westminster.[4] A similar poll for *Scotland on Sunday* in January 2000 found that 51 per cent thought the Scottish Parliament was the most important institution, compared to 13 per cent for the EU and a more impressive 31 per cent for Westminster.[5] Such beliefs placed the Parliament at the centre of Scottish political life, albeit in an exaggerated fashion. Second, there is evidence that the public supports greater powers for the Scottish Parliament. The Scottish Parliamentary election survey of 1999 found that voters wanted the Parliament to have more influence than Westminster, and, among adherents of a Scottish identity, 62 per cent supported increasing the powers of the Scottish Parliament.[6] These are issues that all Scotland's parties will seek to address, not just the SNP.

– CONCLUSION –

Scottish electoral behaviour and parties have undergone significant changes in recent years, and such changes are set to continue with devolution. For example, the existence of the Parliament meant that parties were required to accommodate and manage another set of elections, with implications for candidate selection, campaigning, policy manifestos and organisation. Similarly, balancing the competing demands on parties in Edinburgh and Westminster was likely to prove problematic, with potential fissures between the party at the Scottish and UK levels. Thus, the Liberal Democrats face problems in opposing Labour at Westminster while co-operating with them in coalition in Edinburgh. Labour has to balance its Scottish and British image and appeal, in the context of a Scottish Parliament seeking to assert its autonomy and a centralising Blair admin-istration. The Conservatives in Scotland are challenged by the need to appear as a moderate, Scottish party in contrast to the image of a more right-wing, populist Conservative Party at Westminster, highly Euro-sceptic and favourable towards an English Parliament and restrictions on the voting rights of Scottish MPs. Finally, the SNP has to unlock the door to success at Westminster to mirror its electoral gains in the Scottish Parliament. All the parties must operate within a new multi-party and coalition system against the background of considerable social change and the continued impor-tance of class and national identity. Devolution therefore brought as much of a process of adjustment to the parties as to other institutions and organisations in Scotland.

– NOTES –

1. Scottish Executive, *Scottish Statisics 2000*.
2. Figures from the Scottish Parliamentary Election Survey 1999, *Scotland on Sunday*, 20 February 2000.
3. *Scotland on Sunday*, 30 January 2000.
4. *The Economist*, 6 November 1999.
5. *Scotland on Sunday*, 30 January 2000.
6. Lindsay Paterson, 'What Does Scotland Want?', conference on 'New Scotland, New Politics?', National Museum of Scotland, Edinburgh, 25 February 2000.

CHAPTER 11

The media in Scotland

– INTRODUCTION –

The existence of a distinctive Scottish civil society has become a constant theme in the literature on Scottish politics (Paterson, 1994). Much has been written about the church, legal system and education system being distinctive institutions which survived the Union between Scotland and England in 1707 and helped to retain a sense of Scottish national identity (Kellas, 1984). However, it is not just Kellas' holy trinity of institutions that exist as components of civil society. The media also exists as a distinctive aspect of Scottish life through the fact that newspapers, television and radio programmes are all produced in Scotland for a Scottish audience, and are able to reflect Scotland's distinctiveness in areas such as education, religion, legal system, politics and government structure. The existence of a distinctive media has a number of functions in relation to the transmission of Scottish national identity, providing a forum for political debate and operating as a critical fourth estate within Scottish politics.

Indeed, it can be argued that before the creation of the Scottish Parliament, the media was effectively where Scottish politics existed. It was the forum for Scottish politics on a daily basis, covering both developments at Westminster and in Scotland in relation to the parties, pressure groups, local authorities and civic Scotland. In spite of this, the media remained a reserved power at Westminster after devolution, although the Scottish Parliament debated broadcasting issues on a number of occasions in its first year. This chapter examines the main features of the media in Scotland, with an analysis of the newspapers and broadcasting. It also provides an assessment of the role of the media at the 1999 Scottish election and of its coverage of the Scottish Parliament in its first year of existence.

– THE MEDIA AND SCOTTISH POLITICS –

The media has a number of roles within politics. Sometimes it can be seen as the fourth estate, acting independently as a critical force in political debate. At other times, it can be seen as a more neutral forum for politics, providing space for civil society to discuss political issues, or reporting on political issues to create an informed electorate. Finally, the media can act as an agenda-setting institution through its own political viewpoints, which may veer towards partisanship at elections or in referendum campaigns (Denver, Mitchell, Pattie and Bochel, 2000), or through campaigning investigative journalism or reporting. All of these roles can be found in the Scottish media to some extent, with the partisan elements common in the press but not broadcasting.

Media adjustment to devolution has been limited, because coverage of Scottish politics was already well established in the Scottish press. Some special features were developed to deal with the new Parliament, but few papers had to make substantial changes to their political coverage to accommodate devolution. They increased staff and coverage and perhaps reduced coverage of Westminster, but were hardly starting from scratch in covering Scottish affairs. The position of the broadcast media was somewhat different, especially in the case of the BBC which had to alter its centralised service to adapt to regional changes such as devolution. The BBC made a number of limited adjustments such as the change of language for the 'nations and regions' dealt with by the *Changing UK* stylebook (the BBC stylebook sets out the terms used by BBC newscasters and journalists, and these terms were altered to accommodate the new climate of devolution), the changes to the *Six o'Clock News* and the debate over the *Scottish Six* and the *Newsnight* opt-out (see Case study 12). The BBC's main programming response to the Scottish Parliament was to institute the *Newsnight* opt-out (*Newsnight Scotland*) instead of creating a separate Scottish *Six o'Clock News*. However, there will be continuing pressure on the BBC to make deeper adjustments to the new reality of devolution. To some extent, the introduction of *Newsnight Scotland* and denial of the *Scottish Six* made two points clear. First, despite having two years between the general election of 1997 and the Scottish election of 1999 to adjust to the reality of devolution, the BBC largely avoided the topic and adjusted as minimally as possible (Schlesinger and Tambini, 1999). Second, *Newsnight Scotland* was dragged out of the BBC as a substitute for the *Scottish Six*, which the corporation sought to resist at all costs. In some ways, this situation resembles the history of devolution itself. Rather than a Parliament, Scotland was offered a Royal Commission, the Scottish Development Agency, a stronger Scottish Office, a Scottish Grand Committee, and so on; the BBC followed suit. Of course, there is a great irony in the BBC's response to devolution given the wider context of broadcasting in the UK. Just as the BBC faces pressures to devolve to the regions, the ITV companies, which operate on regional franchises, face mergers and consolidations under the pressures of the UK, European and global media markets. Thus, ITV is centralising just as the BBC is decentralising.

Politicians and the media enjoy a difficult relationship, sometimes positive, sometimes negative. For some academics, this relationship is viewed as 'symbiotic' (Franklin, 1994), with journalists dependent on politicians for access and stories, and politicians dependent on journalists for the oxygen of publicity. Two things are worth pointing out about the Scottish media. First, the political journalists in the Scottish press have often been viewed as an awkward squad, particularly by New Labour. For Prime Minister Tony Blair, the Scottish media were 'unreconstructed wankers', who would ask difficult questions and not simply report positively on Labour in office or opposition. Second, while specialist political journalists deal with many political stories, the founding of the Scottish Parliament has meant that political stories are now covered by a much wider range of journalists, commentators, news desks and editorialists. The symbiotic relationship has therefore become fragmented and problematic. Despite this, there are close links between politicians and journalists, partly because Scottish politics is a small world in which everyone knows everyone else. This situation is even more evident in relation to the Executive and Parliament, which *The Herald*'s Robbie Dinwoodie referred to as a 'village'. Journalists and politicians regularly meet formally and informally and swap titbits of information and gossip. Moreover, politicians brief the press on an off-the-record basis. The Scottish Executive's first year in office was punctuated by a number of briefing wars between Labour ministers over policy, evident in the cabinet row over reallocating the Health Department's £34 million underspend in June 2000.

– THE SCOTTISHNESS OF THE MEDIA –

Although the exact nature of the relationship between the media and national identity is problematic, nationalism and national identity are key aspects of the media in Scotland (Meech and Kilborn, 1992). Television, radio and newspapers all seek to stress the fact that they are serving a nation with its own identity and institutions and, over time, the media has been one institution capable of reproducing Scottish national identity (Kellas, 1992). This reality is manifested in the features and coverage of the electronic and written media, the types of stories and programmes, sports coverage, and news and current affairs in general. But the Scottish media also use national identity in a more instrumental way. First, they use it in competition within each other, to attract and retain viewers/readers by stressing their Scottish credentials. A quality paper such as *The Scotsman* describes itself as 'Scotland's national newspaper'. For a long time, the *Daily Record* masthead pronounced that 'Real Scots read the *Record*', an implicit criticism of its largest competitor *The Sun*, and later its masthead declared it was 'Scotland's champion'. *The Sun*, in its pro-SNP phase, distributed car stickers around Scotland that cried out 'Rise now and be a nation again' and declared itself 'Fighting for independence' on its masthead. In its post-SNP phase, *The Sun* was merely 'Dedicated to the people of Scotland'. Similarly, BBC Scotland styles itself as 'the national network' while Scottish Television seeks to promote itself as the truly Scottish TV station, not merely a regional division of a UK TV station.

Second, the newspapers have used national identity to differentiate themselves from non-Scottish papers or alternatively to repackage themselves as Scottish newspapers. In recent years, the British press has experienced a circulation war between quality and tabloid newspapers, involving price-cutting measures and special sales promotions. Large metropolitan papers such as the *Daily Telegraph*, *The Times* and the *Independent* reduced their cover prices with some impact on Scottish newspaper titles. In general, the Scottish press could not replicate such a price-cutting strategy (although *The Scotsman* attempted to do so in 2000), but responded to the challenge of non-Scottish papers' increased circulation by reasserting their Scottish identity and ability to cover Scottish news and features. Also, a number of non-Scottish newspapers sought to boost circulation by styling themselves as Scottish, changing their titles and content to compete with genuine Scottish titles. *The Sun*'s efforts to take on The *Daily Record* by appearing more nationalist was a case in point, and meanwhile *the Daily Mirror* became the *Scottish Daily Mirror*, the *Daily Star* became the *Daily Star of Scotland*, the *Daily Mail* became the *Scottish Daily Mail* and the *Daily Express* transformed itself back into the *Scottish Daily Express* nearly two decades after it stopped publishing a distinctive Scottish edition.

– THE SCOTTISH PRESS –

Historically, Scotland has enjoyed an indigenous press for several hundred years. *Aberdeen's Journal* was established in 1747 and later became *The Press and Journal*; *The Glasgow Advertiser* of 1783 became *The Glasgow Herald* in 1805; *The Scotsman* was established in 1817, and the *Daily Record* was launched in 1895 (Linklater and Dennistoun, 1992: p. 127). The existence of an indigenous press continues to this day and has become more pronounced than ever. Anyone who picked up *The Scotsman* or *The Herald* on the same day as *The Times* or *The Guardian* could not fail to notice the difference in coverage, with a fairly clear contrast between a Scottish news agenda and a London one, extending all the way through politics, culture, sport and features. Such distinctions mean it is justified to talk of the existence of a Scottish newspaper industry and market, which can be characterised by four features: the regional/local nature of the Scottish paper market, the impressively high circulation figures attained by the Scottish papers, the partisanship of the press, and the highly competitive environment for Scottish papers.

– A SCOTLAND OF THE REGIONS –

The first defining feature of the Scottish press is that it is characterised by regional rather than national newspapers. Among the quality newspapers, such as the big four *The Courier, The Herald, The Press and Journal* and *The Scotsman*, sales are heavily regionalised in spite of the claims of *The Scotsman* that it is 'Scotland's national newspaper'. All four papers can be considered as city-state newspapers (Smith, 1994), in that they sell well within the cities of Dundee, Glasgow, Aberdeen and Edinburgh and their respective hinterlands, but perform badly outside their city-state. *The Scotsman* sells badly in Glasgow and the West, *The Herald* sells few copies in Aberdeen and the Northeast, and *The Courier* sells little outside Dundee and Tayside. *The Press and Journal* remains a North East paper, although it sought to increase circulation by publishing a central Scotland edition in the late 1990s. While none of the quality papers can lay claim to being a truly national newspaper, a number of the tabloids can: the sales of the *Daily Record, The Sun, Sunday Mail* and *Sunday Post* are such that they could legitimately claim to be Scotland's national newspapers on the grounds that their audiences far eclipse the qualities. However, it remains the case that individual circulation figures of the Scottish quality press are far ahead of those of the London broadsheets in Scotland. Finally, the Scottish press is not only heavily regional but also markedly local, with many local papers outselling some of the London broadsheets in Scotland.

– HIGH READERSHIP AND CIRCULATION –

The second defining feature of the Scottish press is its high readership and circulation figures. By contrast with England and other countries, Scottish newspaper readership is impressive. Five million people are reading an awful lot of newspapers and many appear to be reading several each day in addition to a local weekly paper. The scale of the circulation figures become apparent when one considers the small size of Scotland's population. For example, if the *Daily Record* were as popular across Britain as it is in Scotland, it would sell around six million copies per day, whereas the largest selling UK paper, *The Sun*, sells only 3.5 million copies per day. If *The Press and Journal* were selling across Britain as it does in Scotland, its daily circulation would overtake that of *The Times*, *The Guardian*, *The Independent*, *Financial Times* and *Daily Telegraph*.

Table 11.1 National/regional newspaper readership in Scotland, February 2000

Title	Circulation
The Courier (Dundee)	93,406
The Herald (Glasgow)	100,603
The Press and Journal (Aberdeen)	104,548
The Scotsman (Edinburgh)	75,648
Daily Record	625,820
Greenock Telegraph	19,701
Evening Express (Aberdeen)	65,607
Evening News (Edinburgh)	80,754
Evening Telegraph (Dundee)	30,413
Evening Times	108,838
Scotland on Sunday	112,312
Sunday Mail	747,929
Sunday Post	684,749
Sunday Herald	54,316

Source: National Newspaper Data, Audit Bureau of Circulations, February 2000

– PARTISANSHIP AND THE SCOTTISH PRESS –

The partisanship of the press has been a distinctive aspect of the Scottish newspapers, although this distinctiveness has lessened in recent years. In the 1980s, when the London press appeared uniformly pro-Conservative, the Scottish press was largely anti-Conservative. At the 1983 election, only *The Courier*, *Daily Express* and *Sunday Express* supported the Conservatives. Newspapers that were dissatisfied with Labour, such as the *Evening Times*, *The Herald*, *The Scotsman*, *The Press and Journal* and *The Sunday Standard* moved to support the Alliance (Kellas, 1984). Then, as now, the *Daily Record* and *Sunday Mail* supported Labour. Such pluralism in partisanship was a clear contrast to the 'Tory press' in England, where almost all tabloids (except the *Mirror*) and qualities were pro-Conservative. However, in time, the Scottish press came to resemble the London press in its partisan affiliations. As the London press moved to support Blair and New Labour in 1997–9, so did sections of the Scottish press, especially Scottish editions of London tabloids. The decision of *The Sun* and *Scottish Daily Express* to shift to supporting Labour was a clear reversal of their previous outlook. By the 1999 Scottish elections therefore, the Scottish press appeared either pro-Labour or neutral, a situation with clear implications for competitive politics in Scotland.

Table 11.2 Partisanship and the press in Scotland

Newspaper	1992 UK election	1997 UK election	1999 Scottish election
The Herald	Lib Dem	None	None
The Scotsman	Labour/Lib Dem	None	None
The Courier	Conservative	None	None
The Press and Journal	None	None	None
Evening Times	None	None	Labour
Daily Record	Labour	Labour	Labour
The Sun	SNP	Labour	Labour
Scottish Daily Express	–	–	Labour
Scottish Daily Mail	–	–	None
Scottish Mirror	–	Labour	Labour
Daily Star	–	–	None
Sunday Mail	Labour	Labour	Labour
Sunday Post	Conservative	None	None

Historically, the partisanship of the press has changed and changed quite radically, although no paper has matched the political somersaults of *The Sun* from Conservative in 1987 to SNP in 1992 to Labour in 1997. For example, the *Daily Record* was a supporter of the Conservatives until switching to Labour in 1956 (Seawright, 1999: p. 183). *The Herald* supported the Conservatives until 1983, when it supported the Liberal/ SDP Alliance before becoming a pronounced anti-Conservative and pro-devolution paper. *The Scotsman* abandoned its support for the Conservatives in the 1960s to support the Liberals, before supporting Labour at the 1997 general election. The decline of a Conservative-supporting press obviously played a part in the electoral demise of Scottish Conservatism from the 1950s onwards. By the late 1980s and the 1990s, leading Conservatives businessmen were keen to purchase *The Herald* and *The Scotsman* on two separate occasions in order to increase media sympathy for the party (Smith, 1994; Seawright, 1999). Finally, in terms of partisanship, there was the issue of Labour pressure on *The Herald* at the 1999 Scottish election. Labour decided to withdraw political advertising worth £100,000 from *The Herald* because it did not like the paper's coverage of the election, a story first reported in *The Observer* during the election campaign (Ritchie, 2000).

– COMPETITIVENESS –

The final characteristic of the Scottish press is its high level of competitiveness. This phenomenon has resulted from the existence of a large number of titles competing for a shrinking readership and limited advertising revenue. Indeed, the market may have reached saturation point in terms of readership and available titles. For example, in 1981 *The Scotsman* had a circulation of 98,943, while *The Courier* had 135,566 and the *Daily Record* had 726,506 (Kellas, 1984: p. 198), much larger than they are today (see Table 11.1). As in the rest of the UK, Scottish newspaper readership has declined in favour of television. In addition, the number of titles competing in Scotland increased with the entry into the market of London tabloids publishing Scottish editions such as *The Sun, Daily Mirror, Daily Mail, Daily Star* and *Daily Express*. Put simply, there are now more titles competing for fewer readers. The competitive nature of the Scottish market also saw examples of newspaper failures such as the *Sunday Scot, Scotland Today* and *Sunday Standard*. The development of free newspapers, largely consisting of advertising rather than news content, also contributed to a decline in newspaper readership at the local level. The competition between rival titles for the same readers progressively brought a more cut-throat element into the Scottish press. *The Scotsman* attempted to increase its circulation figures in 2000 through a price-cutting strategy and redesign which pushed daily sales up to 100,000. The daily tabloid battles between the *Daily Record* and *Sun* are legion in Scotland, particularly as *The Sun's* circulation has increased and that of the *Record* has declined. The nature of journalism has also changed with the new competitive environment. Chequebook journalism, media feeding frenzies and tabloid excesses have all become a way of life within the Scottish press (Boyle, 1998), just as they are in the rest of the UK.

– THE LOCAL NEWSPAPER MARKET –

The Scottish newspaper industry is not merely national and regional, but distinctly local. There are a vast number of weekly and fortnightly newspapers in Scotland and innumerable free newspapers paid for by advertising. Since much of the academic focus on the media has concentrated on the national press, the local press has gone unrecognised. There are several ways of understanding the significance of the local press in Scotland. First, it is clearly extensive in terms of titles and circulation (see Table 11.3). The local papers are widely read in their areas and political coverage of any sort has an audience. Second, the political significance of the local press is different from that of the national press. While the national press is important to the central party organisations and leaderships, the local press is important to local parties, councils and councillors, backbench MSPs and MPs. Coverage of the success or failure of local councillors affects parties, as do sympathetic or critical stories about MSPs or MPs. For most MPs and MSPs for example, the local press is the centrepiece of their media strategy for communicating with constituents and voters. Indeed, backbenchers have often been advised to concentrate on the regional and local media as their most important vehicle for communication (Franklin, 1994: p. 19). Since their hopes of gaining a profile through the national media are slim, they use local/regional papers to develop a media profile. Local papers are inundated with press releases from local representatives, particularly from the mixture of constituency and list MSPs competing for attention. Whether it is coverage of a debate in Parliament or a photograph with children at a local primary school, elected representatives will look to the local press and freesheets for coverage (see Case study 11). Indeed, individual MSPs used members' motions in Parliament as one mechanism for generating coverage in the local newspapers (see Chapter 5).

Table 11.3 Local newspaper readership in Scotland 1999

Title	Circulation	Publications per year
Airdrie and Coatbridge Advertiser	20,771	24
Alloa and Hillfoots Advertiser	7,778	50
Annandale Herald	3,144	25
Annandale Observer	6,803	25
Arbroath Herald	10,259	25
Ardrossan and Saltcoats Herald	21,088	50
Ayr Advertiser	6,875	50
Ayrshire Post	27,683	25
Banffshire Journal	4,421	50
Berwickshire News	5,717	25
Blairgowrie Advertiser	3,801	25
Buchan Observer	9,609	26
Campbeltown Courier	7,053	25
Central Fife Times	6,757	50
Clyde Weekly Press (Ardrossan)	5,400	50
Clydebank Post	8,492	50
Cumbernauld News and Kilsyth Chronicle	12,718	25
Dumbarton Lennox Herald	12,662	25
Dumfries and Galloway News	9,569	24
Dumfries and Galloway Standard	12,011	24
Dunfermline Press	20,531	25
Dunoon Observer and Argyllshire Standard	6,069	26

East Fife Mail	11,971	25
East Kilbride News	16,489	24
Ellon Times and East Gordon Advertiser	2,210	26
Falkirk Herald	31,867	25
Fife Free Press	20,309	25
Fife Herald News and St Andews Citizen	13,655	25
Forres Gazette	3,252	50
Fraserburgh Herald	5,854	26
Glenrothes Gazette	6,641	25
Hamilton Advertiser	27,345	25
Helensburgh Advertiser	5,870	50
Highland News	9,926	50
Inverness Courier	18,732	50
Irvine Herald	8,119	25
Irvine Times	6,832	50
John O'Groats Journal	9,077	50
Kilmarnock Standard	19,208	25
Kirkintilloch Herald	12,069	25
Lanark and Carluke Gazette	11,933	25
Largs and Millport Weekly News	5,400	50
Linlithgowshire Journal and Gazette	7,544	25
Lochaber News	3,259	50
Milngavie and Bearsden Herald	7,176	25
Moffat News	1,102	25
Motherwell Times and Belshill Speaker	15,442	25
North Star	6,038	50
Northern Scot	19,103	50
Northern Times	5,090	50
The Orcadian	11,090	25
Oban Times	17,843	25
Paisley Daily Express	10,232	155
Paisley and Renfewshire Gazette	9,000	50
Perthshire Advertiser	19,667	50
Rosshire Journal	10,870	50
Rutherglen Reformer	5,927	24
Shetland Times	11,276	25
Southern Reporter	17,314	23
Stirling Observer	13,300	50
Strathearn Herald	2,923	24
Strathspey and Badenoch Herald	4,596	50
Stornoway Gazette	12,551	26
West Highland Free Press	10,009	26
West Lothian Courier	21,051	25
Wishaw Press	12,163	24

Source: National Newspaper Data, Audit Bureau of Circulations, February 2000. Based on period 28 June 1999 to 26 December 1999

Case study 11 The local press and local politicians

The utility of the local press to local politicians is evident from scanning any of the local newspapers in Scotland. For example, the *Stirling Observer* of 5 April 2000 and the *Alloa Advertiser* of 6 April 2000 both contained extensive opportunities for local political figures. The *Stirling Observer* covered the transfer of local hospital services out of Stirling with quotes from the Provost of Stirling Council. Inside the paper, there were three photographs and stories about one of the local MSPs, coverage of Stirling Council and of the political dispute between Clackmannanshire Council's SNP leadership and the local MSP, Richard Simpson, which had a prominent place in the letters page. The *Alloa Advertiser* also covered the closure of hospital services in Stirling on its front page, with quotes from local MSPs and councillors, as well as reaction to Finance Minister Jack McConnell's visit to Clackmannanshire. This story featured a number of photographs. In addition, the paper covered the party campaigns for a local by-election in Clackmannanshire, several pages of local authority matters, coverage of the Scottish Transport Bill, and the Scottish Executive's financial support for rail projects, and the prospects for restoring the Stirling–Alloa rail link. Such stories are the weekly fare of Scotland's local press and are replicated up and down the country especially where there is competition between the different types of MSPs. For example, the *Stirling Observer* will not only feature local MSP Sylvia Jackson, but also MSP Brian Montieth who contested the seat for the Conservatives in 1999 and was elected on the regional list for Mid-Scotland and Fife. Similarly, the *Alloa Advertiser* features the Ochil MSP, Richard Simpson, as well as MSPs George Reid and Nick Johnston who contested the constituency in 1999 and were also elected on the Mid-Scotland and Fife list.

Of course, the local press faces as competitive an environment as the national and regional press, if not a more competitive one. It not only faces local competitors but also the spread of free newspapers across Scotland: advert-driven papers with a minimum of news coverage, mostly limited to community events and photographs. There are free newspapers available across most of Scotland and they provide ample space for soft, uncritical political stories and photo-opportunities for MSPs, MPs and councillors, mostly devoid of editorial comment. The distribution of these papers is extremely high. *The Edinburgh Herald and Post* had a verified free distribution of 177,531 from 28 June to 26 December 1999, compared to 107,247 for the *Aberdeen Herald and Post*, 56,363 for the *West Lothian Herald and Post*, 22,916 for the *Dumfries Courier*, 50,771 for the *Dunfermline Herald and Post* and 19,249 for the *Inverness and Nairnshire Herald*. Of course, it's not just the local press that is threatened by the free sheets: the emergence of the free commuter newspaper *Metro* challenged the national and regional papers and became a competitor for the *Daily Record* and *The Sun* in 2000.

– THE ELECTRONIC MEDIA IN SCOTLAND –

Compared to the press, the electronic media in Scotland is less distinctive but its programming and output reflects its existence in Scotland and the need to serve a Scottish audience. For example, television in Scotland is structured around two main institutions: the Scottish regional branch of the BBC, BBC Scotland, and the three independent regional television companies, STV, Grampian and Border. These organisations provide a range of news, current affairs and political programmes for a Scottish audience as well as acting as the transmitters of UK programming in these areas broadcast from London. This dual function has been an area of tension for many years, particularly for the BBC, with nationalism and devolution creating pressures for more Scottish news programmes within a British service. In simple terms, this pressure has created a Scotland-London conflict within the BBC over news coverage of Scottish affairs. The temporary resolution to this conflict, the Scottish opt-out from *Newsnight*, is discussed in more detail in Case study 12.

Case study 12 The *Scottish Six* **and the** *Newsnight* **opt-out**
The most prominent area of the media affected by devolution was BBC TV. While Radio Scotland and the BBC's local radio stations could easily adapt to the new climate of devolution, BBC TV faced a major challenge. There was pressure for more TV coverage of Scottish affairs before devolution and such pressure escalated after the devolution referendum in 1997. As a Parliament was on the horizon, there was concern about its treatment on BBC since news programming was dominated by London. The BBC sought to revamp its main *Six o'Clock News* to include more news from the different nations of the UK, but Scottish campaigners sought to create a fully-fledged Scottish *Six o'Clock News* which would deal with all UK, international and Scottish news stories at peak time. The BBC's wish to preserve its central control over the *Six o'Clock News* slot put it on a collision

---

course with the Scottish Broadcasting Council and a large section of the Scottish media, including many in BBC Scotland. The BBC was concerned at losing the uniformity of service provided by the national news and worried that the *Scottish Six* would involve a descent into parochialism. Supporters of the *Scottish Six* were concerned about the inability of BBC Scotland to report effectively on Scottish issues, especially as the main news team in London would steal their strongest stories for the *Six o'Clock News*. Instead of the *Scottish Six*, the BBC established a twenty minute opt-out from *Newsnight*, which was broadcast on weekday evenings from 10.30 to 11.20. The Scottish section would begin at 11.00, but was bedevilled by a range of problems. First, the opt-out was viewed as an unwelcome compromise compared to a full Scottish service, especially because it was scheduled so late. Second, the opt-out did not deal with the problem of replication of news stories between the BBC's *Six o'Clock News* and the *Reporting Scotland* programme that followed it. Third, Scottish viewers who wished to see the pre-existing *Newsnight* service, with more international news coverage, could no longer receive it because of the opt-out. Finally, the opt-out itself faced numerous problems of low audiences and a feeling that UK *Newsnight* staff and presenters were sabotaging the handover to Scotland to damage the opt-out programme. Despite such problems and political criticism, *Newsnight Scotland* did establish an audience, although its future was questionable given the strength of support for a *Scottish Six*.

– THE BBC IN SCOTLAND –

Although the BBC developed as a centralised national service, it did take account of territorial features and the distinctiveness of different parts of the UK. London may always have been the dominant centre of BBC broadcasting – a fact which generated conflicts in itself – but regional and local TV and radio stations have grown across the UK to provide a more complex territorial broadcasting network. The BBC began to develop its regional broadcasting network in the 1920s, and although the whole of BBC radio was centralised during the Second World War, the regional broadcasting structure was restored after 1945. The BBC was initially divided into six regions: the three national regions of Northern Ireland, Scotland and Wales, plus three large English regions. This structure was reorganised in 1970 to provide a more decentralised regional structure in England, with eight English regions established in order to boost regional television and radio coverage. This was intended to enable the BBC to produce a more coherent regional broadcasting system and to compete more clearly with the ITV companies.

The recognition of regional broadcasting and the creation of BBC stations in Scotland, Wales and Northern Ireland preceded the growth of mobilised nationalism in these territories, but since the 1960s territorial politics and regional broadcasting have fed off each other. The prospect of devolution for Scotland and Wales raised hopes of greater internal devolution within the BBC to give more finance and autonomy in programming and production to the regions. The increased salience of legislative devolution won BBC Scotland more staff and greater resources in the 1970s, with more journalists and researchers to cover new political developments. The pinnacle of BBC devolution in this period involved the creation of Radio Scotland as a full-time national radio station in 1978. The changing political context created by devolution since 1999 created similar pressures on the BBC, with demands for a new Scottish news service, in addition to changes by BBC Scotland to accommodate coverage of the Scottish Parliament.

The centralised nature of the BBC and its impact on programming has traditionally been a sensitive issue in the BBC network, and concerns about a London bias have existed since its formation. As early as the 1930s, BBC staff in Scotland expressed concern about the Scottish contribution to radio in Scotland compared to the level of programming coming from London, and this contributed to BBC plans for decentralising power over programming and production to the regions in 1936 (McDowell, 1992). The regional aspect to broadcasting within the BBC not merely created its own devolutionary dynamic, it also brought about the establishment of territorial structures within the BBC. Following the restoration of regional broadcasting after the Second World War, the BBC decided to establish representative structures for the national regions and instituted nominated Broadcasting Councils for Scotland and Wales in 1952. These two bodies have since operated as territorial representatives within the BBC structure, taking on the role of overseeing the development of BBC services in Scotland and Wales while also acting as lobbyists for resources and programme access with the BBC in London. Scotland, Wales and Northern Ireland also have territorial representation through the staffing arrangements for the national regions – with controllers for BBC Scotland, BBC Wales and BBC Northern Ireland – in addition to national governors for Scotland, Wales and Northern Ireland who chair their respective Broadcasting Councils and serve on the BBC's Board of Governors. There was the expectation that the national governors would act primarily as territorial lobbyists, promoting and representing Scottish and Welsh interests within the BBC network (Hetherington, 1992), although it is difficult to determine the extent to which they have fulfilled this function.

BBC Scotland had an income of £94.3 million in 1998–9 and was responsible for providing 716 hours of programming on BBC TV in Scotland and 8,909 hours of radio in Scotland. It was also responsible for 172 hours of network programming, largely children's and daytime programmes (BBC Scotland, 2000). In Scotland, 364 hours were given over to news and current affairs, including thirty four hours of parliamentary broadcasting. Such figures will have increased with devolution. BBC Scotland was pledged to spend a total of £10 million covering the new Parliament from 1999–2000, which involved approximately fifty new jobs. BBC Resources in Scotland also won the contract to provide broadcast facilities for the Parliament, so there was income as well as expenditure from devolution. BBC Scotland provides live parliamentary coverage in relation to Scottish Executive question time and First Minister's question time, as well as general coverage of parliamentary debates and committee meetings. TV programmes such as *Holyrood* and *Reporting Scotland* present the bulk of BBC's Scottish parliamentary output, while Radio Scotland's news programmes – *Good Morning Scotland* and *Newsdrive* – and political programmes such as *Politics Tonight* also utilise the parliamentary output. BBC Scotland also produces *Frontline Scotland*, an investigative current affairs programme, although it seldom features Parliament or MSPs.

Many of BBC Scotland's political journalists are well-known and respected commentators such as Brian Taylor, Colin McKay, Derek Bateman, Iain McWhirter and John Morrison. BBC Scotland can also draw on Kirsty Wark for a variety of political programmes as well as Gordon Brewer and Anne McKenzie of *Newsnight Scotland*. Besides its own programmes, BBC Scotland contributes to BBC's digital television output with news and programmes for BBC News 24, BBC Knowledge and BBC Parliament. Finally, BBC Scotland is responsible for Gaelic programming such as the European and international current affairs programme, *Eorpa*, and a range of programmes through *Radio nan Gaidheal*.

– INDEPENDENT TELEVISION IN SCOTLAND –

Independent television was introduced in the UK in the 1950s with a distinctive territorial structure, consisting of regional television companies broadcasting to regional audiences. This structure made it easier for the ITV companies to accommodate pressures for regional programming and deal with the impact of devolution than the more centralised BBC. The development of independent TV in Scotland was particularly significant because it involved the creation of two Scottish TV stations rather than a uniform Scottish service. Grampian was created in 1961 to cover the Highlands and North East of Scotland, and Scottish Television was established in 1957 to cover the central belt. In addition, parts of South and South West Scotland received Border TV from 1961 onwards, a regional station that also covered the North of England.

As part of the ITV network, these stations featured both regional and national news and programmes, with production centres in Scotland producing programmes for their region as well as seeking access to the ITV network for their programmes. STV's evening news programme *Scotland Today* provides thirty minutes of Scottish news, while Grampian's *North Tonight* offers the same service for the North East and Highlands. The ITV network also developed governing structures which institutionalised territorial representation – given the regional structure of the independent network, this was perhaps unavoidable. There were Scottish, Welsh and Northern Irish representatives on the organisation's central executive (the Independent Television Commission), playing a similar representative role to the BBC's lay national governors, in addition to a Scottish committee of the ITC which was first established in 1957 (McDowell, 1992: p. 127). Such structures contrast with later developments in independent television such as the establishment of Channel Four and Channel Five as non-territorial UK-wide TV stations.

STV is the most prominent of the television companies in Scotland. It covers the bulk of central Scotland and, as a company, branched out as the Scottish Media Group. It acquired control of *The Herald* and the *Evening Times*, followed by Grampian TV and Ginger Media. Thus, it has expanded from being TV company into a modest media empire, an expansion all the more ironic given that STV only paid £2,000 to renew its franchise in 1991. However, this expansion has brought problems. The merger with Grampian brought economies of scale to advertising and production, but also criticism related to the deterioration of distinctive regional programming in the North East. Senior executives from the Scottish Media Group and Grampian TV were called before the Scottish Parliament's Education, Culture and Sport Committee in March 2000 and were subjected to intense questioning from all parties, especially from North East MSPs.[1] Subsequently, Grampian was strongly criticised by the Independent Television Commission (ITC) for its performance in 1999. The ITC investigated the operation of the Grampian licence following complaints from MPs, MSPs and the broadcasting unions, and pressured Grampian into producing and airing more of its own programmes, maintaining its own production facilities to support its output, and increasing its Gaelic output.[2] Significantly, the

ITC pledged to monitor Grampian's future performance in terms of its capacity to fulfil its obligations as a regional broadcaster.

In the sphere of news and current affairs, both STV and Grampian provide coverage of Scottish politics. STV has a small but able team of political journalists, most notably Fiona Ross and Bernard Ponsonby. Besides servicing *Scotland Today*, the half-hour Scottish news bulletin on STV, and other STV news programmes, the political journalists and correspondents also provide material for STV's main political programme, *Platform*, and the lighter current affairs and entertainment programme, *Seven Days*. Grampian TV produces *A Week in Politics* and *Crossfire*, in addition to political coverage for *North Tonight* and *Grampian Weekend* on Sundays. Both TV stations also produce Gaelic programmes, with STV making around twenty-six hours a year and Grampian making about forty-six hours a year.

– NATIONAL AND LOCAL RADIO –

Radio is also a significant feature of the electronic media in Scotland, through both BBC Radio Scotland and independent radio companies, many of which are owned by Scottish Radio Holdings. Significantly, through changes to radio franchising in recent years, the number of local, regional and national radio stations in Scotland has grown. Not only does BBC Radio Scotland provide local services, but there are two channels of Radio Tay, Radio Forth, Radio Clyde and North Sound, in addition to Central FM, Scot FM, Westsound FM, Moray fifth, Kingdom FM, Borders, Beat 106 and QFM. BBC Radio Scotland may be the only station that provides sustained and detailed current affairs coverage, but other radio stations provide important arenas for political debate. Like the local newspapers discussed above, local radio has a function as the site of local political debates for MPs, MSPs, councillors, pressure groups and community organisations. Phone-ins, news programmes and election coverage are all provided on local radio at various times.

– THE MEDIA AND THE SCOTTISH ELECTION OF 1999 –

The first Scottish election was extensively covered by the media in Scotland. Usually, general elections mix Scottish and UK issues and coverage, but the stand-alone nature of the Scottish elections allowed a more focused approach to the election by the Scottish media, as well as encouraging substantial coverage from the rest of the UK and the international media. Television, radio and newspapers all gave a prominent role to the election in their news and current affairs coverage. Newspapers dealt with the election on a daily basis, with special election pages, analysis of issues and constituency profiles. The media also followed most staged aspects of the campaign such as party press conferences, manifesto launch and photo-opportunities. Television coverage of the campaign was particularly strong. BBC Scotland spent around £1.8 million on the Scottish election, with TV programmes such as *Campaign 99*, a special Scottish *Panorama*, *Cross-Examination* and *From Here to Holyrood*, in addition to the *Vote 99* election night special. Radio Scotland broadcast *Select Committee*, in which party figures were questioned by their opponents as well as a number of *Hustings 99* programmes across Scotland, and a number of special election phone-ins for *Now You're Talking*. STV and Grampian produced *Vote 99* and *Crossfire*. The extent of the coverage was such that there was an election special on at least one channel, usually the BBC, every night for the last two weeks of the campaign.

The election campaign also received prominent coverage on the two main evening news programmes, BBC's *Reporting Scotland* and STV's *Scotland Today*. On most evenings during the election, these programmes led with the campaign itself or with political issues related to the election. For example, both BBC and STV led with the manifesto launches by the SNP and Conservatives on 8 April 1999, By contrast, Labour's manifesto launches was fourth on the running order on STV and third on BBC on 12 April. STV and BBC also led with coverage of the STUC conference which featured criticism of Labour's proposals for the Private Finance Initiative on 19 April. The SNP faced similar discomfort when each news programme led with the fall in support for the party in opinion polls on 22 April. *Scotland Today* led with this story for eight minutes, and included an interview with Alex Salmond.

Issues of relevance to the election also gained prominent coverage such as the closure of the Kvaerner shipyard in Govan on *Scotland Today* and the effect of the trade war over bananas on the cashmere industry in the Borders on *Reporting Scotland* on 9 April. The issues covered by the media during the campaign occasionally favoured 'hot topics' rather than particularly relevant issues. For example, one of STV's *Vote 99* debates featured extensive discussion of the war in Kosovo and Economic and Monetary Union. Around half of the BBC's one-hour programme, *From Here to Holyrood*, featured a discussion on the war in Kosovo. These issues had some relevance to the election campaign but absolutely none to the Scottish Parliament itself, and they illustrated the ease with which topical issues could dominate election coverage to the exclusion of all else.

The political parties adopted a range of approaches to the media and campaigning at the first Scottish election, and they spent considerable amounts of money on media and advertising, with varying results. The Tories spent money on billboards and newspaper advertising, as did Labour. The SNP paid for leaflets within the main newspapers rather than meet the cost of full adverts within the press. The Liberal Democrats also had a modest campaigns budget which was not used for much of the mass media advertising employed by the other parties. During the campaign, the parties' slickness in relation to the media sometimes faltered, and despite careful media strategies, staging of press conferences and attention to public relations, things did go wrong. New Labour's professional approach to communications was somewhat lacking when it came to organising a press conference on investment in sport with an SNP-supporting Scottish football manager, Craig Brown. The Conservatives managed to organise a press conference for William Hague at Hampden Park in Glasgow at which the UK Conservative leader was roundly booed by workmen at the stadium – certainly an arresting media image of modern Scottish Conservatism at the time when the party sought to wrap itself in the saltire. The SNP spent thousands of pounds on a press conference suite in Edinburgh only to abandon press conferences late in the campaign and launch its own expensive daily newspaper, *Scotland's Voice*.

– THE MEDIA AND THE SCOTTISH PARLIAMENT –

Traditionally, the media has been regarded as a critical fourth estate in modern democracies, separate from church and state and capable of independent and critical analyses of politics and society. Certainly, in relation to the Scottish Parliament, the media has fulfilled this critical function, although its criticism has often been exaggerated. Indeed, certain sections of the media seemed to portray an almost exclusively negative image of the Scottish Parliament that concentrated on negative stories, scandals and political divisions within the Parliament, Executive and the parties. 'Knocking copy' epitomised some media coverage of the Parliament, for example, the holiday arrangements for MSPs over the summer of 1999 were greeted with a front-page story in *The Sun* titled 'You Skivers' on 24 June 1999, and the *Daily Record* followed suit on the same day with 'Time Off For Bad Behaviour'. Subsequent newspaper treatment of the Parliament followed a similar tone, particularly in the *Daily Record* (see Case study 13). Such criticism led the Parliament's Presiding Officer, David Steel, to make a formal complaint to the Press Complaints Commission in September 1999.[3] Much criticism of the Parliament and Executive – which were mostly indistinguishable – related to the Parliament's organisational teething problems in May–July 1999, but it continued with the debate over

Lobbygate, the section 2a/28 issue and many other issues (MacWhirter, 2000; Schlesinger, 2000). Despite the negativity, it would be fair to say that media coverage of the Scottish Parliament was extensive in 1999–2000. Most coverage was devoted to the Scottish Executive, party leaders and spokespersons, and events such as Scottish Executive questions. Parliamentary committees occasionally gained coverage with high-profile meetings such as questioning of ministers. However, the nature of the coverage was extremely mixed. The quality press tended to present factual analysis, while the tabloids were able to rely on dramatic events in the Parliament to provide some sensational coverage of the new politics in action

---

Case study 13 The *Daily Record*

The *Daily Record* has been a Labour-supporting newspaper for decades. It gave extensive coverage and editorial space to Labour at the 1997 and 1999 elections and also played a substantial role in supporting the Yes campaign at the 1997 devolution referendum (Denver, Mitchell, Pattie and Bochel, 2000). However, since the 1999 election the *Daily Record* has turned into one of the sternest critics of the Executive and Parliament. Its coverage of the Parliament's opening ceremony on 1 July 1999 – 'Hooray for Holyrood', with eight pages of pictures and positive coverage[4] – can be contrasted with the many negative stories that followed. The adverserial relationship between the *Daily Record* and the Scottish Executive was at its highest over the section 2a/28 issue, and it gave extensive coverage and support to the *Keep the Clause* campaign. The newspaper regularly denounced ministers over the Executive's position, provided space for special letters page features on section 2a/28,[5] commissioned its own poll to demonstrate support for keeping the clause,[6] and published the Keep the Clause petition on a number of occasions alongside encouragements to its readers to get behind the campaign.[7] The *Daily Record* shaped its attacks to reflect its support for Labour, stating in one editorial that 'allowing the promotion of homosexuality in schools is not what the loyal Labour rank and file want or expect'.[8] The party thus attacked Labour, while still supporting it, and carefully used its agenda-setting role within the media to align itself with a high-profile political campaign that had huge interest within its readership – clever positioning for a tabloid and also important in retaining readers against the market penetration of *The Sun*.

– CONCLUSION –

The media, especially the press, is a distinctive aspect of Scottish life that continues to function as one of the main arenas of politics in Scotland. It is central to political parties, the Executive and the Parliament both as a medium for communication and as a critical forum for political discussion. On occasions, this critical function has been exaggerated, leading to tensions between some newspapers and the new political institutions, tensions that threatened to sever some of the partisan links between newspapers and the parties. However, the media's response to the Parliament was extensive in its first year of existence, and to the annoyance of Scottish MPs, coverage of events on the Mound eclipsed coverage of politics at Westminster. While the role of the press as a distinctive Scottish institution continued post-devolution, the role of broadcasting was more variable. The case of *Newsnight Scotland* and the BBC's attitude to the provision of a distinctive Scottish news bulletin will remain high on the political agenda as the BBC and other UK institutions struggle to cope with the post-devolution environment.

– NOTES –

1. Education, Culture and Sport Committee, *Official Report*, 1 March 2000.
2. Independent Television Commission, *Grampian Complaint*, news release, 10 May 2000.
3. Scottish Parliament, news release, 6 September 1999.
4. *The Daily Record*, 1 July 1999, pp 6–7, and 2 July 1999, pp. 1–8.
5. *The Daily Record*, 20 January and 24 January 2000.
6. *The Daily Record*, '2–1 poll against gay sex lessons', 19 January 2000, p. 1.
7. *The Daily Record*, 22 January 2000, p. 9, 27 January 2000, p. 11, and 28 January 2000, p. 9.
8. *The Daily Record*, 20 January 2000, p. 8.

CHAPTER 12

Beyond the Mound:
local government and Scottish politics

– INTRODUCTION –

Scottish local government has been subject to a continuous process of reform since the 1970s. Structurally, it has experienced three different models of local government since the early 1970s, with the counties and burghs giving way to the two-tier system of regional and district councils in 1974–5 (in addition to the special arrangements for the islands councils of Orkney, Shetland and the Western Isles), before the 1995 reorganisation of local government which instituted single-tier authorities. Financially, Scottish local government has also undergone considerable change, with three different financing regimes rates, poll tax and the council tax – since the 1970s – in addition to a raft of central financial controls on local government. Scottish local government has also experienced considerable changes in relation to political control as a result of three main factors: the decline of the Conservative Party in local elections, the decline of independents in local government in key areas, and Labour's domination of local elections and political control from the 1980s onwards. Finally, there is the prospect of change associated with the new Scottish Parliament, evident in the work of the McIntosh Commission on Local Government and the Scottish Parliament, the Kerley Report on electoral reform, and evolving relations between the Scottish Parliament and Scottish local authorities. This chapter considers each of these developments in addition to the modernisation of local government through its efforts to encourage citizen participation and decentralisation.

– THE STRUCTURE OF LOCAL GOVERNMENT –

The structure of local government has changed substantially in recent years. While Scottish local government seems to have settled into a relatively tidy system of unitary authorities following the merger of regional and district councils, the new system contains significant complexities. The 1995 reforms may have established a unitary system of local government but they did not impose a system with unitary characteristics. The size of the post-1995 authorities in terms of population (see Table 12.1), territory and tax base were all different and the councils themselves are internally quite distinctive. For instance, the thirty-two councils can be subdivided into various types: the three distinctive island councils of Orkney, Shetland and the Western Isles; other unitary authorities based on former regions such as Dumfries and Galloway, Fife, Highland and Scottish Borders; authorities almost completely based on former district councils such as Argyll and Bute, Dundee, Glasgow, Perthshire and Kinross, Stirling and West Lothian; and councils based on amalgamations of former councils such as Aberdeenshire, East Ayrshire, North Lanarkshire and South Lanarkshire. Reorganisation brought about different challenges for each of these groups of councils.

Table 12.1 Scottish local authorities by population

Local authority	Population
Aberdeen	125,000
Aberdeenshire	227,430
Angus	110,230
Argyll and Bute	90,550
Clackmannan	48,810
Dumfries and Galloway	147,300
Dundee	153,710
East Ayrshire	123,820
East Dunbartonshire	110,679
East Lothian	89,000
East Renfrewshire	88,644
Edinburgh	450,000
Falkirk	143,040
Fife	348,400
Glasgow	611,600
Highland	208,600
Inverclyde	86,500
Midlothian	80,206
Moray	86,030
North Ayrshire	139,780
North Lanarkshire	326,520
Perthshire and Kinross	133,250
Renfrewshire	178,260
Scottish Borders	106,100
South Ayrshire	114,870

South Lanarkshire	307,400
Stirling	83,580
West Dunbartonshire	95,690
West Lothian	147,870
Orkney	19,840
Shetland	22,757
Western Isles	28,880

Source: Population figures from *Municipal Yearbook 1999*

Local government reorganisation in 1995 also had the effect of making local government structurally more complex in Scotland in two different ways. First, the abolition of the regions and the transfer of their powers to smaller authorities necessitated the creation of joint arrangements between authorities in some public services, particularly those which involved strategic functions or cross-authority services. This development manifested itself in the establishment of a considerable number of joint boards between authorities to recreate a regional, cross-authority dimension to council decisionmaking to sit alongside existing cross-authority structures such as the police and fire boards. Such boards make sense functionally in order to ensure adequate service delivery, but they blur democratic accountability as a council's involvement in a joint arrangement is seldom subject to public scrutiny, and parties tend to concentrate on what policies they will pursue when in control of an authority rather than the joint policies that will be instituted in conjunction with adjacent authorities. In addition, joint arrangements can be seen to disadvantage smaller and weaker authorities by allowing larger councils to dominate boards by dint of their larger resources, population and council tax bases (Kerley and Orr, 1993).

Second, the creation of new authorities based upon former regional councils in Dumfries and Galloway, Fife, Highland and Scottish Borders was accompanied by internal decentralisation initiatives within the new councils. For instance, the new Dumfries and Galloway authority replaced four district councils: Annandale and Eskdale, Nithsdale, Stewartry and Wigtown. In order to prevent the new arrangements appearing as a measure of centralisation within the region, with decisionmaking concentrated in one authority rather than more locally dispersed as under the pre-1995 structure, the new council established eight area committees of elected councillors to take decisionmaking closer to the localities. These committees meet monthly to identify local issues and problems, monitor service delivery, spend locally-designated budgets and generally monitor council activity in the area. Highland Council followed a similar practice, establishing eight area committees to replace the eight former district councils within the region, and this arrangement enabled the creation of area management offices and managers to oversee local service delivery.

– THE ISLANDS COUNCILS –

The existence of islands councils, which have enjoyed different powers from other local authorities, has added to the diversity of Scottish local government. Between 1975 and 1995, the Orkney, Shetland and Western Isles councils were the only unitary authorities in Scotland, as a result of their distinctive economic and geographical status. Although these councils have become a permanent fixture in Scottish local government, their establishment was certainly not a forgone conclusion of local government reorganisation in the 1970s. The Royal Commission on Local Government initially suggested that Orkney and Shetland be amalgamated into one large Highlands and Islands region, although this was later overturned to allow each council to enjoy special status as an individual council (Macartney 1985: 10). This status was significant because it allowed the two Northern councils to have access to oil revenues in their areas, which was of considerable benefit to local government services. The case of the Western Isles council was entirely different. While Orkney and Shetland had their own councils before reorganisation, the Western Isles was actually split, with Lewis part of the county of Ross and Cromarty while the rest of the isles were part of Inverness (Macartney, 1985: p. 11). The cultural as well as the geographical distinctiveness of the Western Isles certainly played a part in its designation as a unit of local government. The local government reorganisation of the 1990s brought the three islands councils more into line with other authorities – they are no longer the sole all-purpose councils – but they still remain distinctive.

Both Orkney and Shetland experienced the rise of political movements supporting greater autonomy for the islands in the 1980s, as a consequence of the devolution debate in the 1970s and the prospects for island autonomy within Scotland or the UK in line with the Faroes. The Shetland Movement was established in 1977 as a loose pressure group supporting the broad goal of more autonomy for Shetland. It was not hostile to Scottish devolution and its initial strategy consisted of seeking to influence existing Shetland councillors rather than challenging them at elections. Initially, the Shetland Movement downplayed the autonomy issue, but gradually it became more vocal and populist in its demands for more powers for Shetland. The movement's organisers became more confident about island autonomy following their tour of Shetland in 1979, and public support for Shetland autonomy was strong enough for the movement to come out in favour of Shetland Home Rule in 1980 (Dowle, 1980: p. 207). Subsequently, the movement began to adopt a more electoral strategy to pursue its aims, and decided to contest council elections from 1982 onwards: a strategy which was somewhat confused by the fact that twelve of the twenty five Shetland councillors at the time were already supporters of the movement.

The high point for the Shetland Movement came in 1987, when it combined with the Orkney Movement to contest the Westminster elections. The movements' joint candidate, John Goodlad, gained a respectable 15 per cent in a contest in which the SNP stood aside on behalf of the islands' autonomists. The Orkney Movement was founded in 1980 and adopted a much more directly political strategy in its early days. It decided to contest the council elections in 1982 and was successful in electing Spencer Rosie as the first non-independent councillor on Orkney Isles Council. However, the fortress of the organisation have fluctuated since then, with little electoral success. Neither it nor the Shetland Movement contested the Scottish elections in 1999 either on the FPTP or list sections, and their absence offered, a notable contrast to new regional parties such as the Highlands and Islands Alliance. However, as both organisations were movements and pressure groups rather than simply parties, their political strategies and influence extended beyond elections. Indeed, there was little point in seeking to use the electoral process to challenge existing islands representatives as they were also supporters of islands autonomy. Much of the isles' arguments are with Edinburgh and London, not with local politicians.

– LOCAL GOVERNMENT FINANCE –

Local government finance has been an issue of controversy for many years. The economic and political implications of local financial systems have engendered a variety of different financing schemes for councils over the past thirty years, including the infamous poll tax. The current financing system, the council tax, was introduced to replace the poll tax in the early 1990s. It operates through each council setting a council tax rate based on banding of property values, with households rather than individuals responsible for paying the tax according to their property value. The council tax level is determined by local authorities on an annual basis within budgetary guidelines laid down by the Scottish Executive (previously by the Scottish Office). However, the operation of the council tax is only one aspect of local government finance, much of which is extremely obscure to the public. For example, it has been estimated that only 20 per cent of council spending is financed by the council tax, meaning that 80 per cent comes from a complicated system of central government funding formulae (Commission on Local Government and the Scottish Parliament, 1999: p. 18), which ensures that most council spending is centrally financed (see Table 12.2). As local government is a devolved power, the Scottish Executive is able to set financial limits on local authority budgets to constrain their budgets and tax-raising abilities through legislation established by the Conservatives. In addition, the Scottish Executive controls the business rate through the mechanism of the uniform business rate.

Table 12.2 Government-supported local authority expenditure 1998–9

Service	£m
Education	2,436.8
Social work	1,049.7
Other services	616.7
Police	691
Roads and transport	322.5
Leisure and recreation	230.6
Fire	170
Capital financing	728.9
Total	6,246.2

Source: Scottish Executive (2000), *Investing in You: the Annual Report of the Scottish Executive*

Scottish Executive limits on local spending have been one constraint on local autonomy and service provision in recent years, but two other factors are relevant. First, the UK government's decisions to stick to Conservative spending guidelines after the 1997 election and the Scottish Office/Scottish Executive decision to allocate Scottish spending away from local government towards health and education brought about a deterioration in service provision within Scotland's councils. Second, the local government reorganisation of 1995 established smaller authorities which lacked economies of scale and had to cover the costs of reorganisation at a time of fiscal stress. In particular, the abolition of the larger, redistributive regional councils, which enjoyed large tax bases and economies of scale, had considerable impact on the single-tier authorities created after 1995. These changes led to substantial financial problems for most local authorities in their annual budgetary cycle, resulting in increases in council tax levels and cuts in local services, especially in Glasgow (Mair, 2000). The fact that most Scottish local authorities are Labour, presided over by a Labour administration at Westminster and a Labour-led coalition in Edinburgh, did not improve the financial situation of Scotland's local authorities from 1997–

2000, although some aspects of local government finance were under review when this book was completed. The Scottish Executive established a strategic working group with the Convention of Scottish Local Authorities (COSLA) to come up with proposals for three-year budgets for each local authority; simplified arrangements for distributing resources between authorities; and an approach to agreeing outcomes which reconsiders the scale of hypothecation (which involves the levying of taxes for specific purposes) and ring-fencing of local government resources.[1] Despite this, both the Commission on Local Government and the Scottish Parliament and the Local Government Committee of the Parliament called for an independent review of local government finance.

– POLITICAL CONTROL OF LOCAL AUTHORITIES –

Patterns of political control in Scotland's local authorities have undergone considerable change over the past thirty years. First, local government became more partisan. The number of authorities run by independents declined, largely through local government reorganisation and the popularity of the parties. Before reorganisation in 1995, independents controlled three district councils in Borders, four in Dumfries and Galloway, and eight in Highland, in addition to the regional councils for these areas. The demise of these authorities not only reduced the importance of the independents, it, also contributed to Labour's dominance of Scotland's councils and COSLA. Second, the Conservatives declined markedly as an electoral force at local elections to be eradicated from many councils and replaced by all other parties (see Table 12.3). Despite an increase in support in some areas in 1999, the Conservatives remain a marginal force in Scottish local government. They control no local authorities and have experienced an absolute decline in their share of the vote, number of councillors and control of councils since the 1970s. Formerly, the Tories controlled Angus, Edinburgh, Stirling, Perth and Kinross, and the former districts of Kyle and Carrick and Berwickshire and even had a decent enough showing in the former regional councils to control Grampian and Tayside in the 1980s and run Lothian from 1982–6 in coalition with the Liberals. The party was usually third in district elections behind Labour and the independents until 1984, but since then has been eclipsed by the SNP.

Labour has been the most consistent performer in Scottish local elections, in terms of winning seats and controlling councils. It benefitted from the FPTP electoral system and did not suffer from the 1995 reorganisation of local government which removed the regional councils. At the 1999 election, Labour emerged as the strongest party in local government, despite slipping back in key areas. The party lost ground to the SNP in Clackmannanshire, Dundee and East Ayrshire, to the Conservatives in Stirling and South Ayrshire, and to the Liberal Democrats in East Dunbartonshire (Denver and Bochel, 2000). Finally, Labour suffered in Falkirk through the combined impact of the SNP and a group of former members who were elected as independents following the dispute over Denis Canavan's failure to be selected as a Labour candidate for the Scottish Parliament. However, despite losing control of five councils, Labour still dominated Scottish local government.

Table 12.3 Party performance at local elections 1974–99

Election	Lab		Con		SNP		Lib/Lib Dem	
	Votes Seats (%)		Votes Seats (%)		Votes Seats (%)		Votes Seats (%)	
Regional 1974	38.5	72	28.6	112	12.6	18	5.1	11
Regional 1978	39.6	177	30.3	136	20.9	18	2.3	6
Regional 1982	37.6	186	25.1	119	13.4	23	18.1	25
Regional 1986	43.9	223	16.9	65	18.2	36	15.1	40
Regional 1990	42.7	233	19.6	52	21.8	42	8.7	40
Regional 1994	41.8	220	13.7	31	26.8	73	12	60
District 1974	38.4	428	26.8	241	12.4	62	5.0	17
District 1977	31.6	299	27.2	277	24.2	170	4.0	31
District 1980	45.4	494	24.1	229	15.5	54	6.2	40
District 1984	45.7	545	21.4	189	11.7	59	12.8	78
District 1988	42.6	553	19.4	162	21.3	113	8.4	84
District 1992	34.1	468	23.2	204	24.3	150	9.5	94
Unitary 1995	43.6	613	11.5	82	26.1	181	9.8	121
Unitary 1999	36.6	545	13.7	108	28.9	201	13.6	148

The other parties have enjoyed mixed fortunes in local elections. The SNP has had sporadic success in some councils, but consistent success only in Angus. It has occasionally challenged for or won control in Clackmannanshire, Cumbernauld, Falkirk, Moray, Perth and Kinross, Renfrewshire and West Lothian, before and after reorganisation, but its performance has generally been inconsistent. The Liberal Democrats have had a similarly patchy record in local elections. Before reorganisation, they only controlled North East Fife council and found that their areas of support coincided with areas of independent support in the Highlands and Borders, thus restricting the party's performance at local elections. However, in the 1999 elections, the Liberal Democrats consolidated their position as the main opposition party in Aberdeen, Borders, Edinburgh, East Dunbartonshire, Fife and Inverclyde, in addition to making a strong showing in Aberdeenshire, where they emerged as the largest party. Of course, political control will alter markedly in many authorities if the Scottish Executive introduces a more proportional electoral system for local elections (see below).

THE INDEPENDENT TRADITION IN SCOTTISH LOCAL GOVERNMENT

The existence of a substantial block of councillors and councils controlled by independents rather than political parties remains a distinctive aspect of Scottish local government, albeit to a lesser degree than previously. Certainly, the period since the reform of local government in 1975 saw a reduction in the number of independent councils and councillors, and most local authorities were subject to creeping politicisation which had a homogenising impact on the political control of Scottish local government. The independent tradition made a significant contribution to the internal differentiation of Scottish local government, especially in offering clear contrasts between rural and urban areas. Its contribution to the diversity of local government had implications for the reform efforts associated with the Scottish Executive and McIntosh Commission on Local Government and the Scottish Parliament (see below), as the existence of independents created difficulties for proposals to adopt PR for council elections and new political management arrangements (Orkney Islands Council, 1999).

The decline of the independent tradition is evident from consideration of the number of independent councillors elected over successive elections (see Table 12.4), the changing number of local authorities under independent control, and the consequent increase in the number of party political councillors and councils in rural areas. Election results for the two-tier system of regional and district councils which existed from 1974 to 1994 clearly indicate the decrease in the role of the independents in local government. In 1974, 28 per cent of local authority candidates were independents compared to 13 per cent in 1994. Similarly, while independents controlled 33 per cent of council seats in 1974, this figure had declined to 21 per cent by 1994 (Bochel and Bochel, 1998: p. 30). In addition, the period from 1974 to 1994 saw a substantial decline in support for independents in traditional non-partisan regions such as Borders, Dumfries and Galloway and Highland. For example, when comparing regional council election results in these three regions in 1974 and 1994, Denver and Bochel calculated that the combined support for independents had declined from 69 per cent and eighty-three seats in

1974 to 42 per cent and fifty-seven seats at the last regional elections in 1994 (Denver and Bochel, 1994: p. 78).

Table 12.4 The independent tradition in Scottish local government 1974–99

Election	Vote %	Seats
Regional 1974	12.4	114
Regional 1978	4.9	89
Regional 1982	5.1	87
Regional 1986	4.8	79
Regional 1990	4.5	73
Regional 1994	4.2	65
District 1974	14.1	345
District 1977	9.8	318
District 1980	6.7	289
District 1984	6.8	267
District 1988	6.4	231
District 1992	7.4	228
Unitary 1995	7.7	155
Unitary 1999	11.8	135

Indeed, by 1994, it was determined that both Borders and Dumfries and Galloway had largely lost their independent tradition as parties gained the upper hand. While 55.2 per cent of voters supported independent candidates in Highland region in 1994, support for independents in Borders had slipped to only 32.7 per cent, and to 31.6 per cent in Dumfries and Galloway (Denver and Bochel, 1994: p. 74). The extent of the decline is evident in the fact that independents gained 52.2 per cent of the vote at the regional elections in Border in 1974 and even 56.7 per cent in 1986, while independents gained a staggering 81.7 per cent in Dumfries and Galloway in 1974 (Parry, 1988: p. 130). In addition, outside these three non-partisan regions, electoral support for independents was substantially reduced, particularly in Grampian and Tayside which had previously been characterised by a sizeable tradition of independent voting (see Table 12.5).

The reorganisation of local government in 1995 also removed a large number of district councils formerly controlled by independents in the three main non-partisan regions of Borders, Dumfries and Galloway and Highland. For example, independents controlled fourteen district councils following the 1992 elections and remained the largest party in three councils (Bochel and Denver, 1993: p. 118), many of which were districts within the three non-partisan regions. Following local government reorganisation in 1995 and the replacement of districts by larger authorities in the non-partisan regions, independents controlled only two councils – Argyll and Bute and Highland – and were in coalition with the Liberal Democrats in Aberdeenshire and Border and part of a four-party administration in Dumfries and Galloway. Outside these five councils, there was little electoral support for independents.

Table 12.5 Support for independent candidates at regional elections

	1974 (%)	1978 (%)	1982 (%)	1986 (%)	1990 (%)	1994 (%)
Borders	52.2	52.7	34.7	56.7	32.2	32.7
Central	10.5	5.1	3.9	1.1	2.3	5
Dumfries and Galloway	81.7	67.4	51.1	45.7	42.4	22.1
Fife	7.8	3.6	5.9	1.6	2.3	2.7
Grampian	24.5	7.0	3.9	5.6	7.4	2.2
Highland	72.1	83.4	70.9	73	59.1	55.2
Lothian	3.5	1.5	0.7	0.8	0.1	0.1
Strathclyde	4.9	0.7	1.6	1.8	1.0	1.8
Tayside	19.9	3.4	4.6	2.7	1.2	1.7

Sources: Richard Parry, *Scottish Political Facts* (1988: pp. 130–1) and David Denver and John Bochel (1994: 74)

In 1999, the situation for independent councillors declined further, perhaps because of the politicisation of the council elections through their connection to the Scottish Parliament elections. However, as indicated above, the partisan challenge to the independents has been a trend since the 1970s.

In 1999 the contest between parties and independents continued with Conservative, Labour and Liberal Democrat growth in Aberdeenshire and the Scottish Borders at the expense of independents; SNP and Liberal Democrat growth in Argyll and Bute at the expense of the independents; Conservative and SNP success in Dumfries and Galloway over the independents; and Conservative, Labour and Liberal Democrat success in Highland over the independents and the SNP. In contrast, Moray was one case in which independents gained in dramatic fashion over the SNP, to make the council independent-controlled in 1999 (see Table 12.6).

The position of the independents was also undermined to some extent in Scotland's islands councils, with Labour as the sole party contesting and winning seats in the Western Isles against the independents in 1994, and Labour, Liberal Democrats and Shetland Movement councillors challenging independents on Shetland council to win ten of the twenty-six council seats. In 1999, the Liberal Democrats achieved a measure of success in

Shetland at the expense of the independents and the Shetland Movement; while the Western Isles saw a small increase in support and councillors for Labour and the SNP over the independents. However, in Orkney the position of the independents and the parties remained the same in 1999 as in 1994, with all seats and nearly all votes won by independents.

Table 12.6 Support for independent candidates 1995–9

Mainland councils	1995		1999	
	Votes (%)	Seats	Votes (%)	Seats
Aberdeenshire	26	13	14	10
Argyll and Bute	50	21	43	20
Dumfries and Galloway	39	28	25	13
Highland	62	49	55	48
Moray	20	2	33	13
Scottish Borders	40	29	31	14
Island councils	**1994**		**1999**	
	Votes (%)	Seats	Votes (%)	Seats
Orkney	100	26	99.8	21
Shetland	71.4	15	71	13
Western Isles	89.8	24	74	22

– Devolution and local government –

The establishment of a Scottish Parliament has had a considerable impact upon the role and functions of local government. Under the Scotland Act 1998, the new Parliament is responsible for local government, which itself is responsible for a large number of issues of concern to the Scottish Parliament. The new Parliament will control local government finance, structure, elections, and so on, and also key policy areas such as education, environment, housing, transport, planning, police and fire service, social work and a host of smaller council responsibilities contained in the White Paper, *Scotland's Parliament* (Scottish Office, 1997: pp. 3–6). Significantly, the Parliament's powers extend into almost every area of local government, with few local powers left in the hands of Westminster through the reserved powers of Schedule 5. Broad policies developed at the Scottish Parliament in relation to economic development, training, inward investment and the natural heritage, will also be policy areas with implications for local authorities. The Scottish Parliament also impacts upon more recent local government policy interests such as Europe and involvement in European policymaking, and there is an awareness that local authorities must share their EU role with the Parliament in the future (COSLA, 1998).

Essentially, two opposing views can be adopted in relation to the impact of devolution on Scotland's councils: that devolution undermines local government, and that it aids local government.

Devolution undermines local government

Critics of devolution have often asserted that devolution merely involved swapping centralisation from London for centralisation from Edinburgh, with a Scottish Parliament representing the economic and political interests of the central belt and the activities of the Parliament limiting the autonomy of local government. Such views were particularly evident at the devolution referendum in 1979, and to a lesser extent in 1997. In addition, there is an assumption that the Scottish Parliament will operate as an active, interventionist legislature in those policy areas within its domain. Given its legislative focus on domestic Scottish issues and its inability to deal with large socio-economic and financial issues, the parliament will be left to concentrate on issues such as education and housing which are key local government functions. The Parliament will flex its muscles by passing detailed legislation that allows limited scope for local authorities, ushering in a new relationship in which local councils are seen to act merely as the implementation agencies of the Scottish Parliament, which designs policy in a top-down direction. There is also some potential for the Scottish Executive and MSPs to adopt a highly interventionist approach to local government, evident in the former Secretary of State's attempts to close down the Direct Labour organisations of East Ayrshire and North Lanarkshire councils in 1998. These organisations were responsible for local authority construction and maintenance, but had run into severe financial deficits at a time when government was seeking to limit local government spending and demonstrate its financial probity. The deficits were made worse by the fact that they involved Labour-controlled authorities, being disciplined by a Labour government. Although the DLOs were threatened with closure, new financial management measures were introduced. All in all, the exercise was severely embarrassing to Labour.

Devolution aids local government

There is scope for the Scottish Parliament to develop a more constructive relationship with local authorities than has existed in recent years. Rather than taking powers from councils, there are opportunities for the Scottish Parliament to strengthen local authorities by transferring powers to councils by reallocating functions previously transferred to quangos. Thus Scottish Homes' powers over housing, the economic development and training functions of the local enterprise councils (LECs) and the three regional water boards' control over water and sewerage services could all be candidates for strengthening the role of local government. Similarly, there is scope for the Parliament to seek to enhance local government representation on various quangos in an attempt to make some bodies more accountable to and representative of the local communities they seek to serve (Geddes, 1996). The fact that many MSPs will have a local authority background, will assist the Parliament's work in relation to local government, providing a pool of experienced legislators with a familiarity and commitment to the role of the councils. Similarly, the Parliament has the opportunity to redefine central-local relations in Scotland in a more constructive manner than in the past.

Aspects of each of these contrasting scenarios for Scotland's councils post-devolution will probably come to the fore in the new Scotland, and aspects of each will be evident in the future development of Scotland's councils. The relationship between the Scottish Parliament and local government will be an evolving one, in which the role of local government is in flux as a result of devolution and the review of local government by the McIntosh Commission. However, the efforts of some councils to experiment with citizen participation as well as to shed or alter major functions, such as Glasgow City Council's attempts to transfer its housing stock out of council control, mean that councils are undergoing a process of transformation aside from the devolution process.

LOCAL GOVERNMENT AND THE SCOTTISH CONSTITUTIONAL CONVENTION

The manner in which devolution was designed in the 1990s sought to involve local authorities and address the concerns of councils in relation to the design of a Scottish Parliament. Indeed, the extent to which supporters of constitutional change were able to construct a pro-devolution consensus within local government was impressive, particularly as local authorities could be seen as one of the big losers of the devolution process. Local government involvement in the devolution debate was substantially aided by the decline of Conservative councillors and councils, as well as changing attitudes to devolution within Labour and its local authority members. Equally important was the ability of the pro-devolution forces to involve independent councils in the devolution debate and convince them of the merits of constitutional change, which effectively moved the rural areas and island communities into the Home Rule camp. One mechanism for achieving this end was the Scottish Constitutional Convention 1989–95, whose secretariat was hosted by COSLA in Edinburgh.

The Convention involved a range of different parties and interests from across Scotland (Lynch, 1996). It included representatives from the pre-1995 local authorities such as Orkney Islands Council, Shetland Islands Council, Borders Regional Council, Dumfries and Galloway Regional Council, Grampian Regional Council, Highland Regional Council, Annandale and Eskdale District Council, Nairn District Council, Nithsdale District Council and Sutherland District Council. In addition, Gaelic organisations *An Comunn Gaedhealach* and *Comunn Na Gaedhlig* and a representative of the Orkney and Shetland Movements were involved in its work. The Convention involved local authorities in considering proposals for devolution in specific areas such as the islands councils as well as more general discussions about finance and the Parliament's powers (Scottish Constitutional Convention, 1995: p. 11). The extent of Liberal Democrat participation in the Convention as the Westminster representatives of rural Scotland – Argyll, Caithness and Sutherland, Gordon and Orkney and Shetland to name a few – was significant in terms of the final Convention agreement, and in relation to participation in and endorsement of the Convention's proposals by non-urban Scotland.

Case study 14 Devolution and Orkney and Shetland

Scottish devolution has presented difficulties for Orkney and Shetland. On the one hand, devolution was seen to have the potential to limit the post-reorganisation autonomy of the islands councils, particularly in the area of oil revenues. On the other hand, there was some perception that devolution could assist the islands' autonomous status. Among the public, there was lukewarm support for devolution, evident in the 1979 referendum results in which only 27.9 per cent in Orkney and 27.1 per cent in Shetland voted Yes. By 1997, this position had largely changed, with Yes votes of 57.3 per cent and 62.4 per cent respectively, but Orkney opposed tax powers for the Scottish Parliament and also recorded the lowest Yes vote on the first question. Opinion changed, but there remained a mood of scepticism towards Scottish devolution that was not reflected across other parts of Scotland. The Orkney Isles council convenor argued for a referendum in the islands in support of more autonomy following the devolution referendum, while others sought to gain more powers for the council (*The Scotsman*, 13 September 1997).

The position of Orkney and Shetland also played its way into constitutional debates in the 1970s and 1990s. Jo Grimond, the Liberal MP for the islands in the 1970s, successfully amended the

---

Scotland Bill to include a passage committing the government to establishing a special commission to examine the position of the islands and the Scottish Assembly if either Orkney or Shetland voted No at the referendum. The government later produced a compromise position which would establish a Commission regardless of how Orkney and Shetland voted (Macartney, 1985: p. 14).[2] In the 1990s, Orkney and Shetland were given individual seats in the Scottish Parliament, but other concessions were ignored. Jim Wallace sought to amend the Scotland Bill to guarantee the autonomous status of the island councils and extend their powers, but this was rejected by the Labour government despite the agreement to recognise the islands' autonomy in the Constitutional Convention's proposals. However, greater autonomy will remain an important issue in the future, especially in relations with the Scottish Parliament, particularly if it is perceived that the Parliament is overly concerned with the central belt and neglectful of the Northern isles.

Aspects of the devolution proposals of the 1990s explicitly sought to redress perceived political imbalances in Scotland through a range of mechanisms. The most important of these mechanisms involved the design of a mixed electoral system which would prevent the devolved Parliament from being dominated by Labour or by the central belt. The distribution of seats through the Additional Member System component of the electoral system can be understood as a device which ensured greater representation for rural areas than the existing first-past-the-post (FPTP) system used at Westminster elections. Similarly, the fact that coalition was the most likely outcome of the devolved elections meant that the Parliament would not be dominated by a party from the central belt such as Labour (although Labour victory in Inverness and Dumfries at the 1997 general election chipped away at the idea of Labour being purely a party of central and urban Scotland). In addition, measures like providing seats in the Parliament for both Orkney and Shetland can be seen as a measure intended to boost representation for areas beyond the central belt and generate support for devolution in those areas. The island communities were also to enjoy special status within the scheme of devolution through greater autonomy for their local authorities (Scottish Constitutional Convention, 1990: p. 14).

The Scottish Constitutional Convention outlined a number of principles for the Parliament's relationship with local government, based around the need to develop a cooperative relationship between the two sets of institutions (Scottish Constitutional Convention, 1995: pp. 16–17). The

Convention proposed that the government should become a signatory to the European Charter of Local Self-Government, and this was carried out by the Labour government in June 1997. But although the Convention supported the insertion of a clause into the Scotland Bill supporting the principle of subsidiarity for local government (Scottish Constitutional Convention, 1995: p. 17), none was forthcoming in the Scotland Bill or Act. This fact should not have come as a surprise given that the Bill sought to establish a Scottish Parliament rather than seek to fix its relations with local government. Labour decided to leave the issue of local government relations with the Scottish Parliament to future discussions by the Parliament itself (Scottish Office, 1997: p. 19), but it did seek to produce some preparatory discussions over Scottish intergovernmental relations by establishing the Commission on Local Government and the Scottish Parliament – the McIntosh Commission – in January 1998 to prepare a report for the future Scottish Executive.

The McIntosh Commission, devolution and the reform of Scottish local government

The McIntosh Commission undertook an extensive consultation exercise in 1998 with the aim of dealing with local government's relations with the Scottish Parliament, and examining proposals to make local government more responsive and democratically accountable to local people. This latter aspect was part of a reforming agenda for local government, which sought to remedy some of the perceived democratic failings of local government associated with one-party domination of councils produced by the electoral system. This reforming agenda also sought to clear up the general unease with factionalism and suggestions of corruption within Labour local authorities following disputes in Monklands, Renfrewshire and West Dunbartonshire councils and internal Labour problems in Glasgow City Council. The Commission's efforts heralded a second consultation paper in November 1998, which followed extensive discussions with a range of organisations and local authorities and involved over 450 responses to the consultation exercise. This consultation featured submissions from twenty-nine local authorities, COSLA, the SNP and the Liberal Democrats (but neither Labour nor the Conservatives), a range of pressure groups such as the Automobile Association, Scottish Police Federation, Scottish Chambers of Commerce, Church of Scotland, Scottish Trades Union Congress, ninety-three community councils and a variety of other organisations and individuals.

The McIntosh Commission discussed two sets of issues: local government and the Scottish Parliament, and the crisis of local government democracy. On the first issue, it suggested the negotiation of a covenant between local government and the Scottish Parliament to establish a set of ground rules in intergovernmental relations and to ensure a positive partnership between the two sets of institutions dealing with powers and responsibilities, financial arrangements, consultative mechanisms and a regular forum to assess the effectiveness of the Covenant (Commission on Local Government and the Scottish Parliament, 1998b: p. 11). On the second issue, it outlined a series of measures that could contribute to making Scottish local government more responsive, democratic and accountable, a number of which were already in practice in some Scottish councils (see Case study 15 on Stirling Council). The Commission recommended improved mechanisms for local authority consultation with their communities, greater involvement of community councils, where possible, or the use of area committees, citizens' panels, public hearings and local referenda (Commission on Local Government and the Scottish Parliament, 1998b: p. 16). In addition, the Commission entered the debate over the electoral reform of Scotland's councils begun by the Scottish Council Foundation (Adonis, 1998) by suggesting the use of PR for council elections as well as proposing mechanisms to make council deci-sionmaking more open and less subject to party control (Commission on Local Government and the Scottish Parliament, 1998b: pp. 20–1). It raised the possibility of using an executive 'cabinet' system to provide for more accountable leadership within the council, which would be scrutinised by the full council on a more systematic basis.

Case study 15 Local democracy: Stirling Council

A number of Scottish local authorities have sought to become innovators in developing citizen participation within their communities. Stirling Council, which combines urban Stirling with a large number of small towns and an extensive rural area that runs west to Loch Lomond and north to Crianlarich, has developed a range of measures to improve the quality of local democracy in the area. Four distinctive initiatives have been employed by Stirling Council: area forums, Stirling Assembly, the Youth Congress and a range of repre-sentative institutions within primary and secondary schools.

Area forums Before the 1995 reorganisation of local government, the central regional council had developed a range of decentralisation initiatives within its boundaries. Following reorganisation, and in recognition of its geographical diversity, Stirling Council sought to develop a decentralisation strategy based around two different me-chanisms. First, the Council maintained and established a range of council offices across its area, part of the 1980s legacy of 'going local'.

Second, it sought to establish a number of area forums to act as consultative mechanisms to enable greater dialogue between the council and local people. The forums were constituted as open meetings in which councillors, community councillors and local residents would meet to discuss a range of local issues. Over time, the area forums were to enjoy decisionmaking powers to give them a genuine role within the council. By 1998, three area forums had been established, with plans for the whole council area to be covered by such bodies over time (Stirling Council, 1998: pp. 13–16).

Stirling Assembly The Assembly is an open forum involving local people and invited representatives from the business and voluntary sector to give an input into major items of council business. Assembly meetings have mixed plenary discussions, workshops and feedback sessions in order to discuss the structure plan for Stirling, sustainable development in Stirling, local healthcare, young people and civic involvement (Stirling Council, 1998: p. 17). The Assembly operates as a consultative mechanism on major issues of strategic importance to the council and community, and the intention is that it will evolve into an autonomous institution capable of active citizenship.

Youth Congress Stirling Youth Congress was launched in January 1998. It seeks to represent young people from the ages of fourteen to twenty-five, with an elected executive and a range of spokespersons. The Congress meets five times a year formally and has administrative support from the council's department of Youth Services Support. While the Congress remains in its infancy and suffered from significant turnover in its membership – especially especially among those departing for university – it has sought to operate both as a consultative mechanism for young people and a device for political education and participation.

Schools boards and councils The School Boards (Scotland) Act 1988 and subsequent legislation required Stirling Council to establish school boards and mechanisms for devolved school management across the forty-nine schools within its boundaries. The council devolved 80 per cent of its schools budget to School Boards (Stirling Council, 1998: p. 20), in addition to establishing pupil councils in all secondary schools and most primaries. It also created an elected Student Forum from among the secondary schools, with an annual election for a co-opted student representative on the Council's Children's Committee and a similar position for a parents' representative.

In its final report, the McIntosh Commission made a number of recommendations to the new Scottish Executive.

Intergovernmental relations

The Commission proposed the establishment of a covenant between councils and the Parliament which would set out the principles of the relationship between the two sets of organisations (Commission on Local Government and the Scottish Parliament, 1999: p. 14). The covenant would be modelled on the European Charter of Local Self-Government, and the Commission produced a draft covenant as part of its report. The covenant would be reviewed by a joint conference of local government and MSPs, which would exist separately from the Parliament's local government committee (Commission on Local Government and the Scottish Parliament, 1999: p. 15). The Commission also proposed a mechanism to formalise relations between local authorities and the Scottish Executive, legislation to provide councils with a power of general competence, and an independent inquiry into local government finance.

Electing Scotland's councils

The Commission proposed a review of electoral arrangements for Scotland's councils, with more open access to voting, greater use of postal and electronic voting, and a rolling electoral register to facilitate voting. More fundamentally, the Commission called for the introduction of PR for council elections. It did not propose any one PR system but suggested that the system should meet the following criteria: proportionality, the maintenance of the councillor-ward link, fair provision for independents, recognition of geographical diversity, and the need to match council boundaries to natural communities (Commission on Local Government and the Scottish Parliament, 1999: p. 23). The Scottish Executive responded to this aspect of the report by establishing a second committee to consider the issue of electoral reform in Scotland's councils. The Renewing Local Democracy Working Group (Kerley Committee) reported in June 2000 with proposals for using single transferable vote in multi-member constituencies for council elections, with most constituencies comprised of three to five councillors, with a minimum of two councillors per constituency in some sparsely-populated areas (Renewing Local Democracy Working Group, 2000). However, there was no indication of whether this new electoral system would be adopted by the Scottish Executive or instituted in time for the council elections of 2002.

Political arrangements within councils

The Commission proposed that councils undertake a review of their internal procedures for political management to examine the potential for change. The Commission did not recommend the adoption of council cabinets nor individual council leaders, in recognition of the diverse nature of political management arrangements in Scotland, especially in non-partisan councils.

Community councils

The Commission recognised the important role of community councils in the work of local authorities, but did not recommend any major changes. Indeed, it is likely that the consultations over community councils and public participation in local government demonstrated a wide range of participatory initiatives among local authorities, which showed considerable innovation in relation to citizen involvement (see Case study 15 on Stirling Council). Councils were asked to review the resourcing and levels of participation in community councils, with a greater role for councils in providing civic education and reduction of the voting age at community council elections to sixteen.

While the McIntosh Commission sought to address some important issues in relation to local government, it actually ignored two of the main problems faced by Scottish local authorities: structure and finance. These issues were much larger and more complex than the agenda of the McIntosh Commission, and will prove problematic for the Scottish Executive and Parliament. COSLA and a number of member councils sought the establishment of an independent commission to review the issue of local government finance (COSLA, 1998: p. 1), but this was not supported by the Scottish Executive. Indeed, it was significant that the first legislative programme of the Scottish Executive included a bill to improve standards of conduct within Scottish local government, not issues such as local functions, structure or finance. However, the McIntosh Commission proposals were widely debated within the Scottish Parliament's Local Government Committee in 1999–2000 and brought the Executive to consider electoral reform for Scotland's councils, institute a Leadership Advisory Panel to consider decisionmaking within councils, establish a Community Leadership Forum between Scottish Executive ministers and local government leaders, and examine proposals for civic education within Scotland's schools.[3]

– CONCLUSION –

The impact of devolution on Scottish local government was limited in 1999–2000. However, in the longer term the impact is likely to be substantial. First on the horizon is the proposal to reform the electoral system for local elections, which will produce far-reaching changes to local government. The removal of the FPTP electoral system will produce more hung councils and therefore more coalition governments of various political stripes within Scotland's councils. Such patterns will be more complex than the current two-party coalition within the Scottish Parliament, and the new electoral system will have ramifications for Labour's institutional dominance of Scottish local government and politics generally. While the Scottish Executive endorsed many aspects of the McIntosh Commission report and began to press ahead with local government reform, the wider issue of local finance was largely ignored and funding operated on the restrictive pre-devolution arrangements. The modernisation of local government and development of constructive relations between the Executive, Parliament and local councils was therefore a limited phenomenon.

– Notes –

1. Memorandum by Minister of Finance to Local Government Committee meeting of 9 May 2000.
2. This position was later adopted by the Conservative government in the shape of the Montgomery Commission of Inquiry into Functions and Powers of Islands Councils (1984), Cmnd. 9216.
3. Scottish Executive, *Report of the Commission on Local Government and the Scottish Parliament: the Scottish Executive's Response*, 11 July 2000.

Bibliography

Adonis, Andrew (1998), *Voting in Proportion: Electoral Reform for Scotland's Councils*, Scottish Council Foundation Paper 4, Edinburgh, Scottish Council Foundation.

Baggot, Rob (1995), *Pressure Groups Today*, Manchester, Manchester University Press.

Balsom, Denis and Ian McAllister (1979), 'The Scottish and Welsh Devolution Referenda of 1979', *Parliamentary Affairs*, vol. 32, no. 4, pp. 394–409.

Balthazar, Louis (1999), 'The Quebec Experience: Success or Failure?', in F. Aldecoa and M. Keating (eds), *Paradiplomacy in Action: the Foreign Relations of Subnational Governments*, London, Frank Cass.

BBC Scotland (2000), *BBC Scotland Annual Report 1999–2000*, Glasgow.

Bennie, Lynn, Jack Brand and James Mitchell (1997), *How Scotland Votes*, Manchester, Manchester University Press.

Bennie, Lynn, Jack Brand and James Mitchell (1995), 'Thatcherism and the Scottish Question', in Colin Rallings, David Broughton, David Denver, David Farrell (eds), *British Elections and Parties Yearbook 1995*, London, Frank Cass.

Bochel, Catherine and Hugh Bochel (1998), 'Scotland's Councillors 1974–1995', *Scottish Affairs*, no. 24, pp. 29–43.

Bochel, John and David Denver (1970), 'Religion and Voting' *Political Studies*, vol. 18, pp. 205–19.

Bochel John and David Denver (1993), 'Trends in District Elections', *Scottish Affairs*, no. 2, Winter, pp. 106–19.

Bochel, John, David Denver and Allan Macartney (1981), *The Referendum Experience: Scotland 1979*, Aberdeen, Aberdeen University Press.

Bogdanor, Vernon (1979), *Devolution*, Oxford, Opus.

Bogdanor, Vernon (1999), *Devolution in the United Kingdom*, Oxford, Oxford University Press.

Boyle, Raymond (1998), 'Crisis? What Crisis? The Catholic Church and the Secular Press in Scotland', in Raymond Boyle and Peter Lynch (eds), *Out of the Ghetto? The Catholic Community in Modern Scotland*, Edinburgh, John Donald.

Boyne, George, Grant Jordan and Murray McVicar (1995), *Local Government*

Reform: Review of the Process in Scotland and Wales, London, Joseph Rowntree Foundation.

Brand, Jack, James Mitchell and Paula Surridge (1994), 'Will Scotland Come to the Aid of the Party?, in A. Heath, R. Jowell and J. Curtice (eds), *Labour's Last Chance?*, Aldershot, Dartmouth.

Brand, Jack, James Mitchell and Paula Surridge (1993), 'Identity and the Vote: Class and Nationality in Scotland', in David Denver et al. (eds), *British Elections and Parties Year book 1993*, Aldershot, Dartmouth.

Brand, Jack, James Mitchell and Paula Surridge (1994), 'Social Constituency and Scottish Nationalism', *Political Studies*, vol. 42, no. 4, pp. 616–29.

Brown, Alice, David McCrone and Lindsay Paterson (1998), *Politics and Society in Scotland*, London, Macmillan.

Brown, Alice, David McCrone, Lindsay Paterson and Paula Surridge (1999), *The Scottish Electorate*, London, Macmillan.

Burrows, Noreen (2000), 'Relations with the European Union', in Gerry Hassan and Chris Warhurst (eds), *The New Scottish Politics: the First Year of the Scottish Parliament and Beyond*, Edinburgh, HMSO.

Butler, David and Donald Stokes (1969), *Political Change in Britain*, London, Macmillan.

Cabinet Office (1999), *Public Bodies*, London, HMSO.

Commission on Local Government and the Scottish Parliament (1998a), *Consultation Paper 1*, Edinburgh, HMSO.

Commission on Local Government and the Scottish Parliament (1998b), *Consultation Paper 2*, Edinburgh, HMSO.

Commission on Local Government and the Scottish Parliament (1999), *Moving Forward: Local Government and the Scottish Parliament*, Edinburgh, Scottish Office.

Constitution Unit (1996), *Scotland's Parliament*, London, University College.

Consultative Steering Group (1999), *Shaping Scotland's Parliament*, Edinburgh, Scottish Office.

Cornes, Richard (1999), 'Intergovernmental Relations in a Devolved United Kingdom', in Robert Hazell (ed.), *Constitutional Futures: a History of the Next Ten Years*, Oxford, Oxford University Press.

COSLA (1998), *Response to the Commission on Local Government and the Scottish Parliament*, Edinburgh, COSLA.

Craig, Carol (1980), 'COSLA: A Silent Voice for Local Government?' in H. and N. Drucker (eds), *The Scottish Government Yearbook 1981*, Edinburgh, Paul Harris.

Curtice, John (1997), 'A Reply to Michael Dyer', *Representation*, vol. 34, no. 2, pp. 133–4.

Curtice, John (1998), 'Reinventing the Yo-Yo? A Comment on the Electoral Provisions of the Scotland Bill', *Scottish Affairs*, no. 23, Spring, pp. 41–3.

Dahl, Robert (1966), 'Patterns of Opposition', in Dahl (ed.), *Political Oppositions in Western Democracies*, Ithaca, Yale University Press.

Denver, David and John Bochel (1994), 'The Last Act: the Regional Elections of 1994', *Scottish Affairs*, no. 9, pp. 68–79

Denver, David and Hugh Bochel (2000), 'The Forgotten Elections: the Scottish Council Elections of 1999', *Scottish Affairs*, no. 30, Winter, pp. 115–29.

Denver, David, James Mitchell, Charles Pattie and Hugh Bochel (2000), *Scotland Decides*, London, Cass.

Dewar, Donald (1981), 'The Select Committee on Scottish Affairs', in H. Drucker and N. Drucker (eds), *The Scottish Government Yearbook 1981*, Edinburgh, Paul Harris.

Dowle, Martin (1980), 'The Birth and Development of the Shetland Movement 1977–80', in Drucker and Drucker (eds), *The Scottish Government Yearbook 1981*, Edinburgh, Paul Harris.

Dyer, Michael (1997), 'Scotland's Additional Members and the Maintenance of Labour Power', *Representation*, vol. 34, no. 2, pp. 127–32.

Dyer, Michael (1999), 'Representation in a Devolved Scotland', *Representation*, vol. 36, no. 1, pp. 18–28.

Finlay, Richard (1994), *Independent and Free: Scottish Politics and the Origins of the Scottish National Party 1918–1945*, Edinburgh, John Donald.

Finnie, Ross and Henry McLeish (1999), 'The Negotiation Diaries', *Scottish Affairs*, no. 28, Summer, pp. 51–61.

Franklin, Bob (1994), *Packaging Politics: Political Communications in Britain's Media Democracy*, London, Edward Arnold.

Geddes, Keith (1996), 'Local Government and Quangos', in Scottish Local Government Information Unit, *A Scottish Parliament: Friend or Foe to Local Government?* Glasgow.

Grant, Wyn (1989), *Pressure Groups, Politics and Democracy in Britain*, Hemel Hempstead, Philip Allan.

Grant, Wyn (1989a), 'Regional Organization and Public Policy in the UK', in William Coleman and Henry Jacek (eds), *Regionalism, Business Interests and Public Policy*, London, Sage.

Grant, Wyn and David Marsh (1977), *The CBI*, London, Hodder and Stoughton.

Hanham, H. J. (1969), 'The Development of the Scottish Office', in J. N. Wolfe (ed.), *Government and Nationalism in Scotland*, Edinburgh, Edinburgh University Press.

Hassan, Gerry and Chris Warhurst (2000), 'A New Politics?', in Gerry Hassan and Chris Warhurst (eds), *The New Scottish Politics: the First Year of the Scottish Parliament and Beyond*, Edinburgh, HMSO.

Heath, Anthony and James Kellas (1998), 'Nationalisms and Constitutional Questions', in Lindsay Paterson (ed.), *Understanding Constitutional Change*, special issue of *Scottish Affairs*, pp. 110–28.

Hetherington, Alisdair (1992), *Inside BBC Scotland 1975–80*, Aberdeen, White-paper Press.

Himsworth, C. (1998), 'New Devolution: New Dangers for Local Government?', *Scottish Affairs*, no 24, pp. 6–28

Hogwood, Brian (1986), 'If Consultation is Everything, Maybe it's Nothing', *Strathclyde Papers on Politics and Government*, no. 44. Glasgow, University of Strathclyde.

Hogwood, Brian (1999), 'Relations with Other Public Bodies', in Gerry Hassan (ed.), *A Guide to the Scottish Parliament*, Edinburgh, HMSO.

Hooghe, Liesbet (1996), *Cohesion Policy and European Integration: Building Multi-Level Governance*, Oxford, Clarendon.

Hutchinson, Ian (1998), 'Scottish Unionism Between the Two World Wars', in Catriona MacDonald (ed.), *Unionist Scotland 1800–1997*, Edinburgh, John Donald.

Independent Committee of Inquiry into Student Finance (1999), *Student Finance: Fairness for the Future*, Edinburgh, HMSO.

Jeffery, Charlie (1996), 'Sub-National Authorities and European Domestic Policy', in C. Jeffery (ed.), *The Regional Dimension of the European Union*, London, Cass.

Jeffery, Charlie (1996a), 'Regional Information Offices in Brussels', in C. Jeffery (ed.), *The Regional Dimension of the European Union*, London, Cass.

Jones, Peter (1997b), 'Labour's Referendum Plan: Sell-out or Act of Faith?', *Scottish Affairs*, no. 18, Winter 1997, pp. 1–18.

Jones, Barry and Michael Keating (eds) (1995), *The European Union and the Regions*, Oxford, Clarendon.

Keating, Michael (1975), *The Role of the Scottish MP*, Ph.D. thesis, Conference of National Academic Awards.

Keating, Michael (1998), *The New Regionalism in Western Europe*, Cheltenham, Edward Elgar.

Keating, Michael (1999), 'Regions and International Affairs: Motives, Opportunities and Strategies', in F. Aldecoa and M. Keating (eds), *Paradiplomacy in Action: the Foreign Relations of Subnational Governments*, London, Cass.

Kellas, James (1984), *The Scottish Political System*, Cambridge, Cambridge University Press.

Kellas, James (1992), 'The Social Origins of Scottish Nationalism', in John Coakley (ed.), *The Social Origins of Nationalist Movements*, London, Sage.

Kellas, James (1994), 'The Party in Scotland', in Anthony Seldon and Stuart Ball (eds), *Conservative Century*, Oxford University Press.

Kerley, Richard and Kevin Orr (1993), 'Joint Arrangements in Scotland', *Local Government Studies*, vol. 19, no. 3, pp. 309–18.

Land Reform Policy Group (1998a), *Identifying the Problems*, Edinburgh, Scottish Office.

Land Reform Policy Group (1998b), *Identifying the Solutions*, Edinburgh, Scottish Office.

Land Reform Policy Group (1999), *Recommendations for Action*, Edinburgh, Scottish Office.

Lane, Jan-Erik and Svante Ersson (2000), *The New Institutional Politics*, London, Routledge.

Leicester, Graham and James Mitchell (1999), *Scotland, Britain and Europe – Diplomacy and Devolution*, Edinburgh, Scottish Council Foundation.

Leicester, Graham and James MacKay (1998), *Holistic Government: Options for Devolved Scotland*, Edinburgh, Scottish Council Foundation.

Linklater, Magnus and Robin Dennistoun (eds) (1992) *Anatomy of Scotland*, Edinburgh, Chambers.

Lynch, Peter (1996), 'The Scottish Constitutional Convention 1992–5', *Scottish Affairs*, no. 15, Spring, pp. 1–16.

Lynch, Peter (1998), 'Reactive Capital: the Scottish Business Community and Devolution', *Regional and Federal Studies*, vol. 8, no. 1, 1998, pp. 86–102.

Lynch, Peter (1998a), 'Third Party Politics in a Four Party System: the Liberal Democrats in Scotland', *Scottish Affairs*, no. 22, Winter, pp. 16–32.

Lynch, Peter (2000), 'The Committee System of the Scottish Parliament', in Gerry Hassan and Chris Warhurst (eds), *The New Scottish Politics: the First Year Of The Scottish Parliament and Beyond*, Edinburgh, HMSO.

McCrone, David (1992), *Understanding Scotland – The Sociology of a Stateless Nation*, London, Routledge.

McDowell, W. H. (1992), *The History of BBC Scotland*, Edinburgh, Edinburgh University Press.

McIntyre, Donald (1999), *Mandelson: the Biography*, London, Harper Collins.

Macartney, Allan (1985), 'The Scottish Islands Debate', in Macartney (ed.), *Islands of Europe*, Edinburgh, Unit for the Study of Government in Scotland.

MacKay, Peter (1999), Modernising the Scottish Civil Service', in Gerry Hassan and Chris Warhurst (eds), *A Different Future: a Moderniser's Guide to Scotland*, Glasgow, Centre for Scottish Public Policy Big Issue.

MacLeod, Catherine (2000), 'Relations with Westminster', in Gerry Hassan and Chris Warhurst (eds), *The New Scottish Politics: the First Year of The Scottish Parliament and Beyond*, Edinburgh, HMSO.

MacWhirter, Iain (2000), 'Scotland Year Zero: the First Year at Holyrood', in Gerry Hassan and Chris Warhurst (eds), *The New Scottish Politics: the First Year Of The Scottish Parliament and Beyond*, Edinburgh, HMSO.

McCabe, Angela and James McCormick (2000), 'Rethinking Representation: Some Evidence From the First Year', in Gerry Hassan and Chris Warhurst (eds), *The New Scottish Politics: the First Year Of The Scottish Parliament and Beyond*, Edinburgh, HMSO.

Mair, Colin (2000), 'The Executive and Local Government', in Gerry Hassan and Chris Warhurst (eds), *The New Scottish Politics: the First Year Of The Scottish Parliament and Beyond*, Edinburgh, HMSO.

Marks, Gary (1996), 'An Actor-centred Approach to Multilevel Governance', in Charlie Jeffery (ed.), *The Regional Dimension of the European Union*, London, Cass.

Marr, Andrew (1992), *The Battle for Scotland*, London, Penguin.

Mazey, Sonia and James Mitchell (1993), 'Europe of the Regions: Territorial Interests and European Integration – the Scottish Experience', in Sonia Mazey and Jeremy Richardson (eds), *Lobbying in the European Community*, Oxford, Oxford University Press.

Meech, Peter and Richard Kilborn (1992), 'Media Identity in a Stateless Nation', *Media, Culture and Society*, vol. 14, no. 2, April, pp. 245–60.

Meny, Yves (1993), *Government and Politics in Western Europe*, Oxford University Press.

Miller, William (1981), *The End of British Politics? Scots and English Political Behaviour in the Seventies*, Oxford, Clarendon.

Milligan, Tony (1999), 'Left at the Polls: the Changing Far Left Vote', *Scottish Affairs*, no. 29, Autumn, pp. 139–56.

Mitchell, James, David Denver, Charles Pattie and Hugh Bochel (1998), 'The 1997 Devolution Referendum in Scotland', *Parliamentary Affairs*, vol. 51, no. 2, pp. 166–81.

Mitchell, James (1990), *Conservatives and the Union*, Edinburgh, Edinburgh University Press.

Mitchell, James (1996), *Strategies for Self-Government*, Edinburgh, Polygon.

Mitchell, James (1998), 'What Could a Scottish Parliament Do?', *Regional and Federal Studies*, vol. 8, no. 1, 1998, pp. 68–85.

Montgomery, D. (1984), *Report of the Committee of Inquiry into the Functions and Powers of the Islands Councils in Scotland* (Cmnd. 9216), Edinburgh, HMSO.

Moore, Chris and Simon Booth (1989), *Managing Competition: Meso-corporatism, Pluralism and the Negotiated Order in Scotland*, Oxford, Oxford University Press.

Narin, Tom (2000), *After Britain*, London, Granta.

Orkney Islands Council (1999), *Submission to the Commission on Local Government and the Scottish Parliament*, second consultation paper, Orkney, Orkney Islands Council.

Parry, Richard (1987), 'The Centralization of the Scottish Office', in Richard Rose (ed.), *Ministers and Ministers*, Oxford, Clarendon.

Parry, Richard (1988), *Scottish Political Facts*, Edinburgh, T. and T. Clark.

Parry, Richard (1999a), 'The Scottish Civil Service', in Gerry Hassan (ed.), *A Guide to the Scottish Parliament*, Edinburgh, HMSO.

Parry, Richard (1999b), 'Quangos and the Structure of the Public Sector in Scotland', *Scottish Affairs*, no. 29, Autumn, pp. 12–27.

Paterson, Lindsay (1994), *The Autonomy of Modern Scotland*, Edinburgh, Edinburgh, University, Press.

Paterson, Lindsay (1999), 'Why Should We Respect Civic Scotland?', in Gerry Hassan and Chris Warhurst (eds), *A Different Future: a Moderniser's Guide to Scotland*, Glasgow, Centre for Scottish Public Policy Big Issue.

Renewing Local Democracy Working Group (2000), *You Should be Taking Part, Getting Involved, Making a Difference*, Edinburgh, Scottish Executive.

Ritchie, Murray (2000), *Scotland Reclaimed: the Inside Story of Scotland's First Democratic Parliamentary Election*, Edinburgh, Saltire Society.

Rose, Richard (ed.) (1987), *Ministers and Ministries*, Oxford, Clarendon.

Ross, Willie (1978), 'Approaching the Archangelic', in H. Drucker and M. Clarke (eds), *The Scottish Government Yearbook 1978*, Edinburgh, Paul Harris.

Russell, Meg (1999), *Representing the Nations and Regions in the New Upper House*, London, Constitution Unit.

Sartori, Giovanni (1997), *Comparative Constitutional Engineering*, London, Macmillan.

Schlesinger, Philip (2000), 'Communicating to a New Polity: the Media and the Parliament', in Gerry Hassan and Chris Warhurst (eds), *The New Scottish Politics: the First Year Of The Scottish Parliament and Beyond*, Edinburgh, HMSO.

Schlesinger, Philip and Damian Tambini (1999), *Taking Stock: Broadcasting and Devolution in Scotland and Wales*, Stirling Media Research Institute and IPPR.

Scottish Conservatives (1999), *Scotland First*, Edinburgh.

Scottish Constitutional Commission (1994), *Further Steps Towards a Scheme for Scotland's Parliament*, Edinburgh Scottish Constitutional Commission.

Scottish Constitutional Convention (1995), *Scotland's Parliament, Scotland's Right*, Edinburgh.

Scottish Constitutional Convention (1990), *Towards Scotland's Parliament*, Edinburgh.

Scottish Executive (1999), *Land Reform: Proposals for Legislation*, Edinburgh, Scottish Executive.

Scottish Executive (2000), *Scotland the Learning Nation: Helping Students*, Edinburgh.

Scottish Liberal Democrats (1999a), *Raising the Standard*, Edinburgh.

Scottish Liberal Democrats (1999b), *Coalition Framework*, Edinburgh.

Scottish Liberal Democrats (1999c), *Partnership for Scotland*, Edinburgh.

Scottish New Labour (1999), *Building Scotland's Future*, Glasgow.

Scottish Local Government Information Unit (1996), *A Scottish Parliament – Friend or Foe to Local Government?*, Glasgow.

Scottish National Party (1999), *Election 99 – the Manifesto*, Edinburgh.

Scottish Natural Heritage (1998), *National Parks for Scotland: a Consultation Paper*, Perth.

Scottish Natural Heritage (1999), *National Parks for Scotland: Scottish Natural Heritage's Advice to Government*, Perth.

Scottish Office (1991), *The Structure of Local Government in Scotland: the Case for Change – a Consultation Paper*, Edinburgh, HMSO.

Scottish Office (1992), *The Structure of Local Government in Scotland: Shaping the New Councils – a Consultation Paper*, Edinburgh, HMSO.

Scottish Office (1993), *The Structure of Local Government in Scotland: Shaping the Future – the New Councils*, Edinburgh, HMSO.

Scottish Office (1993), *Scotland in the Union: a Partnership for Good*, Edinburgh, HMSO.

Scottish Office (1997), *Scotland's Parliament*, Edinburgh, HMSO.

Scottish Office (1998), *A New Ethical Framework for Local Government in Scotland*, Edinburgh, HMSO.

Scottish Office (1999), *Targeting Excellence – Modernising Scotland's Schools*, Edinburgh, HMSO.

Seawright, David (1999), *An Important Matter of Principle: the Decline of the Scottish Conservative and Unionist Party*, Aldershot, Ashgate.

Select Committee on Procedure (1999), *The Procedural Consequences of Devolution*, HC 185, London, House of Commons.

Sloat, Amanda (2000), 'Scotland and Europe: Links between Edinburgh, London and Brussels', *Scottish Affairs*, no. 31, Spring, pp. 92–110.

Smith, Martin (1999), *The Core Executive in Britain*, Basingstoke, Macmillan.

Smith, Maurice (1994), *Paper Lions*, Edinburgh, Polygon.

Stirling Council (1998), *Local Democracy and Community Leadership*, Stirling.

Surridge, Paula, Lindsay Paterson, Alice Brown and David McCrone (1998), 'The Scottish Electorate and the Scottish Parliament', in Lindsay Paterson (ed.), *Understanding Constitutional Change*, special issue of *Scottish Affairs*, pp. 38–60.

Wheatley (1969), *Royal Commission on Local Government in Scotland 1966–9*, Edinburgh, HMSO.

Whiteley, Paul (1982), 'The Decline of Labour's Local Party Membership 1945–79', in Kavanagh (ed.), *The Politics of the Labour Party*, London, Allen and Unwin.

Index